On Days Like These

By

Phil Collard

First published: September 2014

Copyright © Phil Collard 2014

ISBN : 9781849145411

Table of contents

Just call me "slacker" – November 30th, 2013

Saturday Night's Alright For Fighting – December 3rd, 2013

Hunting elephants, pools and PBs – December 10th 2013

Time to get mushy!! – December 13th 2013

Search for the hundred inside yourself – December 17th, 2013

Oh the weather outside is frightful... - December 21st, 2013

Bring on 2014 – December 28th, 2013

Rear-view mirror – January 4th, 2014

Cometh the hour... loseth the hour – January 9th, 2014

Back on the horse... err.. bike... – January 12th, 2014

Is vanity really where it's at? – January 16th, 2014

Where are the brakes on this thing? – January 21st, 2014

If I need anything, I'll ask! – January 25th, 2014

The Jack and Grace Cotton Audax – 28th January, 2014

All in a week's work – February 4th, 2014

Getting your CV in order – February 8th, 2014

Weather the weather, whatever the weather – February 13th, 2014

Rough winds do shake the darling bike of February - February 17th, 2014

I'm a team player – February 24th, 2014

Gospel Pass Audax – March 1st, 2014

The BIG announcement – March 9th, 2014

If the bike fits – March 14th, 2014

Come out from the cold – March 19th, 2014

It's nice to go a'travelling – March 27th, 2014

You bustin' ma baws? – April 2nd, 2014

Mind, body and splashing in puddles – April 7th, 2014

A picture paints a thousand words – April 15th, 2014

And now for something completely different – April 18th, 2014

It makes me sick, it does – April 23rd, 2014

World in slow motion – April 28th, 2014

It's not all about the winning – May 3rd, 2014

And... breathe! – May 7th, 2014

Tell Lisa; "I love her" – May 16th, 2014

And then it hit me – May 22nd, 2014

Quantifiable progress – May 29th, 2014

What's in a name? – June 6th, 2014

Call me Colin Jackson – June 10th, 2014

I just want to be alone – June 27th, 2014

He shoots... he scores. – July 2nd, 2014

A weekend of ups and downs – July 9th, 2014

Ironman blues – July 14th, 2014

From dusk til dawn – July 17th, 2014

Ticking off and ticking over – July 23rd, 2014

Tapertastic training – August 1st, 2014

Preface

This book started life as a blog-site and, with that being so, you'll need to appreciate that, throughout the pages that you are about to read, there will be references to it as such – I've deliberately kept the "book" version as faithful as practically possible to the original, so as to preserve it as it was written rather than trying to manipulate it too much just so that it will fit this new format.

Before I leave you to it, though, here is a little bit about me.

In 1976, I was diagnosed with cancer but, if truth be told, I feel a bit of a fraud when I use the word "cancer" in relation to myself.

You see, I was just a kid... an eighteen month old baby, to be precise.

To me, even the word "cancer" wouldn't have meant anything at all, let alone the actual condition.

In a very real sense, then, it was my parents who both had cancer.

After all, they were the ones whose world was torn apart whilst a doctor gave them the news and they were the ones who were left wondering; "why us?"

They were the ones for whom the fragility of life was brought into sharp focus.

For me, "cancer" is just something that I know appears as a written word on a piece of paper towards the beginning of my medical file.

If cancer were a single event, then, it would be a battle where I was given a 50/50 chance of victory, but which I fought and won before even my earliest memories were formed.

But, of course, cancer isn't a single event, is it?

Cancer leaves its mark on all whom it touches long after it is seemingly defeated and so, whilst I can't really talk about what it is like to have cancer, I can certainly claim to understand the aftermath.

Despite the fact that everyone tried to give me a "normal" childhood, it was impossible to escape the fact that I was wrapped in cotton wool by all who surrounded me. No-one wanted me to endure any more suffering and I can understand that.

I genuinely don't know how my parents did it… as a father myself, I'd be terrified to face what they did.

Growing up, though, it felt as if my history of cancer had singled me out as someone who needed extra protection from anything that might be just a little bit dangerous and, as a result, I felt like I was missing out on a lot of the fun things that the "other kids" were getting up to.

But cancer left me with much more than just a sense of "living in a protective bubble".

It gave me a whole childhood of regular check-up visits to the hospital.

It gave me a whole childhood of not really knowing what to tell my friends (I didn't even understand it myself).

It also gave me a "corrective operation" at around 13 or 14 years old and, at an age when everything seems more dramatic than it is, I genuinely remember having lonely moments in a hospital bed believing that I was going to die before the week was out.

Pretty terrifying.

All of the to-ing and fro-ing from hospitals, being protected from excessive risks and general secrecy made me different to other kids at school and, I don't know if you realise this, but kids aren't too keen on "different"… Kids can be cruel.

I had a good circle of friends but it was fairly small and for every one friend there were at least two or three kids who made me feel uncomfortable in my own skin. I am hesitant to use the word "bullied" but I was certainly the target of some cruel behaviour.

This, in turn, exacerbated matters, causing me to retreat even further into my shell, and I was into a bit of a spiral during those teenage years, which are tough enough to get through for any kid without having anything else to make them harder.

It wasn't helped then that, just as I discovered something that was helping me to "find my place", cycling, the cancer stepped in again to try to take that away from me.

It turns out that my radiotherapy as a baby had damaged my hip such that, at 15, I was being told that I might not walk again, let alone ride a bike.

10

"I might not walk again" is a tough concept for anyone to get their head around… for me, at 15, it was devastating.

An operation to pin my hip back together saw me go from "facing life in a wheelchair" to "operation table" to "learning to walk all over again" in the space of a week and, whilst I recovered fully, I was now even more "different" to all of those kids at school.

Some kids could have made that a feature of a "cool" persona - I wasn't that type of kid. I was the introvert and self-pity came easier to me than self-promotion.

At around the age of 16, the protective bubble around me started to disappear and my love of cycling, to which I had been able to return, was replaced by a love of motorsport.

Having watched the heroes of the day on the TV and on tracks around the country, I really wanted to race.

My parents allowed, and even supported (both financially and emotionally), my desire and I went on to have a good few years competing. I even won a National Championship.

I was "Phil Collard, winner of a National Motor Racing Championship"… Not "Phil Collard, owner of a dodgy hip and cancer survivor".

That was huge to me.

Sadly, my cancer still had something in store for me.

Slowly but relentlessly, my hip that had been damaged by radiotherapy all those years before, and repaired in my teens, was deteriorating again.

Its rate of deterioration was very slow.

It might be tough for you to understand this but it got to the point that I could hardly walk before I really noticed its decline!

I had to find my own unique ways to do even the most simple things… like sitting down in a chair, dragging myself up stairs or even lying in bed.

All of my childhood memories of what living in the aftermath of cancer meant came flooding back when, during a meeting with a specialist, I was once again told that I should start preparing for life in a wheelchair.

I wasn't going to be beaten.

It hadn't got me as a child and, at 33 years old, it certainly wasn't going to take my life away from me now.

I wasn't about to accept the idea that my little boy would be known as the "one whose Dad was in a wheelchair".

I sought a second opinion from a man who, I think, saw me as something of a project and who has since gone on to be a family friend.

So... another operation, this time to completely replace my dodgy hip (at which point, it was also dropped on me that even my "healthy hip" was far from healthy – although, at the date of writing this, it still seems fine to me), and I was learning to walk again... again.

This time, I found support in my wife, Lisa, and son, Angus.

We soon had another son, Evert (named after the surgeon that replaced my hip), and my life since has been nothing short of amazing.

I became a regular cyclist, as I had been in my teens and, in my spare time, I even qualified as a fitness instructor.

I then turned at least part of my attention to triathlons. For those that don't know what triathlons are, they involve a swim, a bike ride and a run... in that order.

I entered triathlons of the "sprint" variety.

Again, for the uninitiated, a "sprint triathlon", in terms of distances involved, is pretty much the shortest option available and I chose this route into the sport specifically off the back of medical advice to steer clear of running on my replaced hip – but even a Sprint Triathlon, which includes a 3 mile run, meant running 3 miles further than I really should!

I was a fairly regular triathlete at the "sprint" distance before I decided to take on the challenge of becoming an Ironman triathlete!

In terms of mainstream sports, the Ironman Triathlon is widely considered to be the most challenging endurance event around where the run bit alone is equal to a marathon – 26.2 miles.

Even a 26.2 mile run is tough enough for anyone... but, after a 2.4 mile swim and 112 mile bike, for someone who is not supposed to run at all, it is not really welcome on the "to do" list... but I wasn't going to let that stop me!

Outside of my sporting life, I love my family, of course, and, collectively, we are hugely keen on embracing every opportunity to experience life. I think that we all appreciate what "living" means.

As a parent, I reckon that my cancer and subsequent hip issues have had a positive impact on me.

Lisa and I are bringing the boys up to be confident, healthy, aware and outgoing.

We allow them to find their own limits and, within reason, to hurt themselves in that search.

As a result, they are becoming everything that I would love to have been as a kid and we really hope that this gives them a more conventional route to happiness than I had.

Does my medical history have anything else in store for me?

I am pretty sure it does... Hip-replacements don't last forever, for a start, so I know I'll find myself on an operating table at some point in the future and that is quite aside from anything else that might unfold.

Am I bothered by that? Not really. I'll get through it, with help from family and friends, just as I have before.

And therein lies the key. Support.

I am not humble enough to say that I haven't contributed towards my own successes - I have worked really hard to achieve everything that I want to achieve and I tend not to let anything stand in my way - but I'm very aware that, without the unwavering support of my wife and boys, as well as that of my wider circle of friends and family, I would still be stuck in a spiral of self-pity.

The sense of "why us?" that my parents must have felt right at the very beginning of my life would have transferred to me and I would certainly be a very different person both physically and emotionally were it not for the support I enjoy.

Despite my dubious start in life and a few unfortunate episodes en-route, my challenges haven't been all that bad for me, though.

13

In fact, I'd go as far as saying that the things I have gone through have been pretty good and that I'm grateful to my "medical history" for having chosen me.

To say otherwise would imply that I'm in some way unhappy with where I am in life and since I am completely happy with the road that I am travelling, I need to thank everything that has set me on this incredibly exciting journey, including the challenges which have had an impact on shaping it all.

What would I say to someone who has their own challenges in life and for whom the prospect of winning the battle is good?

I would tell them not to confuse winning the battle with winning the war. There is a good chance that the war will continue for the rest of their life in some way, big or small.

But I would tell them that the war is, bizarrely, enjoyable.

With support, focus and goals, the fact that they have these challenges could mean that they go on to enjoy a heightened sense of life that they might never have achieved without it.

I've got it – August 26th, 2013

I've always wanted to blog but never really understood what I would write about.

Until now!

Quite a while ago, I was involved in a Twitter conversation and was asked a specific question about my triathlons:

"Do you do Ironman distances events?"

I should really have just replied; "No"... and left it there.

Instead, for some bizarre reason, I tapped out the words; "Not yet" and hit send.. having planted this seed of an idea in my mind.

Towards the end of last week, then, I entered the Ironman Triathlon event being held in Sweden in August 2014!

Suddenly, my reason for blogging was clear – I would document my Ironman journey to have something to help me remember it later in life, and, along the way, hopefully my endeavours might entertain others or even inspire them to embark on their own mad challenges!

For those that aren't in the know, entering an Ironman Triathlon means that I have committed to a 2.4 mile swim followed by a 112 mile bike ride and finished off with a 26.2 mile run (yep, that'll be a marathon).

Am I mad? Probably... Particularly given my own medical history.

So, there you have it...this blog will be a dedicated diary of my Ironman adventure.

By way of a bit more background for you, I completed a sprint triathlon yesterday (25th August) and:

- It took me 10 minutes to swim 400 metres. I'm not a fast swimmer and rarely swim much further than this!

- It took me 44 minutes to ride 13.5 miles. I'm okay on a bike, I guess, and my longest ride to date was 190 miles which makes the Ironman distance look fairly straightforward.

- It took me 28 minutes to run 3 miles. I'm not a fast runner, then, and my back-story is such that I shouldn't run at all (my orthopaedic consultant will be.. err.. "interested" when he finds out what I'm up to!!)

So... there is quite a lot of work to do and somewhere around 354 days to do it in.

Stick with me and follow my progress through its inevitable ups and downs!

An insane journey – August 29th, 2013

I know, I know, I know - it is only a few days since my first blog. This means that, to keep up this frequency, I'll either have to put in a lot of work or I'll get fed up and stop bothering after only, oooh, 2 weeks.

Well - the answer is "neither". I have no intention of keeping up any particular frequency of these blogs. Sometimes, I may even blog on consecutive days - sometimes I may disappear for a week or two.

Now that we have that cleared up, I thought I would just update you a little and, in the process, let my back-story unfold just a little bit more.

I went for a little bike ride last night… it was a gentle affair covering 24 miles in a little over 1 hr and 23 minutes.

It was a lovely ride for a couple of reasons.

1) Because I like cycling - I am one of the lucky ones who even manages to ride to work (albeit on a much heavier bike with panniers - it all counts as good training in my opinion!)

2) Because it got rid of the last remnants of soreness in my legs following the sprint Tri run I did at the weekend.

"Whoa" I hear you say… "Soreness after a 3 mile run?" you continue… "You're planning an Ironman and suffer leg soreness for three days after a 3 mile run?"

Well - the answer is… err… yes.

Let's make this clear - I managed a 300k bike ride a few weeks ago and still had enough in me to teach a Spinning class the next morning so my legs are reasonably "cycle fit"… but they are not "run fit" for the following very good reason.

A few years ago (for the second time in my life), I faced a decision between browsing wheelchair brochures (is there such a thing? I guess there must be) and a fairly serious operation - in this case it was for a hip-replacement due to a severely poorly hip.

My hip had deteriorated since a previous operation (the first instance where I faced the wheelchair) and it had become difficult for me to walk, drive, sit, lie down.. anything really. I hadn't been able to get on a bike for 7 years, let alone ride one and playing with my little boy (I had just the one son at that time) was almost impossible.

Hip replacement it was then!

Now - you shouldn't really run too much with a hip-replacement - any specialist will tell you that - so the sprint Tri that I did at the weekend was the first time that I had broken into even a jog since the previous sprint Tri I did which was... oh... A WHOLE YEAR BEFORE!

So, I hope you understand how my legs, with no running in them at all, might have held on to some soreness having been forced to run three miles from zero (and they did run it.. no walking - honest!)

How am I feeling about the last 26.2 miles of the Ironman? A mix of "terrified" and "confident".

My regime can't change - I can't train to run.. at least not in the same way that a "normal" marathon runner might train. I just have to trust that, from a cardiovascular perspective, I'm fit enough and rather hope that the rest just comes together!

So - there is another dimension to this blog for you - I might just be one of only a few Ironman contestants out there who won't really have trained for the run bit!

And now - an appeal:

1) If anyone out there can suggest any non-impact tips to train for running, then get over to the "contact me" page that I have added and let me know

2) If you want me to drop you an e-mail every time I update this blog then, again, just drop me a "contact me" message, and I'll do that!

See you all again soon!

Blue Lines, White Lines and Tan Lines – September 3rd, 2013

A pretty successful few days have passed and I thought I'd pen the next instalment of my blog (do you say "pen" any more - now that, strictly speaking, I'm typing it? - oh well, I'll leave it for now). Last Thursday, I kicked off my swimming training.

You might recall from my earlier blog that I rarely swim more than 400 metres - the distance I tend to do in the sprint triathlons that I take part in - so the Ironman swim of almost 10 times that distance seems like a million miles away. Well... it does and it doesn't really.

Built within me is a confidence that I can't really describe - it may or may not be misplaced, I don't know - but I have an overwhelming sense that I can do this. Time might erode this confidence a little but I'll keep you updated!

Anyway, back to the swim. I have decided to increase my swimming distance by 400 metres each week until I am up to swimming 2km - this will be in a few weeks' time. I will then hold my swim-training at that distance until, realistically, sometime in the new year.

So, last Thursday, I set myself the target of 800 metres and, as I pushed off for the start, I started my stopwatch - I'm pretty anal when it comes to assessing my performance and I need a guide of my progress.

400 metres takes me 10 minutes in a sprint Tri and so, as I got through the 400 metre mark last Thursday, I pushed the "lap" button on my stopwatch (just so that I could work out how long each of the two blocks of 400 metres took me) and swam on into, if you'll excuse the pun, unfamiliar waters.

800 metres came without any drama. My front crawl and breathing technique didn't really miss a beat.

My time for the first 400 metres was 10 minutes, as expected, and for the second 400 was somewhere around 10 minutes 40 seconds.

But that doesn't tell the whole story - the second 400 metres included a prolonged stopped period having to negotiate a couple of other people standing in the lane (long story). My genuine feeling was that my two 400 metre blocks were completed at almost identical pace and, at that rate, I'm covering the Ironman distance in sub 1hr 40 which, in all fairness, I'll be happy with - and this doesn't take into account natural improvements in my swimming strength/speed that should occur over the next year, I would imagine.

So far so good then - In a heartbeat, I have doubled my normal distance and didn't start to slow. I certainly didn't feel any different at the end of 800 metres to how I feel after 400 metres. Later this week, I'll do 1,200 and we'll see how my consistency looks then.

My swim did throw up an interest question, though.

I spent 20 minutes staring at the blue line along the bottom of the pool, using it as a guide to make sure that I was swimming in a straight line. I am assuming that no-one will paint a blue line at the bottom of the Baltic Sea next year so the one thing I do need to learn is the ability to look forwards to check my direction so, again, if anyone has any tips for that then let me know!!

On to Sunday and I was switching blue lines for white - It was the day of a cyclosportive bike ride - 155km in all although I rode up to the start (around 6 miles away) so as to push my day's mileage through the 100 mark.

I did the ride with a mate, Tom, who, to my knowledge, has never ridden a 100 miles before (or at least, he hasn't for years) and so the target was just to get around and have fun. We did both of those things so mission accomplished

I think I have one word that best describes the route - "hilly" - just over 7,000 feet of climbing. Within that, there were some real "legs almost stalling" sections to really test us but I was pleased with my own ability to drag myself up them, passing others for whom the urge to get off and walk had proven overwhelming.

Tom did great too and, despite suffering from cramp throughout, he pushed through and, I hope, found it enjoyable enough to do again some-time soon.

I promised that I would be honest through this blog and I would be breaking that promise if I didn't go on to say that I was a little disappointed with my average speed around the route. Or at least, I should say, I was disappointed with how the online logging programme that I was using calculated it! (I know, a bad workman blames his tools!).

The app I was using on my phone to record the ride credited me with a 15.5 mph average which, all things considered, I was okay with but then, on uploading exactly that data to my laptop, the chosen site knocked a whole "mph" off of this. I checked the timings and it seems that the online site "thinks" I was "stopped" for less time than I was meaning that my average "moving" speed was skewed lower - I can't quite understand it but, hey ho, it doesn't really matter.

The most reassuring thing for me was that, at the end, I felt fresh and, for as an experiment, I broke into a light jog within a few minutes of getting off the bike, just to see if my legs felt like jelly - they didn't.

They also didn't ache the next morning for my cycle to work, my cycle to a leisure centre where I teach Spinning after work, the Spinning session itself and then my subsequent cycle home.

And, as I write this, they're still not aching... so DOMS has been avoided which, again, I'm pleased with although, I should add, I didn't expect anything else.

In fact, the only negative to have come from the week is that, despite spending much of the summer battling the cycling tan lines that come from having clothes which grip your biceps/thighs like an elastic band, the beautiful sunny conditions for Sunday's ride mean that, yet again, I look like I'm wearing a white T-shirt and shorts even if I'm not wearing anything at all.

I'll leave you with that rather unsavoury thought and the confirmation that, all in all, nothing that has happened this week has shaken my confidence. Onwards and upwards!

It's like being in a nightclub in here!!! — September 6th, 2013

My Ironman Triathlon adventure continues and this week has been no less successful than last week.

Wednesday night was ride night and so I, and a group of local cyclists, took to the roads. The nights are drawing in a bit now and by the end we just looked like a group of flashing lights... so much so that I think we can thank our lucky stars that a plane didn't land on us.

We embarked on a fairly flat and "brisk" ride.

The ride, at an 18.5mph average speed, was especially pleasing as I can really say that I didn't feel my legs had that performance in them.

I know that I said in my earlier blog that the 100 miler hadn't tired me (and I wasn't lying) but, at the same time, I just guessed that the combination of that ride and my subsequent cycle commutes to work, might leave me a little slower. But, that fear proved to be unfounded.

It was starting to become clear that, with the nights drawing in, some of the cycling group were planning a winter break from our evening rides and, truly, I am enjoying cycling (the proper, outdoor kind) so much that I just don't want to have a nature enforced break.

It was a nice relief, then, when a few of the group showed themselves to be as mad as I am by saying that they are happy to ride in the dark through the winter... phew - I'll have company!

Last night (Thursday) was swim night and, as you may recall from my earlier blog, my target was to add another 400 metres to my swim distance. To remind you: Before I committed to this Ironman Tri, I rarely (read - never) swam more than 400 metres in one go (the distance required of me in the Sprint Triathlons that I take part in) so I recognise the need to step this up pretty damn quickly if I am going to get 'round almost 10 times that distance in Sweden next year.

I doubled that distance last week without drama and last night I was targeting 1,200 metres. When I say "targeting", I am not really referring to simply swimming 48 lengths of our local pool in any way that I can... I mean swimming it in full front crawl with no stopping or breathers. This probably sounds like small-fry to some of the people reading this blog but the thing that few people realise is that, at the beginning of this year, I was over the moon if I could keep up front crawl for only 25 metres.

I remember flashing my wife a huge smile at just having managed two lengths of the pool in front crawl mode without stopping... That was only around 9 months ago. I used to pootle up and down the pool in "head-up" breast-stroke mode for all of my Triathlons - I really didn't like swimming!

And then, like someone flicking a light switch, my biggest obstacle, breathing, was gone and suddenly I could just.. well... do it. I had had swimming lessons a couple of years ago which Lisa, my wife, had given me as a birthday present but the tips I picked up in those lessons remained locked away until almost 18 months later. They showed their faces eventually, I suppose!

Now, I'm not saying I'm Michael Phelps all of a sudden - a 10 minute time to swim 400 metres is enough to tell you that. Compared with some, I swim about as well as a rock but I'm at least a rock that can go forwards now!

So, last night, I pushed off the side with 1,200 metres in my sights. I wasn't in the best frame of mind (long story but it would end up with me looking like a right grumpy git so I'll exercise my option to leave it out!) and I can't really say that I was feeling confident.

That said, within a few lengths, I was enjoying myself.

As before, I'd started my stopwatch with the intention of timing each section of 400 metres just to see if my pace dropped off at all.

The first 400 metres went well (on this note, my next 400 metre Triathlon swim should be a breeze, it hardly feels like I have started at this distance now). My second 400 metres went just as well.

My third 400 metres was marginally less successful - I started to feel a bit panicky that the pool was closing within a few minutes and that I needed to press on quickly - this, in turn, disrupted my technique for a length or so but, crucially, I managed to psychologically get myself back into order and recover my swimming - that, in itself, was a huge win for me.

I touched the end of the pool at 1,200 metres and stopped my watch at the same time - 30 minutes, 31 seconds. Each of the first two lots of 400 metres were 10 minutes or so with the last lot being only marginally slower - thanks, I assume, down to my "wobble". I am over the moon with that and, next week, I'll go for 1,600 metres and see what happens!

I do have another question, though. As I got out of the pool, I did quite quickly get a bit of a headache. Now, in my "laymans terms" head, I have put this down to one of the following

1. I hadn't eaten enough before starting

2. I wasn't breathing properly and need to improve the technique

3. (This one is going to sound a bit odd) - When I am breathing out, the "noise" of thé bubbles is, well, loud! I'd get a headache if I stood next to a speaker at a night-club (which I've not done for a lot of years!!) so is this any different?

Has anyone out there suffered from the same and, if so, what would you suggest?

Anyway, I think I'll finish off by throwing in a few photos of me at recent events that I have taken part in!

Stay tuned for more!

I can see clearly now the rain is here... – September 12th, 2013

Another few days have gone by and some stellar training too so it must be time for an update.

Last night was wet. Last night was cold. Last night was windy. Last night was dark. Last night was misty. Last night was Wednesday evening bike ride time with the local cycling group that I ride with.

I actually take some bizarre pleasure from riding in dubious conditions - there is something about that self-righteous feeling that you get as you are battling the elements that makes it all worthwhile... that sense that you are out there whilst others have wimped out and are sitting in front of the television.

Well, by that logic, last night I was simply oozing "self-righteous" and we covered 25 miles in a little under 1 hour and 40 minutes!!!

Now, let's get some facts behind those stats.

The visibility, in places, was so poor that, actually, riding any faster than 15mph even going down a steep hill, was scary to say the least - my light's beam was bouncing back off of the fog in the same way that a car headlight does, making it even more difficult to see where I was going - on otherwise pitch black country roads, that is tough going. Every now and then, I managed to see a blinking red light of a mate up ahead or a faint white light of a mate behind but, for the main part in those foggy sections, I might just as well have been alone even though I was no more than metres away from four other people.

Add to this the fact that the chap who "de-facto leads" the group is a mad-man (sorry Spencer, but you are!) who aims at the steepest hills in the area (and we have a few of them in North Somerset) rather than riding around them and, all in all, you have a tough ride.

The group are a great bunch though and it's great to ride with them - I would have gone out alone but having company (when you can see it, at least) is great for pushing you on as well isn't it.

Did I enjoy it? Oh yes - it was great! I got back home and had to peel my cycling gear off. Furthermore, I expect that my bike will need some TLC before I get on it again (I ride a different bike to work) but, you know, aren't these just the battle scars of a war being won?

Without wanting to sound too soppy or, for that matter, mental, there is a clarity of mind that comes from being out on the bike in poor weather which, bizarrely, I don't really get in the nice weather. Sure, riding in the sun is lovely and, as a rule, preferable - I found myself saying, the other day, of cycling, that "It is fast enough to get you places but slow enough to take in the view".

This is true and a beautiful sunny day is great... but the bad weather gives you a heightened sense of isolation - you can almost hear your own heart beating and lungs heaving - very therapeutic stuff.

On to today and I have decided to switch my weekly swimming sessions to Thursday mornings. On a Thursday, the best day of the week for me to swim, the pool is only open in the evenings for the general public between 9 and 10. As I step up my swimming distances, this simply won't be a long enough period of time for me and you may even recall from before that the sense of feeling rushed somewhat put me off my swim last week.

So, a switch to Thursday mornings was on the cards and I turned up at the pool at 7 this morning (I should say that Lisa, my VERY understanding wife, does put up with a lot doesn't she? Out until goodness knows when last night and then up within a few hours to desert her and the boys once again - thank you Lisa, I really appreciate it).

The issues that I really wanted to overcome with today's swim, as well as the simple process of stepping my distance up by yet another 400 metres (to 1,600), were:

1. The boredom that comes with more distance

2. The difficulty in counting my lengths. This really isn't as easy to me as I guess it should be. I seem to lose count very easily and have to focus to make sure I don't get it wrong

3. You may recall from an earlier update that I suffered something of a headache after my 1,200 metres so part of me wondered if, by swimming on a further 400, my headache would be proportionately worse on getting out of the pool

To conquer the boredom, I gave myself little projects to think about as I swam... that seemed to work.

To conquer the counting issue, I purchased a little counting device that fits on my finger which I can click with my thumb at the end of each lap... that didn't work.

As early as two laps in, I couldn't remember whether I had clicked the button or not!

Honestly, I felt ridiculous! Still, I will perservere with that as I think, in principle, it seems like a good idea. For this morning, I just had to return to the bog standard "count in your head" method which I seem to find tough!

To conquer the headache, I wasn't sure what to do.

Some of you lovely readers gave me great ideas as to WHY my last swim had left me with a headache.

They ranged from "inadequate pre-swim nutrition" to "breathing technique" and, interestingly, the "idea that if I go from horizontaly swimming to vertically getting dressed, this may throw out my inner ear a bit". There wasn't much I could do about that last suggestion so I focused on eating before the swim and then really making sure that I was breathing properly during it (that was one of the projects that I gave myself to think about to conquer boredom - you see, I can multitask!!!).

It worked. I did my 1,600 metres, a mile as good as makes no difference, and there was no hint of the headache that had taken the edge off of last week's swim a bit.

Now to my time. People who have followed this blog since day one will have read that, previously, a 400 metre sprint Triathlon distance was as far as I would EVER swim and I have worked really hard to get it down to a few seconds under 10 minutes (that made for some odd looks from fellow swimmers as I got into the pool and then, ten minutes later, got straight back out).

Regular readers will also know that, even in January of this year, swimming two lengths of full front crawl before reverting to "head up" breast-stroke, was deemed a "win" and now, here I am, doing nothing but full front crawl!

Whilst out riding last night, I mentioned to one of the group that I was stepping my distances up by 400 metres each week and that "tomorrow" was when I hit the mile mark. He asked me to estimate how long that would take and I responded with 40 minutes.

I was way out... let me tell you. I should be ashamed of my poor estimation skills.

It actually took me 40 minutes and 4 seconds - you know, 4 whole seconds different to my guess!!

In all seriousness, I was REALLY pleased. Each block of 400 metres was, with the exception of the first where I was 15 seconds or so faster, completed within 5 seconds of each other so, thus far, my swimming pace, whilst hardly blistering, is metronomically consistent. I am still on for the sub 1hr 40 swim come the day of the Ironman which is what I am aiming for.

This week hasn't all been good though. I have also purchased some aqua-jogging shoes on the advice of some very kind helpers - the theory being that I can train for the running bit of the Ironman in the water and achieve my goal of avoiding impact on my hip at all costs.

I did take them with me into the pool. I even put them on at the end of the swim AND got back into the pool. But then a whole sense of self-consciousness swept over me and I just couldn't bring myself to run up and down the lanes with the swimmers. It sounds ridiculous even writing that... no-one would have taken any notice, I know, but there you go. MUST... TRY (or should that be "Tri")... HARDER.

A bit of a mish-mash – September 15th, 2013

A bit of a mish-mash blog today, really, as there were a few things I wanted to put in here and I just didn't want to stagger them over a few different blogs.

I had a bit of a realisation yesterday whilst talking to a mate - that is to say that what he said made me see this Ironman in a slighlty different and, dare I say, more exciting and challenging way. You see, some of this underlying confidence that I have had about the Ironman has been down to basic maths. The speed I reckon I could cycle at, with improvement that should come between now and then, and the speed I "reckon" I can end up swimming at would be giving me somewhere around 7.5 hours to complete the 26.2 mile run before the cut-off renders me a non-finisher!

For those not entirely familiar with Ironman (and I count myself in this bracket), I understand that, to be qualifed as a finisher, you need to complete the challenge in 17 hours or less. Now, with 7.5 hours to complete a Marathon, I'd like to think that I could pretty much walk it (briskly) and still be classified as a finisher thus removing any worries that I might have regarding running on my hip. (If you are new to this blog, you can get a feel for this concern in the preface section).

Would I be elated if I crossed the line, even if the clock read 16 hours, 59 minutes and 59 seconds? Oh yes... absolutely. Would I be "more" pleased if I completed it any quicker? Err... probably not... or so I thought, before a chat that I had with my mate.

I pretty much said all of the above to him and he reminded me (as if it were needed) just how competitive I was and suggested that my Ironman "competition" was going to end as I get off the bike.

By this, he meant that I "must surely be setting myself a target time for the swim and the bike and then, yes, if the run takes the remainder of the 17 hours then that is fine" - you know what? He was right.

I can still turn this into a competition but one in which I only stand to "compete" in the swim and bike!! It seems so obvious and you are probably sat there reading this wondering why it has only just occured to me when it was a "given" to you and everyone else.

So - my target time for the swim remains at 1hr 40 mins (a time I know I have already talked about on these pages).

I have never really thought about a target time for the bike bit but I'm going to set an initial target of 7hrs 30 mins. That is, basically, a 15 mph average which, all things being equal, I would be happy enough with if I set off on a similarly long ride right now so, after a 2.4mile swim, I think that this target is sufficiently stretching so as to be worthwhile.

So, combined, that is an elapsed time of 9hr 10 mins.

Now, I have no idea how long the transitions take but I get the feeling that they are slower than that of a Sprint Triathlon (please, anyone, chip in here with comments) so let's say that I will also target a total time elapsed, including transitions, before I set off on the run, of 9 hrs 30 minutes.

There, I have something very tangible to aim for which, aside from the distances and the overall 17 hours, I didn't really have before. That feels good.

These targets, I should add, are flexible (downwards, I should hope) because I don't want to start the event either knowing that the targets are easily achievable or that they are so far outside of my capabilities that I have no hope of hitting them. Either way, they are a start and already add a different dimension to my challenge.

I've spent longer on that subject than I thought so I will just briefly mentioned something else that I wanted to get down here.

I have had a bit of an enforced two day rest period where I have literally done no training at all - not even as much as my normal commute to work.

"Enforced" because, on Friday, I had the fortune to go to the Goodwood Revival event.

Motorsport is my other love so this was certainly no hardship!

Yesterday, I simply had too much on to train - My wife runs a local village market for my oldest son's school and I sell ham... add to that an afternoon out with the boys and yesterday was busy enough without me trying to squeeze in a session.

The break, actually, was lovely... and helpful too: I had a tiny twinge in my thigh muscle after I wrote my blog on Thursday so I think my body was grateful for the rest and, touch wood, it cleared up as quickly as it appeared.

Back on it today though.. I have a Spinning class to teach!

Until next time!

Every Cloud – September 20th, 2013

Today's blog will have a general theme in keeping with the title "Every cloud" - we all know the end to that saying but is it really true that every cloud does, indeed, have a silver lining?

Well, probably not I suppose - I could think of a few pretty dire situations to which this wouldn't apply but actually, yesterday morning, did seem to support the saying!

I am talking about my Thursday morning swim and, whilst I fully intend to start taking some of your well founded advice to vary my swim sessions (largely to combat the boredom factor), I really wanted to get myself up to regularly swimming the 2,000 metre mark with no stops for breathers.

Regular readers of this blog will know that, until I entered this Ironman, I never swam further than 400 metres and I have only been able to do all of that in full front crawl mode for a matter of months. They will also know that, as soon as I entered this Ironman, I knew I needed to step that up quite quickly so I have been adding 400 metres to my weekly swim every week. Basic maths tells you that, now that I am five weeks into this strategy, yesterday was to be my 2,000 metre attempt.

I got into the pool full of confidence having experienced no real dramas with the weekly 400 metre increase to date. Quite the contrary, actually, I have found that each additional 400 metres has been barely any different to the last and my pace for each 400 metre section (I time them all separately, such is my anal approach to this stuff) has been pretty metronomic.

Yesterday, however, I swam the first three lengths of my intended eighty and, like a switch, I started to lose concentration. My confidence completely disappeared with my concentration and, for the next half a dozen lengths, I was having to fight the urge to give up. My breathing was eratic and stroke was all over the place. (That, for clarity, is the "cloud")

I am really not sure why it all started to go so horribly wrong but I suspect that my mind was pre-empting boredom. I knew that I was going to be staring at the bottom of the pool for ages and I think I just got myself all tense about it.

Anyway, here's the silver lining - I dragged myself through the mental issues and pressed on. I consciously told myself to concentrate and to stop being ridiculous. Just as quickly as it started to go wrong, it turned itself around and returned to plain sailing once again. The silver lining, of course, is that I learnt something

31

about my ability to push through the urge to give up and I imagine that that might well come in handy on more than one occasion over the next 11 months leading up to (and during) the Ironman event.

Another interesting point was that I actually felt strongest during the last 400 metres which I felt hugely uplifted by. I almost had to force myself to stop when I reached 2,000 metres. I could have gone on but I have promised myself that I would swim certain distances at certain points and I really want to stick to my plan. I had no aches or pains after the swim either.

My pace was 51 minutes 45 seconds so the almost metronomic 10 minutes (ish) per 400m is maintained despite my "dark 150 metres shortly after the start. I am pretty pleased with that to say the least. Again, if you've read this blog before, I am fully aware that my pace is hardly blistering BUT I don't slow down with distance, and that is my goal at the moment!

On the speed thing, let me reveal something else about me! I think I could be quicker if I only used my legs more efficiently... well, let me be honest.. I know I could be quicker if I used my legs AT ALL.

I have tried kicking sessions but I really go nowhere with just my legs - and I mean nowhere! I think that this will be something to do with trying to kick from the hip (which I am reliably informed is the correct form) with very little by way of hip strength.

My hip-replacement has made it very difficult to build hip muscles - primarily as a result of so many years where they were deteriorating through total lack of use. My surgeon has told me that I won't be able to build these muscles so I think I just have to accept, I reckon, that kicking in the swim is just something that other people will do. (Just to be really explicit, that'll be another one of those pesky clouds).

The silver lining, of course, is that when I get out of the pool, my legs are completely fresh - there isn't even a hint of leg fatigue. This helps me in the Sprint Triathlons that I take part in (next one in just over a week!!) but the benefit I get from this otherwise negative fact will surely be enhanced when I am multiplying the distances up to Ironman magnitude.

Don't get me wrong, I know I won't be the only Triathlete who doesn't go for the full swim kick - I have learnt over the last couple of years (correct me if I'm wrong) that it is a "Triathlete thing" to do - i.e swim with minimal kicking to preserve the legs - but I might just be taking this strategy to the extreme - mine just seem to trail behind me!

So, there you have it - two clouds and two silver linings proving that, at least some of the time, bad things can give rise to good results.

In other news, I managed to get another bike ride in on Wednesday night - thanks to, as always, Lisa, my understanding wife!

It was a fairly steady affair in terms of pace - with plenty of slower, sociable style, riding but, at the same time, we dragged ourselves up a good few climbs in the twenty odd miles that we did. The views were lovely looking out over the lights of the City of Bristol and the training was very welcome indeed!

Lessons learned – September 26, 2013

I was watching the highlights of the Ironman in Wales a week or so ago (I had recorded them and it took me a wee while to get around to watching them!).

To generate more of a "story", they followed the fortunes of one particular contender.

I forget his name and, as at this very moment, I am nowhere near my Sky+ box / Television so going back over the recording to find out is not really an option.

Besides, it is irrelevant!

This chap was a favourite to win from the start. I guess he must have been to have had television crews following him around before the event. As a viewer, we were treated, in the build up section of the programme, to an insight into his training regime and there were plenty of emotionally charged images of him walking along deserted beaches and riding alone in the middle of nowhere.

It was amazing to see what these "elites" put themselves through.

This chap was on top of his game. His fitness level was supreme and he was going to win. He was a very impressive individual.

Somewhere during the event itself things started to go wrong for the guy and, during the run section, he slowed to, well, my kind of pace (which is clearly unacceptable!) and stopped.

He pulled out of the event that he had hoped to win and I'm not sure whether the pain on his face was down to physical pain or disappointment - a bit of both, of course.

I took quite a lot from watching this.

The first thing I took from it was that things can go wrong. I guess I hadn't considered this prospect in respect of my own Ironman next year.

What if I had a whole series of mechanical problems on my bike (it happened to me on a short ride the other day so there must be a chance it could happen in the space of 112 miles!)? What if I suffer from something that slows my "run" pace to "even slower than my normal walking pace"?

I have had this confidence (and target) that if I can complete the swim in a certain time and the bike in another particular time then I will have enough scope to even walk the marathon and still get done within the 17 hours maximum.

This confidence has led me to REALLY not worry about the marathon bit (first time visitors to this blog might not realise that I really shouldn't be looking to "run" all the way in the marathon section - see previous blogs or the "preface" section).

But, what if things went so horribly wrong that I got off the bike with only five of the allowed 17 hours to go? I'd have to run just to be classified as a finisher!

So many permutations and very little that I can do about most of them.

There is, however, one thing I can do. I can get myself as ready as is realistically possible for all three disciplines so that any unexpected time spent in one of them can be made up in the others.

This will certainly mean that I need to train more for the run section that I might previously have intended... something I know that Lisa, my wife, will be happy about - she was the happy to voice her concern at my "I won't bother to train for the run bit" strategy. Now, where did I put those aqua-joggers (a previous attempt at aqua-jogging failed for vanity reasons and, for the same reason, I haven't tried since).

What else did watching this chap's misfortune in Ironman Wales teach me?

It taught me that everyone can be a winner just by crossing the line. Every single person who got to the end that day beat this elite athlete.

Every person who was overcoming their own challenges was listed above him on the finishers list.

That is not meant to single this guy out as some kind of loser.

Goodness, even with his issue he could still have finished the Ironman in a time that I couldn't even dream of, I know that - he chose to stop because, for him, it was win or nothing. As soon as he knew a win wasn't on the cards, there was little point and he only risked compounding an injury which would have cost him, perhaps, more than that one event.

The act of finishing itself isn't a big deal to him.

I know all of that but I still couldn't help seeing his misfortune as a reminder that, just by getting to the end, your achievement is immense and I for one can't wait to experience what that must feel like.

A triathlon, ahem, debrief – September 30th, 2013

I took part in my last Triathlon of 2013 yesterday so, given the nature of this blog, if that isn't a good reason to sit down and type, I don't know what is!

For me, the day started at 2am. I had meant it to start at 5am but, sadly, a nasty cough had other ideas and waking in the wee-small hours with little prospect of getting back to sleep meant that I was up just a few hours after I went to bed. It wasn't the best start to the day, I'll give you that.

So, I had four and a half hours to kill before I needed to set off to Tockington, North Bristol, where I was due to start my Triathlon at 8:15am. It was a sprint triathlon with distances as follows - a 400 metre swim / a 20km bike ride / a 5km run.

Despite the massive amount of time I had to get ready (and the fact that I had packed my box for transition with everything I was going to need the night before), I still managed to nearly forget something. Not just anything, either. I actually got into the car and was about to drive off before I remembered that I hadn't put the bike on the roof!

Anyway, I turned up at Tockington with plenty of time in hand. I felt relaxed and supremely confident. I was aiming for a time of sub-1hr 25 and I knew what times I needed to put in for each section to get it.

The swim was a pool swim, in waves, and then what followed gave this blog it's title (admit it, you just scrolled back to the top with your eyes to check the title, didn't you?!).

I was milling around the transition area just doing those last minute checks when the first wave of swimmers, having finished their swim, came running in to collect their bikes. Two of them, in fairly close proximity to me, had clearly never heard of two things: Triathlon clothing and the no nudity rule!

These people didn't seem to be "together" but both of them (1 male, 1 female) proceeded to strip off... Out of their swimming costume... Completely naked... before donning cycling gear for the ride.

The chap even treated us to the full towel dance! It was as if he'd just got out of the shower. Quite aside from the spectacle of it all, his "transition one" time must have been horrendously slow - he took as much time as you might if you were getting ready for work in the morning!

Anyway, moving on... I arrived at poolside with a couple of minutes to spare. I looked at the water which, with my increased swimming training that you will have been following through this blog, no doubt, now looks like a second home to me. I was just so confident. I've been swimming 2,000 metres in full front crawl with no problems at all. 400 metres was going to be an absolute breeze.

I jumped in with three other people in my allocated lane and I was due to be the second of the four to start. The whistle went for the first chap who promptly pushed off and then, rather sooner than I had expected, it went again to signal my start.

I quickly fumbled my stopwatch to start timing and pushed off. Within about 15 metres, I was staring at the chap in front's legs and I tapped him on the heel to signal that I wanted to go past. Etiquette, for those who don't know, is that the chap would reach the end of the length and let me through at the turn-around point.

I then had a flashback to when I had done that in a previous Tri only to find that the chap who was in front on that occasion had sped up over the course of the swim and I had ended up breaking my own rhythm just to let him back past me. With this in mind at the end of the length, then, whilst I was correctly gestured through, I think I confused him by signalling for him to carry on ahead of me.

He didn't speed up and I had the choice of either another length behind him, out of rhythm, or I could try to overtake in the narrow lane where I risked a head on collision with people coming the other way.

I went for the overtake and promptly took in a mouthful of water, from a "wave" being thrown out by the adjacent lane's swimmers, and had to duck back in behind him. Such was his pace that I had to flick to breast-stroke for the remainder of the length. I was broken. My swim suddenly turned into a disaster just 1.5 lengths in!

I sat behind him for another 8 or 9 lengths doing a combination of front crawl / breast stroke depending on whether I was catching him or needing to slow down so as not to hit him. I suddenly lacked the confidence in myself to tap him on the heel even though I knew he would let me through - all I was thinking was that, if he did let me through, I could very well end up holding HIM up so what was the point?

Somewhere around length nine, I did pluck up the courage to tap his heel and he did allow me through at the turnaround. I thought that that was my chance to get my rhythm back and to front crawl the rest of the way. But no. My front crawl deserted me and I'm not sure I even managed 1 full length of it. I hauled my very,

VERY, disappointed body out of the pool at the end of the swim, glanced at my watch as I crossed the transition line just outside the pool and my head hung very heavy at the sight of the time - 10:44 including the short run to transition. I hadn't swam that slowly for ages and I was gutted.

One thing that I am good at, though, is the act of moving on from failure and move on I did.

As I was preparing for the bike, I let my mind consider what I needed to do to get back on track for my sub-1hr 25 target. I had cautiously banked on 10 minutes for the swim (half expecting a 9:30 result) so, in the grand scheme of things, the extra 44 seconds was hardly a disaster and I had targeted a 17mph average on the bike. Ok, so now I would target 17.5 mph average and, rather than just "make up" the 44 seconds, actually get AHEAD of my original target. That would make me feel better.

I set off on the bike at a great pace... Quickly getting up to almost 30mph down a very gradual descent away from the pool and out on to the country roads of the route itself.

I overtook a few competitors on the subsequent climb which was long (ish) and grinding... Not steep, just a bit sapping.

Then followed a left turn along a main A-road at the top and I was into a headwind. Wow! This just wasn't looking like it was going to be my day as a headwind is the one thing I hate more than any other condition I could face!

My pace into the wind was barely 16 or so miles per hour... Some way short of the target average and it felt like I was pushing through treacle. I was getting into full tuck on the Tri-bars but, as streamlined as I might have been, the brick wall of wind was making it tough going.

Another left turn and things started to look up... I was now going to have the wind behind me for a stint! I made the most of it despite the fact that I think the wind chose just that moment to abate (thanks, Mother Nature, for that, by the way!) and I promptly got myself up to the mid 20s in terms of miles per hour on the long, broadly flat, section that followed.

I was surprised when one chap, whom I recognised from his Triathlon gear as being a member of the same Tri club (BADTri) as me, overtook me at this point. I'd overtaken him up the hill shortly after the start and he had obviously stuck with me through the wind.

Either way, I was motoring and another left turn dropping us back down towards the end of lap one of this two lap course, sent us down quite a short and steep hill (basically to lose the height that we'd gained in the climb at the start).

As I got to the end of the lap I glanced down at my average speed up to that point - 17.5mph.. I was on target and the disastrous swim was a dim and distant memory. I actually smiled "out loud", if that makes sense, and pushed on with legs feeling good!

Again I caught and passed the BADTri chap on the drag up hill at the start of the lap but this time I was determined to keep him behind me.

I pushed with everything I had into the wind that had mysteriously sprung up again just in time for me to take it on (thanks, again, Mother Nature, you really know how to treat me!) and, in predictable fashion, I sensed an easing of the wind when I took that turn left out of it for the second and final time.

I was pointing back towards the finish and I was conscious that this was where my BADTri companion had caught and passed me on the previous lap. I pushed as hard as I thought I could get away with, to prevent him doing it again, and pulled into the dismount area in transition with him being a little way behind. My average speed? Bang on 17.5 mph. He graciously complemented me on the ride much later after we'd both finished the event.

My cumulative time, as I exited transition to start the run clock going, was somewhere around 54 minutes so I had 31 minutes to run 5k.

In the Westonbirt Triathlon a few weeks ago, I had done the 5k in 28 minutes so nothing short of another disaster was going to stop me hitting my target now, surely?

Before the run, I had consciously told myself that I wasn't going to run "heavy footed" like I think I did in Westonbirt and that, instead, I was going to focus on the "bounce".

I'm not sure what it must have looked like to an onlooker but I tried to run as if my feet were attached to springs and, as I ran, aware, roughly, as to how far I had left to go, I realised that I was setting a good pace (good for me, that is!).

I turned into the home straight and somewhere up ahead I saw a lady who I had chatted with before the start. She was doing her first Tri and had been in the first wave of swimmers.

I could see that I was catching her and to give myself that extra push for the line, I targeted getting to the finish ahead of her. It worked. I did.

My run time for the 5k of 23 mins 40 seconds was something of a surprise, even to me, given the fact that, as regular readers of this blog will know, I really don't EVER run unless it's part of a triathlon (for very good reason, mind - not just because I can't be bothered - see the preface section!)

My overall time was 1 hour 18 minutes and 24 seconds. This is nearly ten minutes quicker than my time at this same Triathlon last year and comfortably ahead of my target time.

Goodness, it's nearly 30 minutes faster than my very first triathlon which I did at this same event in 2009 (although it's not technically like for like since that had a longer 25km bike ride)

Am I happy? I'd be lying if my answer included the word "completely".

I'm ecstatic at the overall result. I'm "pleased", but no more than "pleased", with the bike and I'm over the moon at how the run went (incidentally, I am writing this the morning after the Tri and, unlike after Westonbirt Tri, my legs have no sense of soreness at all - I am putting this down to the deliberately more bouncy running style I tried but I guess I stand to be corrected by you running types out there!).

I am, however, gutted about the swim though and I want to tell myself that it was because the chap in front broke my rhythm and that that had destroyed my confidence etc. The truth is though, that I'd be lying; Firstly, I am not SURE that the chap in front of me is what broke my rhythm as I couldn't get it back when I had a clear lane in front of me and, secondly, I really must get used to my rhythm being interrupted as I'm quite sure that the Ironman swim will be ten times worse.

I would also like to blame the cough and general "less than 100% health" feeling that had got me out of bed at 2am but, again, I think this would be an easy excuse and wholly inaccurate as I would then need to do some more thinking as to how on earth I had managed a good ride and strong run despite this lack of full health.

No, the reality is that, for my swim at least, there is quite a bit of work to do yet.

I'm not going to end this blog there though, as to do so would be ending on a negative even though my mindset is VERY MUCH POSITIVE.

Did I enjoy the day? - yep... and that is surely the main thing! I truly love the feel of a Triathlon - the competition against yourself and others - the thrill of having to attack three different disciplines in quick succession. The changes in mindset as you push yourself through countless subtle (or not so subtle) challenges and the sense of achievement as you cross the line.

I can actually take something positive from the swim too. Last year, the same swim distance in the same pool at the same event took me 12 mins 56 seconds and I remember being genuinely over the moon to get under 13 minutes. It's a stark reminder to me how far I have come that 10 minutes 44 is deemed a total disaster. Put in this context, I really have to say that this Triathlon has been immensely positive.

I never would have dreamed five years or so ago when walking (or even lying down) was becoming increasingly difficult to do, and when a wheelchair was being offered as very real option, that I would be able to even start a Triathlon let alone finsih it at the pace I managed yesterday. It really does make me so proud and grateful to everyone who has played such a huge part in making it happen - my wife and boys are at the top of that list, of course.

There is plenty more news, some of it not so positive, sadly, but this has been a long old blog so I'll save the rest for another day.

Health and Fitness. Two words, different meanings – October 2nd, 2013

I knew about the reason for today's blog before I sat down to type the last one but I didn't want to merge the two. I did, however, allude to it at the end of the last so here goes.

I sat down, all full of my own self-importance, at the end of the day on which I had completed the Tockington Sprint Triathlon and was scanning over some old photos with my wife on the iPad, entertaining us both with images of our two boys when they were even younger than they are now and gasping in disbelief at how much they have grown and changed in just two short years, without us noticing.

Then a text message came through.

It stopped me firmly in my tracks.

I was being informed of the sudden death, from what seems to be a stroke, of a fellow cyclist - someone I had rode a fair few times with and someone who I had shared a good many conversations with.

I am not presumptuous enough to count myself as one of his friends, as such, but I was certainly a "cycling buddy" and the news shocked me to the core and I was rather upset, I don't mind admitting.

Here was a man who certainly wasn't old (I suspect we are talking something around the 50 mark). He certainly wasn't slow on a bike either - he could out-drag me up a hill without any difficulty. He came across as a lovely man, plain and simple.

That is all I'm going to say about him personally, lest I offend anyone for making him the topic of a blog in what must be a truly horrendous period for his family. For that same reason, I won't even name him in this public forum but I will say "rest in peace".

What it served to do, though, is remind me of the difference between "fitness" and "health" - Those two words that tend to be used as one, and which are often almost seen to be interchangeable.

False modesty aside, I consider myself to be a "fit" chap.

I realise, because of how I "market" this blog, that the majority of those that read it are probably "fitter" than I am in that they can swim, ride and run faster or for longer than me but, hey, I can hold my own in terms of a random selection of the general population and, as a rule, I "feel" pretty good.

I haven't got to make "old man noises" when I get up from a chair or sit down in one.

I don't know what it is like to get out of breath doing what are really day to day activities of basic living - walking up stairs etc.

I can play with the boys safe in the knowledge that they will not tire me out before they have had enough.

I bounce out of bed before 6am every morning. Granted, I might sometimes fall asleep on the sofa at night meaning that Lisa, my wife, has to turn the volume up on the telly to hear what's going on over my snoring but, if called for, I can even stay awake late into the night without then compromising my liveliness the following day.

Put bluntly, I am genuinely not familiar with the idea of lacking energy. It is just a problem that other people talk about.

And at what some could consider the more extreme end of activity and endurance, I managed a 300k bike ride a couple of months ago and, for goodness sake, I have entered an Ironman... a prospect that, again dropping any sense of false modesty, would indicate a certain confidence in my own fitness.

So - I'm "fit" then.

Am I "healthy"? I certainly HOPE so and, equally, I certainly THINK I am... but being "fit" doesn't automatically mean that I'm "healthy" and these last few days has reminded me of that.

I could have any number of things wrong with me and be completely unaware of them until it's too late, such is the fragility of life.

Don't get me wrong, I'm certainly not about to become all maudlin and I'm not going to turn into a hypochondriac either. I have no intention of becoming, for that matter, a "born-again healthy living preacher" (I think I have too much of a sweet tooth for that!).

At the same time as trying not to become too introspect about this sort of thing, however, I will make a conscious effort not to confuse the "fitness" word with the "health" word quite so often. I was thinking of booking myself in for a health check and one day I might just do that, but in the meantime, taking as much care of my health as I do my fitness will certainly be on the cards.

I'd respectfully suggest that we all do the same. Just think - if everyone who reads this blog does start to focus on their health a bit more, it seems like a numbers game to me that at least one of you will divert yourself away from a potentially serious issue.. quite a sobering thought when you put it like that isn't it?

Eye Watering Indeed – October 7th, 2013

Off of the back of the last two blogs, I thought I'd just return to a more basic training update for today's since last week was a pretty good week for that!

Wednesday night was bike ride night with the local group - those of us, at least, who are prepared to ride in the dark.

I say "ride in the dark"… you have to remember that we are lit to the point that we are not so much at danger of being hit by a passing car as we are of being mistaken for a runway by a plane coming in to land.

The evening bike rides with the group are an excellent reminder to me of how different my "road bike" is to my "work bike", complete with its panniers etc. I should add that my "road bike" is nothing special - I crave a carbon framed beauty but, since my budget forbids it, my aluminium framed entry level steed does the trick.

Wednesdays nights generally mean that I get home from my cycle commute on my "work bike", have dinner, get changed and then effectively get straight back on to my "road bike". It is then that the difference between the two makes itself known!

Before I am even at the end of the road, I notice just how much more responsive my "road bike" is and how much less effort I need to put in just to get it up to speed. I am never sure if the difference is mainly in my head but let's get things straight, wherever the difference is, there is a difference! I might just train on my commuter bike over the winter though - that has to be good training doesn't it?

The group I ride with on a Wednesday is the group that, sadly, is one member down (see my last post) so it was a fairly quiet night with us all in a pensive mood.

There was some consideration to not going out at all, almost in tribute to our lost friend, but I am pretty certain that the ride was a better way to honour his memory than sitting on the sofa.

The ride itself was quite brisk, albeit flat, and I thoroughly enjoyed it.

You know, some nights, when you just feel "strong" - well this was one of those nights for me. That is despite a mechanical issue though with the bike which I noticed for the first time in the triathlon last week - an odd noise when I put the drive-train under any pressure. I need to look at that before my next ride.

For the stat-crazy amongst you, we covered a little under 22 miles in a little over an hour and a quarter.

Thursday morning is swim morning, as regular visitors to this blog will know, and... disaster... I couldn't find my swim-goggles. I feel sure that I had brought them home with me from last week's triathlon but I had to conclude that they were lost in action by the pool. So I cycled away from my home at 6:30am, "goggleless", hoping that the swimming pool would have some decent quality goggles that I could buy. I am a bit of a wuss when it comes to swimming without goggles I'm afraid.

Goggles, therefore, were my first thought on arrival and was told that the only pair they sold were £4.50. I'm not normally one to judge things by their cost but I figured that, being less than 1/5th of the price of the pair that I've lost, they were unlikely to be top quality!

And so it was, then, I got into the pool feeling a bit negative - not the very best start, sure, but I was there and I needed to get my swim in - if nothing else, I wanted my swim confidence back having had the dreadful swim in the triathlon last weekend. I adjusted the new goggles, started my stop-watch and pushed off.

Within just a couple of metres, they were FULL of water. Cue me stopping, turning around, resetting my stopwatch, adjusting the goggles and pushing off again.

Within just a couple of metres, they were FULL of water. Cue me stopping, turning around, resetting my stopwatch, adjusting the goggles and pushing off again.

I said that bit twice, I know.

It happened twice.

I looked around and the lifeguard chap clearly thought I was trying out a strange training technique.

Suddenly I realised that these goggles weren't even worth the £4.50 that I'd paid for them. By now I was grumpy AND lacking confidence - remember that the triathlon at the weekend had gone disastrously and had severely shaken my swimming confidence. This additional setback really wasn't helping. Already, I could feel myself wanting to get out of the pool and just call it a bad morning. I gave myself a mental talking to and resolved to make the best of a bad job.

I worked out that the only way that these goggles would create a seal around my eyes would be if the annoying bit of plastic joining one eye-piece to the other was pressing into my nose to the point that I was in a degree of pain - needs must though and, hey, it's all character building.

At the third time of asking, I pushed off the side and everything seemed fine.

I'm still not the proud owner of anything technologically advanced enough to count my laps for me so manual counting it was. I devised a maths game to help the counting (it's too convoluted and probably too useless to anyone else to share here so I won't bore you with it!) and took my mind off of the goggle pain through a combination of this odd counting method and a concentrating on my front-crawl "form".

The first 400 metres were actually not that great.. about 20 seconds or so slower than I seem to be able to manage as a rule. This, though, was a legacy of the pain my nose was experiencing and, I reckon, the generally lower confidence levels I had after last weekend's triathlon.

The more I swam, though, the more confident I grew and the more used to the pain in my nose I became... although it started to become more difficult as the pain extended to my whole eye area (it actually carried on hurting for most of the day, long after I took the things off!!)

800 metres came and went without drama, as did 1,600 metres. 2,000 metres (the distance I promised myself I would "stop" at - i.e I would build up to swimming that distance regularly but that I would not go beyond it until the start of the new year) also came and went. I was feeling stronger and stronger as the time passed and I pushed on to 2,500 metres.

Pushing the "lap" button on my stopwatch at the end of each 400 metre stint enabled me to see, after the swim, that my pace for each 400 metre tranche was as metronomic as ever and the complete lack of tiredness gave me confidence that I was only stopping because I was running out of time before work.

I covered the 2,500 metres in 1 hour and 3 minutes and extrapolating this out, this means that I am swimming at a 1 hour 38 minute pace for the Ironman Distance. I am targeting 1 hour 40 minutes so I am, once again, back to brimming with confidence.

This is my normal state and I am more comfortable here!

Sure, I know that the Ironman will be colder - I know it will be choppier - I know it will be more intimidating. At the same time, I know that I'll be more buoyant in a wetsuit - I know that I'll be 10 months further down the line with my training - I know that adrenaline will speed me up.

What with the daily "short burst" rides to work, the three Spinning sessions I instructed (in which I genuinely do push myself) and the resistance gym sessions that I do, last week was a good training week. I am craving a long-distance bike ride though - it's over a month since the last one I did of any "real" distance and that was the 100 mile sportive at the beginning of September.

That last statement is a funny one when taken in context of something I found yesterday. I was doing a general tidy up and came across a list of "written goals" that I had set myself for 2011. Cycling wasn't something that I did then anyway near as much as I do now, clearly, and I was targeting an average of a 12 mile bike ride per week. I seem to remember that seeming like it was going to be a challenge. If I'd told myself then that I would get to the point where I could get past the 100 mile mark (and all the way on to 190 miles) in a single ride, I think I would have laughed.

I'm in danger of going into a whole new blog there about recognising how far you've come, so I will stop and leave that topic for another time!

Procrastinate? Maybe tomorrow... – October 9th, 2013

I read a tweet the other day - I can't recall who it was that tweeted it but, even if I could, I probably wouldn't name the author here anyway just in case they were just having a bad day.

The tweet alluded to the individual in question's tendency to procrastinate about exercise.

I should clarify that the author of the comment is a fitness fanatic, a self confessed triathlon junkie and, from what I have seen, trains as often as I do... and yet, here they were, revealing their natural propensity to procrastinate about exercising in preference to relaxing at home in front of the television.

It got me thinking. Do I do that?

My conclusion was that I don't procrastinate enough...

I just love, for instance, getting out on my bike. I feel energised just walking into a gym and, despite some inherent lack of ability, plunging into a swimming pool ready to start a swim is exciting to me. Put bluntly, I would feel positively grumpy if I didn't get my fix of these things (and I do get grumpy - Lisa, my wife, will tell you that!).

Some of you may think that that makes me sound a bit like a drug addict and, in a sense, I guess I am.

Let me allow a bit more of my own story to unfold now.

The preface to this blog gives you the headline stuff, my "main story" if you like, so take a look there too but a sub-story of mine was that, at around the time I got together with Lisa, I was on the verge of giving up my motorsport and, let's be sensitive about this, I was letting my physical fitness go.

Okay, let's be a little less sensitive, there was a fair bit more of me than there is now... see next picture!

That photo was taken when I was some three stone heavier than I am now, just before I embarked on a fitness regime.

Roughly six months after that shot was taken, this photo was taken of me on holiday:

That was 2004 and, obviously, I would consider myself to have been on an upward fitness curve ever since (wow, that is nearly TEN years!!! - where has that time gone?).

Those two pictures happened to be taken right in the middle of the period during which my hip was deteriorating too but, despite this, I certainly didn't procrastinate about getting fit then. With or without the limits that my hip was imposing on me, I was determined to be as fit as I could get!

I remember completely changing the way I was eating and embarking on my new regime at the same time.

I, complete with my rapidly deteriorating hip, started to go to the gym twice a week. A combination of weights and cardio - I had to choose my cardio machines carefully around motions that my hip would actually perform... that was a challenge in itself.

I then stepped it up to three times per week... then four times.. then five times every week. Each day was varied enough to rest one area of my body while I worked the rest.

I was working hard enough to see and, more importantly, FEEL results and that drove me on to keep doing what I was doing.

Within quite a short space of time, getting and keeping fit became a way of life and, if anything, I would have to procrastinate about relaxing - "Nah, I'll have a rest day tomorrow!"

Even in my darkest days, when my hip had deteriorated to the point that I was in pain just lying down, I still WANTED to carry on. Granted, part of my logic was that it was helping to maintain whatever supporting muscles I had around my hip joint and, therefore, easing the condition from which I was suffering, but, really, I wasn't doing it for that - I was getting fit because I loved it. Again, procrastination simply didn't come into it!

As I said earlier in this blog, I still absolutely love it and to procrastinate about it would be cutting my nose off to spite my face - it just doesn't come into the equation.

Back to our "procrastinor" then, their revelation might even have made me respect them more, now I know that this is how they feel. That they keep pushing themselves through their physical limits despite wanting to put it off is pretty remarkable and not something I think I could do - It takes nothing like that amount of commitment from me to get out of my chair!

People often refer to be as dedicated and disciplined with my training and I tend to reply that it would take more discipline and dedication for me NOT to train on my rest days than it does for me to get out there and get sweaty!

Me? Procrastinate about exercise? I'll think about it tomorrow.

On days like these. – October 12th, 2013

Another week has passed and, again, this will be another training update.

Today's will be interspersed with some learning points though.

Wednesday night, as always, was bike night and I set off on my merry way at around 6:45pm, meeting up with one of our group within a few minutes and the rest around 10 minutes or so later.

It is great, really, that there remains a small, select, group of us that will persist on our bikes in the evening despite the fact that we are now at the stage where we are "lights on" from the very start. Those halcyon summer days where the sun remained high until long after the ride was over and we were all eating our recovery food (biscuits), have gone!

Last night was colder too, and there was talk of rain and wind, but, despite this, a new member to the group chose now as his time to start. He certainly had my admiration for this from the moment he arrived. It's one thing continuing a habit in all conditions but starting it against such a backdrop takes that bit extra doesn't it?

It was a nice ride, too - again, another night, like last week, where I was feeling strong. I shall have to stop saying that soon as it feels like I'm saying it every week - maybe I'm just getting stronger!

On that note, I had a fun moment earlier in the week whilst on my commuter bike - complete with weighty panniers - as I drifted past a huffing and puffing "all the gear" cyclist on his beautiful carbon machine going up a hill in Bristol. I managed to control my breathing enough to clearly articulate a cheery and upbeat sounding "Good evening" and quickly accelerated past him so that I could return to my own breathlessness without him realising just how hard I was pushing.

I think he managed to grunt a reply but I didn't quite catch what he said - maybe I don't want to know!

On days like these, you can't help but smile!

Anyway - back to last night's ride – we covered 23 miles in, as good as makes no difference, an hour and a half.

I certainly don't mean to single out the new chap but the moment where he struggled to keep up with the group to the point that he "offered" to turn back and leave us to it made me realise something that will be the topic of a later blog, no doubt, relating to my own progress.

In short, I learnt that that person at the back USED to be me but, it's on days like these when I recognise that my "progress" has been such that it generally ISN'T me any more.

It wasn't that long ago that I was the one feeling guilty about holding people up, making them wait for me every few miles.

Don't get me wrong, it sometimes STILL IS me and, despite the fact that the group are genuinely welcoming of all, it is difficult to remind yourself of that fact as you come around a bend, gasping for air, and see a load of people stood around waiting for you, looking as fresh as daisies.

I could most definitely relate to our newest member last night but I really hope that he realises that the biggest step has been taken - it will get easier from there.

Thursday morning is my swim morning as many of you will know and, bright and breezy as always, I turned up at the pool at 6:40am there or thereabouts. Readers of the last training update will, no doubt, be delighted to learn that I am back in possession of a well fitting pair of goggles and off I set, on my swim, at around 6:50am.

Something that I am beginning to realise is that, whilst it might be my fastest 400 metres according to the stopwatch, the first 400 metres is the hardest; The hardest to get a rhythm, the hardest psychologically and the hardest physically.

I assume that it is to do with the need to warm up but perhaps some of you readers could give me your thoughts on this?

I got into my stride though, timing each 400 metre stint as I went and settled into my "normal pace". Then came another interesting learning point.

I glanced at my stopwatch after the 1,600 metre mark and saw that that last 400 metres had taken me noticeably longer than the others. I wasn't feeling tired so I concluded that I must have simply "fallen asleep" so to speak - lost concentration, maybe. I took the opportunity to learn whether I had it in me to accelerate and to put in a quick (by my standards) 400 metres stint.

Immediately, I was passing the guy swimming alongside me at quite a rate where, for some 10 minutes or so, I'd basically been swimming at his pace.

Sure enough, my next 400 metres was, give or take a few seconds, swam at the kind of pace that my first (and generally quickest) stint was swam at.

Mission "accelerate" had been a success so I learnt that I am not the "single speed" swimmer that I thought I was.

On days like these, when you realise something new and positive about yourself, life feels good doesn't it?

What else did my little burst of speed teach me? It taught me that the faster I swim, the less time it takes me to swim a length of the pool. That sounds ridiculously obvious, doesn't it?

I guess what I mean is that I hadn't really put two and two together before that, as I swim faster, the lengths feel shorter. I guess I'd always felt that a length would feel like a length, however quickly or slowly I swam. That's not the case at all!!!

Please let me know if that makes any sense to you - I'm not sure if it does to me even! In the meantime, I think I'll work on speed a bit and that means the T word - "technique".

The 2,500 metre swim took me 1 hour and 3 minutes - around 25 seconds faster than last week so, to all intents and purposes, the same - notwithstanding my slower middle 400 metre stint - so I am happy with that.

I did try to work on two other things in the pool, after I'd completed my swim, with varying degrees of success or, should I say, failure.

I currently only breathe to the left in the pool and a few readers / friends have pointed out the benefit of bilateral breathing, especially for open water swimming (the sun might be right in your eyes, for instance, to the left, so you will be thankful for the ability to breathe to the other side). I did 2 lengths breathing to the right and felt like a newbie again! I have some work to do there!

I also tried to develop my "sighting". I am acutely aware that the blue line along the bottom of the pool that keeps me straight won't be painted at the bottom of the Baltic Sea in Sweden (or will it? - nah, I'd better not bank on it) so I ought to develop this "sighting" skill that people tell me about. I think the less said about my attempt at that, the better really so I will leave that topic well alone! Again - a bit of work to do!

On days like these, I realise that I have more to say about swimming than I do about cycling.

I certainly "enjoy" cycling more so this comes as a bit of a surprise - I guess it's just because swimming is newer to me and I seem to learn more about my ability for each hour in the pool than I do for each hour on a bike... Reading that back, it sounds like I'm saying that I have less to learn about being on the bike which clearly isn't the case. Maybe I should take a cue from my desire to "learn" about swimming and apply myself to "learning" about cycling - then you might find me "talking bike" a bit more!

On days like these, I realise that this is as much about learning and application as it is about hard graft.

You are probably wondering why I seem to have a fixation with using the words "On days like these" - It is not a bid to make the title of the blog seem more appropriate, nor is it just a poor memory, using the same phrase over and over having forgotten that I've already said it.

No - I actually realised during both my bike ride (the more lonely moments when the group became fragmented) and the swim that I love the song "On Days Like These" - by Matt Monroe.

I found myself singing it out loud on the bike and am sure that, if it weren't for the basic laws of physics, I would have done so in the pool too!

The song is used in the opening sequence of the film "The Italian Job" which is probably why I like it – for those of you familiar with the sequence, it features someone driving along a Mediterranean coastal road with, apparently, not a care in the world.

That reflects my mindset at the moment whether I am on both the bike or in the pool... it's quite a nice place to be indeed.

Of course, those of you who know the film will also know that, the end of the same sequence ends with the carefree driver crashing and burning in a tunnel that you see him drive into - the less said about that bit the better!

On a less upbeat note, I attended the funeral of the cycling buddy that inspired an earlier blog and, of course, it was a very sad and sombre event, as is only natural.

I learnt a lot about this chap during that couple of hours, not least the fact that he was loved by many.

To round this blog off and tie it up in a neat little metaphorical bow, it's on days like these that you turn your attention to what is truly important in life... Family, friends and health.

I went home from the funeral to all three of these things which made me very happy.

Anything else is just a bonus so be thankful.

The importance of context – October 16th, 2013

At the very end of an earlier blog, I talked about a note that I had found which outlined a target to cycle 600 miles over the year ahead.

The note was made a few years ago and, in that blog, I pointed out, in a round-about way, that that target would be no target at all now.

I have already entered a ride next year, for instance, which will see me get considerably over a third of the way towards that yearly target in a single day.

Having said all of that, I am NEVER one to knock earlier targets and achievements just because they would no longer be challenging now and, co-incidentally, a comment from a friend a few weeks back regarding "how far I'd come" reminded me of that.

Let's talk progression for a moment.

As regular readers of this blog will know - it was less than 5 and a half years ago that I genuinely couldn't sit on a bike (my legs simply wouldn't allow me to get on).

I physically couldn't "run" - and, to explain this further, my definition of "run" at that time was simply to have both feet off of the ground at the same time whilst moving forwards - I couldn't even do a single "one" of those motions - it sounds like an odd thing to say given the fact that I could, basically, "walk" but I did try to "run" a step of two and I just couldn't do it.

And, more through lack of trying than a physical limitation, I couldn't really swim.

Within a year, thanks to my hip-replacement operation and a dollop of determination, I could "do" all of these things so that was a massive shift to have experienced in itelf.

As an aside, I made a "to-do" list of physical achievements that I wanted my new hip to help me do and, as Lisa, my wife, would confirm, the very first thing on that list was "walk up stairs" and, second, was "sit in a chair normally".

As soon as I was physically capable, I recall regularly going out on my bike on a 5 mile route. The first half was up hill and the second half was, basically, down hill back to my home. It used to take me more than 30 minutes and I would crawl back in to the house almost on my hands and knees in a bath of sweat. I genuinely remember feeling that 5 miles was a HUGE distance and it used to make me smile just to even think that I'd done it.

I then graduated up, over time, to a fifteen mile route which, again, had me at my point of exhaustion by the end - I would brag about it to friends.. "FIFTEEN MILES" I'd say - "I cycled FIFTEEN MILES WITHOUT STOPPING"!

At about this time, I remember entering a 28 mile bike ride - a fairly flat route from memory.

It seemed a bit mad to me that anyone would even attempt such a distance but I was game. I assumed that the other entrants were expecting to make a day of it but I said to Lisa, my wife, that I was going to "ride it in one go"... I felt like a nutter.

To cut a long story short, I was so exhausted in the last few miles that Lisa had to track me down in her car, with my boys, and stop to feed me peanut butter sandwiches by the side of the road just so that I could get to the end. I was, apparently, pale to the point that she was worried for my health.

Even when I entered my first triathlon, I was targeting, but rarely hitting, a 15 miles per hour average on a basic, 10-15 mile, flat bike ride and fifteen miles was pretty much the most I would ever do in one go.

Now, I find myself sitting here saying that I don't know what my maximum bike range is (with a record one day ride of 190 miles, I don't really feel as if I have hit it yet) and, in terms of speed, I certainly know I could be faster than I am now but I would currently target, on a like for like short flat ride, pushing myself to the same degree of exhaustion, a 17-18 mph average, I would think.

Looking at the swim - I remember when I first committed to a triathlon and went down to my local pool thinking - "how hard can this be?". Five metres from pushing off, I had to stop, such was the difficulty of the task that faced me. I got out of the pool there and then, and went home. I had a matter of weeks between then and needing to swim 400 metres, which I just about managed in around 13 and a half minutes.

Lisa paid for me to have swimming lessons, which I found useful, but the information I learned failed to stick and my 400 metre swim time was stuck at 13 minutes for what seemed like an eternity. "Head up, dry hair, breast stroke" was my only option.

It was some 18 months later, spent constantly trying (and I mean constantly trying.. and constantly getting frustrated), that I managed to be able to swim two lengths in front crawl. Two whole lengths. I was overjoyed. That was at the beginning of this year, 2013.

Up to this point, I was targeting, but rarely hitting, a 12 minute swim time over 400 metres (by which I mean sub 13 minutes rather than a 12 minute dead time - I was delighted with any result which started with a "12").

Now, I would say that I really don't know what my maximum front crawl swim range is (I don't feel as if I've got close yet to my maximum range and I'm up to 100 lengths, or 2,500 metres, every Thursday morning) and, in terms of speed, I certainly know I could be faster than I am now but I would currently target around 9 minutes 45 over the same distance.

I have no such comparables with runnning due to the fact that I don't train to run, as you all know - but I do know that I can do it now (and that I have 8 minute miles in me as was proven at the last triathlon I did) which is a million miles away from where I was not all that long ago!

What is my point? It certainly isn't to say "look at me, aren't I great!?" - I rather hope that in a year or two's time, what I now deem to be a strong swim or cycle will, at worst, be deemed normality and, at best, slow and clumsy.

I also know that probably more than half of the readers of this blog would feel that hitting MY target would mean falling well short of their own.

No - narcissism through the words of this blog would lead to ridicule, I fear. It is actually something that I think everyone should steer clear of, to be blunt, and I don't care who you are. After all, there is ALWAYS the chance that there will be someone better, stronger or faster than you, whoever you are and whatever you are achieving. Even the Brownlees, Usain Bolt or Lewis Hamilton can attest to that.

No - the point I am making is that, whilst it is so very important to push forward, on to your next goal or target, it is equally important to look back on you past successes in context rather than by comparing them to what you are doing now.

That 28 mile bike ride I referred to above took me three hours...

THREE HOURS!!

I'd be gutted if I couldn't do that same ride in barely more than half of that time now but, still, it remains one of my top 5 cycling moments.

It was almost twice the distance that I had even attempted to ride since being able to get back on my bike after my operation and I've no doubt that, by the time I crossed the finish line, I was just as exhausted as any Tour De France stage winner had ever been before or will ever be again.

What is not to feel proud of?

The medal and map print-out from that day hangs on my wall alongside all of my subsequent triathlon mementos and motorsport trophies - I wouldn't dream of taking it down.

This approach of contextualising achievement also works the other way too - i.e if, for whatever reason (let's say age or injury), you are no longer able to perform at the same level that you used to.

Rather than beat yourself up about getting "worse", you should look back, recognise the advantages that you held then over now, and pat yourself on the back for how close to that hey-day you can still get.

It's all about understanding not just WHAT you are doing but HOW you are doing it and all of the factors that are influencing the situation.

I'd go as far to say that our most impressive performances are rarely the ones that are statistically our best - (after all, we tend to have luck on our sides for those, let's not kid ourselves).

No, the ones that, when seen in context, represented our toughest challenges are the ones that will give us the most satisfaction for years to come and we should cherish them more than any others.

I've got terrible wind! – October 22nd, 2013

Another training update from me, this time around.

As always, I started the week with my daily ride to work.

Commuting by bike is a great way for me to start and, indeed, end the day. My previous job was a minimum of a one and a half hour drive away (given the level of traffic that I used to encounter) and it got so dreary that it actually started to take away from my enjoyment of driving (which, by the way, I love).

These days, the journey to work isn't so much a chance for me to get "wound up" as it is an opportunity to "clear my head" ready for the day.

It's a chance to utter a cheery "good morning" to the other people out and about – the fellow cyclists, the dog walkers and the mums (and dad's – let's not make this a sexist thing) who are taking their little ones to school. My journey home is much the same.

I love it.

And, although it is only brief at around 5 miles each way, it gets a minimum of 50 miles per week into my legs and I'm not one to pootle along (watch out for a later blog on this very subject) so it gives me slightly over 15 minutes, twice per day, of cardio workout before I even start doing anything else by way of training. What can be wrong with that?

Monday night is the night when I "moonlight" as a Spinning instructor so I drag my bike, panniers and ruck-sack up over one of the more notorious climbs of the area near my home to start "cracking the whip" as a fitness instructor.

Again, Spinning is another opportunity for me to work-out. I know, I know, I know – I should be instructing, not working out. I get it. But, actually, I like pushing myself in these classes and I think that the people I'm instructing appreciate it too.

For the last few weeks, I have been leaving my regular Spinning session and hot-footing it down to another leisure centre, a few miles away from the first, to instruct another Spinning class – covering for a friend - and last Monday was no different. So, on Monday alone, I managed around 2 and three quarter hours cycling (including the Spinning) without impacting on my "working day" – it's a win win really!

Wednesday night was, as always, the night that I head out with a cycling group and, on the basis that my main bike was not back from being serviced, I nervously removed the panniers from my commuter bike to give it a go.

I say "nervously" as, whilst it had always been my intention to use said commuter bike as a winter training bike, I hadn't anticipated doing my first training ride on it with a group of other people. I had rather hoped to do it alone lest I go embarrassingly slowly.

It is a heavier and more sluggish feeling bike, no doubt but, to be fair to the old girl, she did me proud on that night – I took her up some pretty steep climbs and I was generally in touch with the pace that I would tend to ride at on my main bike.

We covered 22 and a half hilly miles in around an hour and a half.

I don't cycle as regularly as I would like at the weekend, at the moment, as, again, I instruct a Spinning class on Sunday mornings but, knowing I wanted to get a longer ride in again, an offer from one of my cycling buddies to plan and accompany me on an 80 miler got me texting around for someone to cover my Sunday Spinning class as soon as the opportunity was put in front of me.

Having got someone to agree to cover my class, then, I knew that, irrespective of weather, I was going to make the most of my "Spinning-free-Sunday" and get some distance in my cycling legs.

I did have my main bike back from being serviced in time but, if you'll forgive me my vanity, it looks so beautifully clean that I couldn't face getting it all dirty and wet with the forecast being for such horrendous weather and, given the relative success of my Wednesday foray on my winter bike, I thought that now might be an opportunity to see how she felt over a longer ride.

My winter bike, as well as being heavier, has, ummm, "character": I can only get the front mech to select the inner of the two chain-rings (despite a lot of tampering with the screwdriver – I suspect a new front mech would be needed if I could be bothered), the brakes stick a bit and she makes some odd, as yet undiagnosed, noises as we potter along.

But, for this bike, I am genuinely happy with these little idiosyncrasies and have no desire to fix them until I am forced to, if ever. I am labouring under the logic that it all adds up to a harder training experience ergo I'll be faster on a fully functional model.

And so it was, at 7:30am on Sunday, I turned up at the pre-arranged meeting place ready to set off on our 80 miler (with a café stop en-route). Sure as eggs are eggs, so did everyone else who'd agreed to join us and, in all, 5 of us headed north.

One of our number needed, for reasons of time management rather than fitness, to turn back after about 20 miles, but the remaining band of 4 pressed on and, in the main, we were lucky with the weather in that it didn't rain as was forecast. It was mucky though and, by the end of the ride, I could barely remember what colour my bike was when we'd started.

The bike seemed disappointingly fine!.. I would love to say that I was working gallantly against a plethora of problems and that my sheer hard-work was allowing me to still keep up with the others but this would be a shameful lie - it felt barely any different to my main bike once I had got used to the little differences that I've mentioned above and this came as a surprise – perhaps winter training on it will be as enjoyable as the summer months have been on my main bike and, actually, once you learn to ride around a problem, it ceases to be a problem.

We made great time to our café stop about 40 miles or so in to the ride and promptly got some well earned cake down our throats!

Now, personally, I love the café stops of our bike rides. It is a great chance to chat which you "kind of do" on your bike but it's not really the same. It is also a great chance to see some lovely areas of the country. Having said all of that, and I don't know if this is just me but, I don't half struggle to get going again.

Within a few minutes of getting back on the bike, everyone else's legs seem to be whirring away quite nicely whilst mine seem stuck in treacle for what seems like an eternity and, disappointingly, I never quite get back to how I was feeling before the stop. I eat the same kind of stuff as they do at the stop and I believe that I take on as much nutrition during the moving bit but it's just one of those things that I can't seem to get my head around.

I even experimented last year by doing a solo 75 mile ride non-stop and my legs really didn't suffer anything like the same level of drop-off that I experience if I do have a café stop en-route. Can any techy people out there clarify this for me and give me an idea if I can stop this happening? Please? Pretty please?

To those who I cycle with and who I know read this, please do not take this as a request for non-stop rides (or even for shorter stops) – as I say, I genuinely enjoy the stop bit – but do take it as a thinly veiled excuse for my "second half lull" – perhaps they should start to call me "first half Phil" – that has a nice ring to it!

In all seriousness, my physiological "preference" for non-stop distance probably bodes well for the Ironman as I suspect that café stops won't really be on the agenda!

With this in mind, I will probably throw in a few solo, non-stop, distance rides from the beginning of the new year.

On the way back, it really didn't help that we had a headwind which came as a surprise on the basis that I didn't feel like we were benefitting from a tailwind on the way out. I guess we must have been but I would have liked to have known – I might have made an effort to appreciate it more!

Now, a headwind is the one thing I REALLY detest on my bike.

Many people have suggested that, because I am hardly a "man-mountain", I carry very little momentum to push me through it but, you know, I think that is just being kind – Could you not equally argue that the bigger cyclists act as more of a sail and, in fact, it is they that should struggle in a headwind whilst I merrily cut through it like a knife? Again, techy answers on a postcard please!

No – I just think I need more power so I will be using the winter months to do some resistance training in the gym. I will get these thighs working if it's the last thing I do!

It's an odd thing, though, wind. My speed falls to a nigh-on stall and yet you can still give me a hill and I'll get up it. To support this, I was able to pass the same people that were leaving me for dead into the headwind, once we got to the hills on Sunday.

So, it isn't as if the wind saps my energy then. For the third time in this blog, if a techy sort wants to throw some clarification on this issue my way then I am ready to catch it!

Anyway – we covered 81 miles in a total riding time, not including stops, of 5 hours 20 minutes.

A quick word regarding the swim on Thursday morning: It went well although, as always, I found the first 400 metres to be the hardest.

Having said that, each of the other 400 metre splits were consistently quicker than I had previously done on other Thursdays and I got perilously close to breaking the 1 hour and 3 minute mark for the 2,500 metres that I swam. This compares to pretty much 1 hour and 4 minutes for my first 2,500 metre swim only a couple of weeks ago.

I know that a 1 minute improvement doesn't sound like a lot but it is almost the amount of time that it takes to swim a couple of lengths so I would say that, however small progress seems, progress is most definitely progress.

As before, I felt as fresh as a daisy at the end of the swim and certainly was feeling no physical "need" to stop – getting out of the pool was mainly driven by my need to get on my bike and get into work - which takes me back to the beginning of this blog and, therefore, a nice place to end!

To do is not necessarily to understand - November 7th, 2013

I remember, quite well, Lisa (my long suffering wife) suggesting to me that I take part in my first triathlon.

It was late at night. I was in bed and in that state which falls somewhere between asleep and awake. Lisa was getting in from a very rare night out with friends. It turns out that a husband of one of the friends was a regular triathlete and was due to take part in one a few weeks later. Lisa suggested I joined him. I laughed and fell asleep.

I woke up the next morning and it was one of the first things I thought about so, on that basis, I felt like it warranted further consideration. Me? A triathlete? Really?

I genuinely was the last to be picked for sports teams at school (everyone seems to say that but, for me, it really was depressingly true) and, aside from my motorsport "career" and a period as a cyclist in my teens, I had never really found any form of sport that I was particularly good at. I had found an enjoyment in the gym over the previous few years though, so fitness related stuff wasn't too far from my mind.

Having said that, I was only a year or so on from my hip-operation and was under pretty strict instructions not to run (instructions, I should add, that I was happy to abide by since running is hardly something that I wanted to do).

I barely even knew what a triathlon was either but here I was thinking about it.

I spoke with the husband who'd been the source of this crack-pot idea within a day or so and he re-assured me that the event would not be set up in such a way so as to let anyone fail.

I had no idea what he meant at the time.

I do now.

He was right, of course. I entered that same day.

What I knew about swimming extended only as far as the knowledge that it got you wet.

What I knew about cycling extended only a little bit further and most of that knowledge was gleaned from my first time around as a cyclist in my teens so was consigned to the same part of my brain where trigonometry resides – you know, the bit which is locked away, never to be opened again!

This time around, I had only been riding for a matter of months since my hip operation and "knowing" about cycling was taking a backseat behind simply getting to the end of a given route!

What I knew about running was marginally less than I know about astro-physics (which is nothing, incidentally).

In the short time between entering that first Triathlon and turning up at the start line, my efforts were focussed not so much on "understanding" the disciplines involved as simply ensuring that I could complete the distances required. I even did a bit of training for the run although I don't do that now as regular readers of this blog will know.

You might assume that, now that I have quite a few triathlons under my belt, an awful lot of cycling miles and an ever increasing number of swimming miles, I now "understand" what makes you good at these disciplines and, therefore, I now have a better understanding of how to maximise my performance in the individual disciplines and, for that matter, triathlons.

Sadly, I think you'd be wrong.

What I now know about swimming is probably only marginally more than I knew at the very start of my triathlon adventure. Sure, I can "do it" better now and I have a rudimentary understanding of the basics but a conversation with a friend a couple of weeks ago who, himself, is a very strong swimmer, made me realise how little I do know about performing well at this discipline.

And, I suppose, what I know about cycling is still fairly sketchy. For instance, I sometimes get my nutrition right on longer rides and finish with a flourish whilst, on other occasions, I get it wrong and "bonk" long before I can see my home. This lack of consistency tells me that I need to develop a better understanding in this area, certainly.

I hear people talk about pedalling technique and positioning on the bike but I can't get my head around it... my pedalling technique involves nothing more technical than keeping my legs turning and my positioning is barely more advanced than ensuring that my backside is on the saddle and my hands are on the handlebars!

To an extent, of course, I am using some artistic licence in this blog– I am not quite as backward or ignorant as I am portraying and, actually, have a qualification in anatomy and physiology, albeit a fairly basic one, so I do "understand" more than most, perhaps.

But the point I am trying to make with this slightly exaggerated, humble approach that I am adopting in this blog is that, right now, I consider myself as someone who "does" swimming and who "does" cycling. I don't "do" running regularly but, when called for in a Triathlon, I still feel like I am just "doing" it.

It is becoming abundantly clear to me that I need to become someone who better "understands" swimming, someone who better "understands" cycling and, dare I say it, someone who better "understands" running (even if my capacity to get out there and actually run is stifled).

Above all, though, it seems of huge importance that I become someone who better "understands" Triathlons and what they take from anyone competing in them if I am to make August 16th next year both a success and, let's face it, an enjoyable experience.

I am hugely lucky to be surrounded by knowledgeable and supportive people, though, so I am not on my own in this.

Barely a day goes by without someone volunteering some useful titbit of information or e-mailing me a link to a great source of online material designed to make me stronger, faster, better.

You can bet your bottom dollar that this blog alone will result in me having a whole load of offers of help and I am looking forward to taking you all up on them.

The difference between "pre-this blog Phil" and "post-this blog Phil" though is that I will need to start listening to the advice and, most importantly, acting on it.

The challenge, of course is that the advice and information that I will undoubtedly get put in front of me is likely to vary and, in some cases, it will even conflict with each other. There are many theories out there and every source will have its own underlying ethos with compelling evidence to support it.

It strikes me, then, that the key to acting on advice is not so much working out which bits are wrong and which bits are right, for this is incredibly subjective.

No – the key will be selecting an overall ethos that suits me in as many ways as possible and then sticking to the advice that adheres to that ethos and ignoring that which doesn't.

That, in itself is a challenge, I suspect – it's a good job that I like challenges wouldn't you say?

I'm a Rubik's Cube. November 12th, 2013

Well, it has been quite a week for "hardened and committed" training so I thought it warranted another blog update.

Last Wednesday night, as is always the case on a Wednesday, was bike night and the forecast looked questionable, to say the least, but a surprisingly strong number of us turned up, in the dark, at our usual meeting point ready to brave whatever nature felt like throwing at us.

To be fair, we were rewarded with fairly manageable conditions… right up to the point where one of the group decided to refer to the "better than expected" weather.

That was, of course, like a red rag to a bull for Mother Nature and she summoned up any water she could find and decided to drop, nay throw, it down on us for the whole of the second half of the 25 mile ride!

What made the whole experience even more.. err.. "pleasurable" was the wind.

People who have read a few of my training updates will already be familiar with the fact that I am no friend of wind so Wednesday night, then, was like spending an hour and a half with someone that you really can't abide… you know, the one who gets right on your nerves the minute they walk in the room.

At one point, as we turned into the country lane that would take us up and over the last climb of the night, the wind in my face was sufficiently strong to almost bring me to a stand-still and the force of the rain on my eyes (I'd given up wearing my cycling glasses around mile 15) was actually quite painful.

And yet, it was a ride that I enjoyed. To this day, I am not sure why I enjoy that kind of thing but I actually do. There is a strange satisfaction to be derived from it both during and after the event. Some of you will agree, I'm sure, and some of you will think that I'm mad but, well, there you go!

In stats, we covered a little over 25 miles in a little under 1 hour and 40 minutes riding time.

The next day, Thursday, would ordinarily see me heading to the local pool at the bright and early time of 6:30 am to swim my customary 100 lengths before heading on to work. Last Thursday, however, was different.

A chance discussion with someone I know through my work revealed what a small world we live in.

It turns out that we share cycling buddies (it is amazing that we have never found ourselves cycling together!) and, more importantly, a love of Triathlon. His strongest discipline, it would seem, is the swim and he offered me the opportunity to swim with him one night so that he could give me some much needed guidance.

The "date" was fixed for Thursday night at a time when we would pretty much have the pool to ourselves, 9pm, and so, notwithstanding an awful bike ride down to the pool which left me with a destroyed rear rim after I hit a pothole so big that you could have been forgiven for thinking that we had come under attack from overhead bombers, I turned up and quickly located my coach for the evening.

Far from it being a night where we both "went for a swim", I was hugely grateful to have one to one coaching for the whole hour. He didn't swim a single length unless it was alongside me for the purposes of observing what I was doing. Amazing!

After I swam a couple of lengths using my normal technique, Ian (for that was his name!) was actually quite complimentary.

His words "you are actually a very good swimmer, Phil" are still ringing around in my head and could easily warm the cockles of my heart on a cold winter's evening. Deep down, I never expected this kind of positive feedback.

Having said that of course, he was able to suggest things that would make me better / more efficient / faster and it all largely revolved around two things; 1) me finding my natural buoyancy and balance as, at the moment, I seem to be battling the water rather than flowing with it and 2) "Gliding" for further – apparently, my arms don't stop moving for long enough and, again, I am not taking advantage of the "glide" phase as much as I should.

I understand what he means and I could certainly see it in practice when he was demonstrating it.

"Doing it" was, as could be expected for my first attempt, much more difficult than "saying it". I did "feel" different and more fluid when I was trying to adopt his guidance but, at the same time, it did feel a little like I was starting again.

In my head, I now liken his compliment of my existing swim technique as being similar to me complimenting someone for having completed 4 sides of a Rubiks Cube i.e It is, certainly, a very impressive achievement but there isn't any way of doing the last two sides without messing up the other four at least a little bit.

It's the same for me in the pool, now, I think – I'm not a million miles away from getting it right but I need to "unlearn" and "relearn" quite a bit incorporating subtle differences as I go.

It's all good though and I will now work on the ideas that Ian gave me. I am feeling "buoyed" (pun very much intended) by the experience and the fact that I now know what I need to do to get to the next level.

I probably need to face the reality that, initially, I will slow down a little (in terms of my pace per length) until such time as I get the technique right and my next swim will be this Thursday so let's see how it goes.

Still on the swimming theme, I managed to convince two friends to join me in an open water swim on Sunday. Without exception, all of my Triathlons have been pool swims and I was quite conscious that, unless I got into open water soon, that whole thing would start to become an "elephant in the room" – I needed to get over this hurdle and quickly.

The weather was sunny but very cold as all three of us (two of us managed to convince our families to go along) turned up at a marine lake near our home town. This lake fills up with sea water as the tide comes in and then, as the tide goes out, you get a ready made "outdoor swimming pool".

Getting undressed and into a wetsuit by the side of this marine lake, with the public all walking past in their big winter coats was a little surreal and quite a few people stopped to watch as all three of us tentatively waded into the water. Lisa and my boys thought I was stark raving mad and as soon as I felt the temperature of the water on my feet, I totally agreed with them.

Then came the precise feeling that I was hoping to foster by getting other people to join me in my first open water attempt. That feeling that you get where you know you want to turn around and go home but where you just know that you can't because other people are there with you. Having other people around is what kept me walking in to the water.

When the water was waist height, we essentially fell in the rest of the way.

Ouch!

The temperature on my body and limbs, where my wetsuit was doing its job very well, was actually okay, surprisingly… cold, sure, but not unbearable.

If only the same could have been said for my hands, feet and face! The feeling on my face of the cold water is pretty difficult to describe but one of the other guys that had got in with me described it as burning. The other likened it to the worst "ice-cream headache" that he's ever had.

I think it was worse.

Something I've not really mentioned before on this blog, I think, is that my inability to breathe out under water is directly correlated to the temperature of the water.

Warm water: no problem. Swimming pool kind of temperature: Normally no problem but if it is on the cold side, it becomes slightly less comfortable. If you get me into properly cold water though, as was clearly the case on Sunday, my mouth and nose seem to go into spasm as soon as they are submerged and breathing out feels nigh on impossible.

Quick straw poll? – Am I alone in this? Please do let me know!

Anyway, this inability to breathe out did hamper proceedings a little as I found myself reverting to any swimming stroke which didn't involve putting my head underwater. Any hopes that I had of practicing technique were dashed of course.

We swam around 600 metres, we reckoned. Stopping from time to time to chat and exchange the kind of laughter and banter that you reserve for moments of extreme stress.

On the swim back towards where we started, I did manage the "head under, breathing out" thing a few times and, whilst it was by no means smooth, it did give me some reassurance that it was physically possible!

Getting out of the water was "fun" too as all three of us realised that our feet were completely numb. Walking on numb feet is harder than I had imagined and, when the time came, it actually felt like I was putting socks on someone else – I really couldn't feel my feet at all!

Pictures of the swim follow (I'm the one in the blue cap):

Having read over that review of my first ever open water swim, it sounds a bit negative and that is entirely un-intentional. Rather than go back over it and re-word what is a very honest account, I would reassure you that my experience was absolutely a good one.

Okay, I might not have got in and swam like a pro but I got in.

Okay, I might have quite a few teething problems to overcome but at least I know what they are now.

Okay, I might have got out of the water and taken ages to get myself warm and dressed which, in a "transition" environment, would have been disastrous but at least I did it.

Overall, the experience gave me confidence rather than took it away and all three of us committed to return on another day to give it another go.

A fair amount of my confidence comes from having braved the cold.

A later online search revealed that the water temperature where I was swimming averages around 13 degrees for this time of year whereas it averages around 18 degrees for the Sweden Ironman that I am doing in August 2014.

That 5 degrees sounds like quite a lot and if I can get used to swimming in much harsher conditions than I will face on the day then that can't be a bad thing, can it?

So, a solid week and plenty of learning points for the future. I moved forward and am pleased to have done so. More importantly, though, was the enjoyment that I got from it all.

If I start losing that, then we really would be in trouble!

Easy rider – November 20th, 2013

I finished a ride to work the other day with my usual huff and a puff.

I glanced down at the iPhone app I use to "map my ride" (it isn't actually, the "map my ride" app, as it happens but I couldn't think of a way of slotting the word "cyclemeter" into the sentence!) and pushed the "stop" button as I do at the end of every ride that I do.

The app immediately tells me whether the ride was the fastest I have ever done the route, faster than average, bang on average, slower than average or the slowest.

How I feel about the ride is largely decided by what that app tells me about my performance when compared with previous efforts over, say, the same route.

It's a little more complicated than this as my mind then ticks over the variables concerned i.e was it windy?... am I carrying a lot of weight in the panniers?... etc but, once I have got my head around these, I quickly decide whether to feel smug at my own success or grumpy at my own failure.

Returning to my point; the morning in question was a good one. I'd done the route in a quicker than average time notwithstanding a slight headwind and a particularly heavily laden commuter bike.

This would normally have me whistle my way into the office with a grin on my face and a spring in my step but, strangely, I didn't have any sense of satisfaction on this particular occasion.

You see, I had set off at the start of my commute, determined to just take it easy - enjoy the ride - take my mind off of the "competition" element, just for once!

Yet, within just a few pedal strokes, I found myself pushing and, clearly, the end time on the stopwatch proved this to be the case.

Let me pause there and, for a moment, take you back to April. It was the day of a group ride that I had organised. I'd managed to persuade 10 parents of children who attend the same school as Angus, my oldest son, to take part in this group ride and to raise money for the school.

Some of these people were non-cyclists.

I mean that they were REALLY non-cyclists.

Two of them even had to BORROW bikes to take part AND YET all 10 of us gamely set off one Saturday morning to ride to Glastonbury and back.

For those not familiar the area of the country in which I live, this is a 62 mile bike ride including a few hills, just for fun.

62 miles for people who, at best, hardly ever ride a bike and, at worst, never let their backsides anywhere near a saddle.

I was the "co-ordinator" of the ride and, as such, I assumed the responsibility of riding up and down the line of cyclists through the day just to make sure that everyone was being kept company and that no-one was about to pass out.

I did the ride on my own, ahead of the big day to "try out" the route, in somewhere around 3hrs 45 minutes and, yes, I was pushing myself when I did it.

On the day of the parent's ride, it took us somewhere around 8 hours. Some of the group were naturally fitter and faster and some were less so but such was our determination to finish together that we stayed as a group the whole time, by and large.

At around 1/3rd distance, one of the group suggested to me that I might be getting frustrated with the pace and my very answer was "Quite the opposite - I am actually really enjoying just riding without having one eye on my speed / heartrate / time / distance etc".

Just for once, I was enjoying the ride for the sake of the ride itself and I loved it. The scenery around me was truly stunning and the lack of "hard work" made the whole thing seem so simple. There was just no sense of wondering how my "time would compare". All I needed to do was to keep pedalling. Simple.

I've only achieved that same degree of simplicity a couple of times since, though, given my natural propensity to push myself even if it simply isn't necessary and sometimes I just wish that I wasn't so bloody-minded about it.

I've tried to cycle without any time / distance measuring device but that doesn't seem to help - I still find myself pushing on to my own personal limits and not being fully satisfied unless I feel like I have achieved more than simply getting from A to B.

I know that I am training for a big year of events in 2014 and I know that, amongst the events that I have entered, the Ironman stands head and shoulders above the rest in terms of likely difficulty.

I also know that my time, in terms of hours per week, that I have available to train, is limited and this means that I tend to have to make those available hours productive, ergo: I need to push myself when I get the chance.

Many of the people who read this blog will be in the same position as I am, I suspect, and will feel the need to make maximum use of every available minute whilst they are training.

Having said that, I would urge you to, from time to time, even if I find it difficult to do myself, slow down once in a while.

Experiencing whatever form of training that floats your particular boat, whether it is cycling, running, swimming or something else, at a more leisurely pace without punishing yourself for not setting a personal best might just give you a new dimension to a sport that you already love.

Okay, it might not satisfy that competitive urge but I reckon that hardly any of the people reading this blog would really lose out if they kept these "slower" days to a minimum, so giving ourselves this permission to take it easy once in a while really won't hurt will it?

What? No Drowning Moment? – November 27th, 2013

A couple of weeks have passed since my last training update so I thought I would fill you in on some of the detail.

I certainly won't go through every bike ride or every swim but I will focus on the one swim and the one bike ride from which I took the most satisfaction.

Last Thursday, as always, was my swim morning and I turned up at the pool, like clockwork, at 6:30am ready to go.

Every part of me exuded confidence for this swim. That isn't always the case. I often go into the swim feeling like it will be boring or like, for some reason, I am going to struggle.

The big difference here, though, was that this was to be the first swim that I was due to trust my new gadget, my swimovate watch, explicitly. For those who don't know, this is a watch with an inbuilt accelerometer which detects changes in direction and, therefore, can count your lengths for you... thus removing the horrible bit of a pool swim.

Until now, I have worn it but still maintained the manual counting. It hasn't missed a beat yet and so I am now comfortable to just trust it and get on with swimming.

Now, within a few lengths (sometimes even after 2 of the 100 lengths), I ALWAYS have a moment of doubt which lasts for a few lengths. I start to wonder whether I can get to the end of the length that I am on, let alone the full 100. My breathing starts to go to pot and I start to flounder. It's is as if I am about to drown!

In an odd kind of way, this feeling of panic doesn't bother me anymore as I know to expect it and I also know that, without fail, I have always got through it within a couple of lengths and then gone on to complete the full 100 lengths without difficulty.

Thursday was different.

I wasn't counting anymore, due to the watch, but I got the sense that 5 lengths came and went without a "dark moment".

A little while later and I reasoned that 10 lengths must have been completed without the customary "dark spell".

A little while later still and I felt that 20 lengths must, by now, have been completed without my "dark spell".

At this point, I started to think that the "dark spell" wasn't going to arrive. And so it didn't... for the whole of the 100 length swim.

I reckon that it has something to do with the lack of counting.

Until now, I suspect that the demoralising feeling of getting to, say, 5 lengths, and realising that I have another 95 to go, has caused a negative mental mindset which has had knock on effects on my confidence etc etc etc. Without this mindset, I just felt good throughout.

I can't tell you how good "not counting" felt. It was very liberating. I could concentrate on my technique or think of the day ahead. I could even play little mental games, knowing that I could rely on the watch which I checked from time to time to see how far I'd got.

I didn't blog last week but, to fill you in on the detail, the previous swim had been my fastest yet (something that I put down to the one to one coaching session that I had from a friend) and this week, over a whole 100 lengths / 2,500 metres, I proved that it was no fluke by matching it (I actually beat my best by 2 seconds! – 2 seconds, over 100 lengths!! – That is consistency for you!)

As always, I had no sense of tiredness at the end so I left the pool and got on my bike for my onward journey to work with, very much, a spring in my step!

On Saturday (23rd November) I was faced with the prospect of either an hour on the turbo-trainer or an hour on the road and, despite the fact that the sun had long since disappeared, the temperature had plummeted to near freezing and the wind had sprung up, every part of me ached with the desire to opt for the road.

I got myself kitted up (remember, there is no such thing as the wrong weather, only the wrong clothes) and, once my boys were in bed and I'd convinced my wife that I was going to be safe, I headed out.

I decided to do a route which I have only done only once before. The route just breaks through the 20 mile mark by a few tenths of a mile. The other time I did the route was back in July and I averaged around 18.3 miles per hour which, for me, is a good pace.

July in the UK, as many of us will recall, was a lovely time. The weather was gorgeous and I distinctly remembered the day that I did the ride. I set off with birds singing, the sun shining and even the wind had seemingly gone on holiday.

Saturday was different and, as I pushed into the headwind and tried to maintain my breathing despite the icy air being pushed into my lungs, I resolved to be content with any average speed north of 17.75 mph (I'm quite precise aren't I?!).

From the off, I was pushing myself as hard as I felt I could given my need to sustain it over 20 or so miles and the omnipresence of those icy and leafy bends.

Happily, that enjoyment that I derive from cycling, seemingly irrespective of weather, was there in abundance.

There has been a spate of cyclist deaths recently, across the UK, and I can't pretend that this hasn't gone un-noticed in terms of my mindset when I hear a car come up behind me on a dark road.

Even though I am lit up like a Christmas tree, then, the whole ride was spent on maximum mental alert, as well as being at the upper end of my physical exertion capabilities.

A little over an hour later, I arrived back at my home and clicked that stop button on my iPhone app.

I was just ten seconds slower than my July effort.

Ten seconds!

So there you have it, a quick update of my training and I'm continuing to take positives from everything I do – long may that continue, I say.

It's not all "sunshine and flowers" though – my next blog will deal with the idea that, in some ways, I am a bit of a slacker!

Just call me "slacker" – November 30th, 2013

I'm a motivated chap. I believe that if you can't find enough time to do something then you just need to get up earlier.

I am not going as far as saying that you can be anything that you put your mind to being; that is just nonsense for, if it were true, I'd be lining up on the starting grid of next year's formula one season in my Ferrari or looking forward to taking Olympic gold in the 2016 Rio Triathlon.

No, that kind of talk is for the delusional, but I do think that, in pushing our own limits, we can achieve much more than we might have ever thought possible and I certainly do push my own limits as far as I can.

My performances may not reach some of the heady heights that some of you aim for but you can trust me when I say that I rarely go easy on myself.

I think it is fair to say, then, that I wouldn't consider myself a slacker (notwithstanding the growing list of DIY jobs around the house that my long-suffering wife, Lisa, has to tolerate).

Against this backdrop, I can almost hear you wondering about what I could possibly write in a blog entitled "Just call me slacker"? Well, are you sitting comfortably? –

Then I'll begin!

Whilst I was out cycling a week or so ago, one of the group with which I ride referred to the "elephant in the room".

I wondered, initially, what he meant but then he went on to explain that he was referring to the Ironman that I am entered and, specifically, the run section.

The "elephant" being, of course, the unavoidable truth that I don't run. (Only a couple of blogs ago, the "elephant" was the fact that I have never done "open water" swimming – these elephants are queuing up, it would seem!)

Everyone who knows me knows that I do not run unless it is the actual run section of a triathlon. I have the very understandable nervousness about doing so with my hip but, at the same time, I know deep down that I can't put it off forever.

If you have been reading this blog since the start, you will be aware that I splashed out (yeah, yeah – an obvious pun) on a pair or aqua-jogging shoes but my initial attempt at using them failed amidst an unusual episode of self-consciousness and, hands up, I've not tried since.

I still think that aqua-jogging will be on the list as one of the ways to go but I am picking my moment for that so watch this space.

None of this reluctance to run, though, is helping my running legs and 26.2 miles is a long old distance to cover if, to extrapolate my current strategy, I end up winging it on the day!

I've probably altered the algorithms of the whole of Google, such is the amount of time I've searched the words "improve your running without running", or variations of the same, but it seems to me that there is no substitute for the real thing.

I did come across an attractive alternative that I might yet try on the day; "run-walking". Again, though, there is no escaping this need to practice, darn it!

Try as I might (or should that be "Tri"?), I am just finding it very difficult to get myself into the mindset of WANTING to run. A huge part of my reluctance, certainly, is due to my hip but that isn't the full story, I don't think. Nope – some of it is just pure, old fashioned, "slacking".

There is some light at the end of the tunnel, though, and it came in the form of an offer from a mate to go walking / jogging with him over fairly short distances at a decidedly leisurely pace.

The offer was very welcome and the idea that someone else is getting their running shoes on ready for me to knock on their door might just be the proverbial kick up the backside that I need.

Mind you, I've not got the first date in the diary yet – small steps, dear reader... small steps! And if you are the mate in question (you know who you are) – I'll drop you a text soon but do chase me!

Another area of my training that has taken a bit of a nose dive of late is resistance work.

My routine, until earlier this year, included an approximate 50/50 mix of cardio and resistance work but then things started changing.

I started cycling on a Wednesday night and, whilst I might not be the most "selfless" husband and Dad in the world, even I recognised that adding something new to my already full routine meant that it was only fair to drop something old to make room for it.

Oh, I am sure that I had the CHOICE to carry on (Lisa would have understood, no doubt at all) but give me some credit, I do WANT to have my family time too irrespective of whether I have their blessing not to!

And so it was that my Thursday night resistance sessions got the chop in favour of my Wednesday night bike rides.

As we got into the summer months, I started heading out on the bike on a Saturday too and such is my reluctance to stop this that I will now either ride on the road or on my Turbo-Trainer on a Saturday even now that the summer is long gone. Almost without thinking about it, then, my Saturday resistance session was gone too.

This left me with just a Sunday morning (before the Spinning class that I instruct) and a Monday night (after a Spinning class that I instruct) to squeeze in some resistance work without letting my weekly routine spill into what was being deemed "non-training" time.

This worked and ticked over quite nicely until the last five weeks or so when a friend of mine has been asking me to cover her Spinning class – on a Monday night, around an hour after (and a twenty minute bike ride away from) my regular Monday night class. Two Spinning classes on the same evening and a short bike ride between the two leaves no time for a resistance session but, hey, "I was just covering, so it wouldn't be too long before I could get back to my routine.. right?"

But then came the offer to take over the second Spinning class permanently – I accepted (I do enjoy it) and, in a flash, my resistance work was down to once per week – a Sunday morning.

Anyone who has met me will know that I am no "man-mountain" but, at the same time, I do like to throw a weight or two around and would certainly class myself as, "pound for pound", pretty capable.

I am also very aware that a degree of resistance work is good for triathlon specific and overall fitness.

So, for the last five or so weeks, I have been slacking... I confess. My resistance work has been negligible and I really have started to notice the difference when I have ventured into the weights section of the gym on a Sunday morning.

What I've not mentioned yet through this blog is that, not so long ago, I was lucky enough to have a fully equipped gym at home.

It had a cross trainer, an exercise bike, a rower and all the freeweights and bench style equipment that you could desire. I could dip into and out of as often as my heart desired – which, as you might imagine, was pretty often!

I sold it all when I was given free gym membership at the club where I instruct Spinning and that came in handy as I really needed to turn the room into an office at the time, being that I spent a reasonable amount of time working from home!

This week, however, I started to make amends.

I don't need an office at home any more, a job change saw to that and, whilst I don't need a "full" gym at home (the cardio stuff, aside from my Turbo-trainer, would be pretty redundant) I have pretty much re-stocked the resistance stuff and am now the proud owner of a pretty comprehensive (enough for me at any rate) set of weights, bars and a bench.

So, let's raise a glass (of whey-powder infused drink, I would think) to being able to do some resistance training to compliment all of this cardio that I do – now I just need to find the time without impacting on my family and that, returning to the beginning of this blog, is what early mornings are for!

Saturday Night's Alright For Fighting – December 3rd, 2013

Whilst Saturday night be well be, as the song goes, alright for fighting, Wednesday night is perfect for cycling in my world and so it was that I found myself doing my standard routine, last Wednesday evening; Cycle home from work, eat dinner, get changed into "lycra" (I refuse to wear it on my commute to work) and get back out for my evening ride.

I am lucky to have the luxury of choice in that I have two road bikes – neither of them are especially flash but, in very simple terms, I have the choice between the "red one" (lighter, feels more responsive and mechanically much more "up together") or the "blue one" (workhorse, heavier, my commuter bike and mechanically not so much up together – I can only select one of the front two chain-rings, for instance).

The choice isn't really about which I prefer to ride though (I would always lean towards "red" if it was simply a matter of preference).

No, primarily, it's a choice based on weather: Dry = Red one... Wet = blue one

It's also a choice between how hard I feel like working myself as, without doubt, the commuter bike is a "harder" bike to ride. This is especially true when I'm cycling with a group of people who will obviously maintain the same pace regardless of which bike I happen to be on.

So, before I select my bike for the ride ahead, as well as looking at the sky, I ask myself; how much hardship do I want to put myself through? In short, I opted to make last Wednesday a "blue bike" night.

The ride itself was pretty good, on paper at least.

We took in a couple of decent hills and, including a few stops along the way just to allow the group to re-form and to consider the route which largely unfolded as we rode, we kept up an average pace of 15.5 mph over the 20 miles we covered and I even managed to get a couple of personal bests on some of the more hilly strava segments – "personal bests" in the darkness of winter and on my workhorse bike?.. pretty good stuff.

To all intents and purposes, then, I should have been content but the odd thing was that, despite the heightened sense of confidence that I had started with, I just wasn't "feeling it" at all.

Instead, for pretty much the whole ride, I felt very "anxious" for some reason. I found myself feeling nervous and overly cautious on the slightly damp bends... I felt like I was focussing too much attention on the mechanical integrity of my bike, listening for any odd noises and probably hearing a whole host of things that didn't exist... I felt physically uncomfortable on my saddle too. I was basically lacking confidence!

All of these things are not just "unusual", they are "unheard of" for me, so I experienced the very odd sensation of being happy when I was able to get my helmet off and declare: "ride over".

Looking at the logged data after the ride, I was very surprised that, statistically, it had been a good night and, ever the optimist, I am choosing to focus on the fact that, despite it being an "off day", my actual performance was still respectable.

Do I worry that I will feel like it again? – not really... I'm not one of these people who thinks like that. Sure, if it happens again then I might start to worry that a loss of confidence might become a more enduring challenge to overcome but, right now, I'm putting it down as a "one-off, never to be repeated" episode.

By contrast to that bizarre biking experience, then; just 9 hours after arriving home from the ride, I was setting off (on the same bike) to head down to the swimming pool for my Thursday morning swim and I was brimming with confidence.

The previous week's swim had seen a consolidation of my effort the week before (two weeks in succession of setting my best ever time over 100 lengths – just 2 seconds of elapsed time separated the two consecutive efforts).

What's more, as you may have read in my earlier blog, my previous swim did not, for the first time ever, feature a "dark spell" where, historically, I have tended to lose confidence for a few lengths towards the beginning.

So I had a very self-assured mindset as I hopped into the pool ready to go and I could tell immediately.

For the first 400 metres, I couldn't help but count lengths despite the fact that I am now trusting my swimovate watch implicitly – old habits die hard - but I got into my stride, focussing on my technique and pushed on, forcing myself to lose count so I could stop worrying about it.

Did I have those few lengths of self-doubt, I hear you ask? Nope – for the second week running.

Rather bizarrely, I even tried to force myself into a "dark spell" by thinking bad thoughts; "I'm not going to be able to do this in the Ironman", "I'm struggling", "My breathing is all over the place".

I'm not sure why I did this to myself. I tried to stop but, in the same way as some people can't help but laugh at a funeral, the devil on my shoulder was trying to make it more difficult for me – trying but failing, happily.

My attempts at self-sabotage just didn't work and before I knew it, I glanced at my watch and I'd covered 54 lengths.

The next time I bothered to look, I'd covered 84 lengths. Exactly 400 metres to go and I noticed that I had more than 11 minutes to swim the remaining 16 lengths if I was to beat my previous best 100 length time.

In the length that followed, I wondered if I'd seen correctly. I would easily be finished inside 11 minutes so I must be on for a PB over 100 lengths by some margin! Could that be right or did I actually have more than 16 to go?

Indeed it was correct and my end time was over a minute quicker than I had swam that same distance the week before which, itself, was a PB. To put this into context, it was over 3 minutes faster than I had taken to swim the same distance less than 2 months ago.

I'm a long way from being a fast swimmer but I am going in the right direction indeed.

As always seems to be the case, I didn't feel tired as I got out of the pool and my onward ride to work didn't give rise to any of the confidence issues I'd experienced the night before.

And now I have got through "that difficult ride" AND had a great swim (despite my attempts at self-sabotage early on), I can now look back at that training week with a great deal of satisfaction that the "scores on the doors" were strong, notwithstanding the obstacles that should have made them less so.

Hunting elephants, pools and PBs – December 10th 2013

In an earlier training blog, I talked about the "elephant in the room" being that I don't run.. at all... EVER.

There is good reason, mind you, but no amount of "reasons" are going to help me finish the marathon section of the Ironman.

So, to continue the "elephant in the room" analogy, this next training update will have the international animal welfare lobbyists hammering down my door for I have put on my hunting attire and taken steps towards making that particular pachyderm as extinct as the dodo.

Pressure has been building for a while, now, with everyone seemingly willing me to at least start to run, even if only for a fairly short distance, and so when I decided to take Tuesday off work, my ever suffering wife pounced on the opportunity to suggest a run together.

Tuesday is her only day of the week when her parental responsibilities are suspended on the basis that both my children are either at school or nursery for the whole day.

We agreed, as a result, to jointly ferry them both off to their destinations for the day before embarking on a route that she and a friend of hers have taken in on a couple of occasions.

It was never going to be at a pace to make Usain Bolt quake in his boots and it was never going to be a sufficiently long run so as to make Paula Radcliffe re-define her understanding of "distance".

Having said all of that, we parked the car up at the local leisure centre and, after a false start thanks to dodgy technology (I do love my data logging apps), we started to jog.

This will have been my only run on a "non-triathlon" day for years (literally).

We headed off along the road and I can't tell you how great it was to be exercising with Lisa. We were maintaining conversation which, itself, was lovely and comparing notes on how we were feeling all the way round.

Lisa "kicked" as we entered the last few hundred metres and suddenly I realised that she is no one speed wonder! – My "jog" turned into a "run" and then, almost, a "sprint" as we closed on the finish line.

The 20 minutes that we were running came and went, seemingly, in the blink of an eye and before we knew it, we were back at the car.

From a pace point of view, it was admittedly some way short of the pace that I know I CAN run when I am in "triathlon mode" (8 minute mile territory) but this is exactly what I WANTED it to be. It was meant to be a pleasurable introduction to "running for the sake of it" rather than a gut-busting, eye-bleeding, thigh-popping sweat-fest.

Those will follow, I'm sure!

Towards the latter half of "couple of mile" loop, I had considered persuading Lisa to go around it a second time but I thought better of it- Not because I didn't feel that I could or because I didn't feel that Lisa could, but more because I didn't want to spoil something that had been extremely pleasurable.

I have a tendency to just push things further than other people want to go and, on this occasion, I really wanted to leave myself, and Lisa, wanting more rather than regretting starting.

Throughout the jog, I felt comfortable, from a cardio-vascular perspective and, knowing my own body pretty well, I expected that I would. From a muscular point of view, I was also within my own limits.

Over the next day or so, I wouldn't say that my legs "ached" in the truest sense of the word but I did feel "aware" that I had put them through something that they don't ordinarily do.

Next week, (when Lisa and I will go again thanks to another Tuesday off work) we may well double the distance and see how we feel but, for now, we're happy with what we achieved.

Wednesday night was the customary group bike ride. The darkness and the temperature are joining forces now to mean that the rides are shorter than we were managing back in the summer and they tend now to be around 20 miles.

I sense that, with quite a bit yet to write about the week's training, this could already be on target to be a long blog and, since there was nothing unusual or remarkable about the Wednesday evening ride, I will not go into any more detail than that.

On Thursday and Friday, I was due to be in Glasgow with work so, with an early flight up, my Thursday morning swim was never going to happen.

Never one to be put off by something as inconsequential as being in the wrong city, staying in a hotel (with a meeting due to kick off at 8am) and not having a faintest clue about local facilities, though, I managed to find a swimming pool within walking distance of where I was staying and, on Friday morning, set my alarm for 4:30am.

I'm an organised monkey and, on Thursday night, had found my way to a supermarket to pick up all of the necessary ingredients to have porridge and a cup of tea in my hotel room before I headed out for the swim.

The swim itself was a little non-representative in that, disappointingly, it was only a fifteen metre pool. This made me quicker than normal over the 2,500 (2,505 to be precise) metres and I finished in under an hour, some 2 minutes quicker than I have ever covered that same distance before.

As I say, though, I'm certainly not getting carried away by this "personal best" given the fact that I am simply not comparing like-with-like. Instead, I will "ignore it" for the purposes of any future comparisons.

Having said that; the swim felt good. I felt strong and I reckon that my technique is continuing to improve.

Those hitherto forgotten demons that I have mentioned before (where I feel like I am struggling after only a few lengths "started") did start to creep back in, surprisingly, but as soon as I sensed it happening, I slowed my stroke down and consciously steadied my nerves to overcome them, which worked well before I pressed on at my normal pace once again.

And to top off the successful start to the day, I made it to my meeting on time and without looking too much like I had just towelled myself off in a hot changing room (which, of course, I had)!

The weekend was a drink fuelled, Christmas party infused, hazy affair – I confess!

I am really NOT a drinker – let me get that very straight.

A couple of glasses of wine is pretty much all it takes to get me singing on a Playstation Karaoke game (or so it turns out – this gives you an insight as to what I ended up doing in the early hours of Sunday morning!) and so Sunday was spent with something of a hangover.

I still managed my early morning ride up to the local gym to take my Spinning session, though, and I don't "think" that any of my class spotted that my complexion was turning a little... well... green!

I think that the effort was well worth it as I'm sure that I saw at least a little bit of my hangover in the puddle of sweat that accumulated on the floor beneath my Spinning bike!

I gallantly dragged myself through the day towards Sunday night, through a birthday party that I took my boys to, all the while fading into and out of hangover mode (these hangovers don't half last longer as you get older don't they?) and, by the time the evening came, I just felt that a bike ride in the fresh air was what was needed to kick the last remnants of my headache into touch – like an alternative to Ibuprofen, if you like.

Fully kitted up, then, I headed out on a route which I did only a week or so ago.

It is around 16 miles long, mainly flattish with a couple of little climbs just to remind the legs what work feels like. Perfect.

Surprisingly, given how I was feeling, I set a personal best time for the route - by over a minute (and the last personal best was the last time I did the ride – itself a minute or so faster than my previous personal best).

When I saw how much quicker I had gone than ever before, nostalgia set in and I started to look through previously logged rides on my iPhone app.

The route is one I have been riding since the days when 16 miles was as far as I would ever ride and I looked back with amazement that, having covered it in around 53 minutes, I am now some 9 minutes quicker around that route than when I first rode it.

Nine minutes!!

At the pace I was riding that is over 2 and a half miles! And to be perfectly honest, the weather was hardly conducive AND I didn't really feel like I was pushing. A little pat on the back to me! Not to detract from those earlier achievements, then, but sometimes the odd reminder as to how far you've come is nice isn't it?

Indeed, this WAS a long blog, as I suspected it would be, so if you are still reading, I thank you!

There WAS a lot to say, though – a run (wow!), a swim in a strange pool whilst away with work (thus supporting either my dedication or my madness – you choose!) and a personal best bike ride all mixed in with copious amounts of alcohol and a dollop of nostalgia.

If you ask me, I did well to keep the blog as short as this!

Time to get mushy!! – December 13th 2013

Hello, my name is Phil and I am NOT an alcoholic.

Indeed, I really can say that, aside from the odd glass of wine, I don't drink alcohol at all.

And yet, last Friday evening, I found myself drinking the stuff in abundance. (AND again on Saturday, but that is a different story!)

So... what was the cause of my temporary change of habit? A Christmas night out with friends.

These weren't just any friends, however. They were "sporty" friends - members of the cycling group that I ride with, specifically.

If this were a video-blog, I would now be pausing on the image of me having my Christmas night out with others, cueing some dreamy music segue and mysteriously transitioning into another image of me from two years ago, almost to the day.

But, because this ISN'T a video-blog, I'm going to have to ask you to imagine it instead!

Now, the image in front of you should be me (or whatever mental image you have of me if we've never met) - I'm sitting next to Lisa and she is showing me a fairly mooted advert in the local paper. It gives the contact details of a chap who is looking to pull together an informal group of people who... well... just like to go out on a ride.

Not a race.

No competition (aside from a bit of machismo that can creep in from time to time).

Nope – just a ride, a chat and a cup of tea half way around.

On the day that we all now have in our minds eye, I contacted the number, arranged to meet the group as they set off for a ride and, unbeknown to me at the time, initiated a whole host of new friendships.

I remember turning up on the corner of the street where the group were going to pick me up en-route. I wasn't alone. Two other group wannabes were already waiting.

Rather poignantly, one of them has since passed away, very sadly (see my earlier blog).

The other, I seem to recall, found the pace a little too frantic and graciously let us go after less than a mile.

We cycled around 45 miles that day and I could hardly believe that we took in places that, previously, I would have only considered going by car.

Friendships were born that day, for me, and they have grown, that's for sure. Let me give you some context as to how much they have grown in the paragraphs that follow.

There was the text message conversation with one of the group deep into the early hours of the morning. One of our number had been ambulanced to the A&E department of our nearest hospital after a crash on a group ride and Lisa, my wife, was sitting with him until he was seen, repaired and sent home.

Having been involved in the incident that put him there, carrying my own minor injuries to boot, I was at home and our boys were both asleep. The text messages that were still coming through to me at 2am offering to take over from Lisa, PLUS the fact that Lisa was sitting in a hospital at all, showed me that these were real "there for each-other in times of need" friendships.

And then there was the time when members of the cycling group attended the funeral of the chap that I referred to earlier – you don't get much more intimate than that. A selection of people who, less than two years before, were almost all complete strangers to each-other were now gathered together at this most sombre of occasions.

And so, to come full circle and back to the present day, the friendships are now such that we all found ourselves sitting in a pub (I think they call themselves a Gastro-Pub but, hey) eating a Christmas meal, drinking alcohol and "making merry". And there wasn't a single square centimetre of lycra anywhere to be seen. We were "off duty" if you like... but together as a group all the same.

What made the evening so great was that we could talk about cycling without fear of an "eye-roll" of pure boredom in response. Goodness, I could even throw in a few swimming stories and the person at the other end was polite enough to listen! Having said that, the whole evening wasn't consumed with "talking sport" and, in that regard at least, our friendships were transcending the very reasons that we knew each-other in the first place.

Outside of the cycling group, I have gained many friends through social media as a direct result of my training for an Ironman. Many of you will be reading this blog, in fact.

I have had countless offers of help, funny exchanges and general chats through Twitter, Facebook and LinkedIn. I would say that I have friends all over the world – a fact that is often brought home to me when I find myself typing the words "good morning" to someone when, in fact, in the UK at least, it is the middle of the afternoon!

I won't name-check you all, for that would take me all day (and probably longer), but I have even gone on to meet quite a few of you.

As with my cycling group buddies, though, a lot of these social media friendships, whilst having been formed off the back of some crackpot sporting endeavour, are now much broader than that.

Now, I am fully aware that when you sign yourself up to something like an Ironman, or any all-consuming sporting challenge, you metaphorically leave your wider personality in the corner of the room and assume that the whole world can think of nothing better to do than discuss your training successes or failures - and regale you of theirs.

On that note, whilst I have always considered myself to have a strong but relatively small circle of friends, I didn't really have any with whom my relatively new ability to link any discussion topic to "training" would sit comfortably.

As it is, I can now rave with my much-enlarged circle of friends about how bright my bike light is (really... that has come up in discussions!), or recount what it feels like to swim in the cold cold cold (yes, I said that three times... for a reason!) sea near my home without fear of being "that" person that no-one wants to strike up a conversation with.

Sport, then, is about so much more than sport. For me, sport has been an "in" to a whole new world – a world in which I feel I belong and a world in which I am made to feel very welcome.

I now feel awash with friends which is an amazing place to be. It has even given me some more non-sporting friends who, whilst not bothered about partaking, are always keen to find out what kind of madman does the things I do!

So when I am sitting with a glass of an alcoholic beverage in my hand, looking across a "party popper strewn" table, eating great food and having a good laugh without needing to "vet" what I say next lest it might come across as boring to the un-interested, I owe it all to my sport (and Lisa, of course, for putting up with it!)

And I am, indeed, thankful for that...

Search for the hundred inside yourself – December 17th, 2013

A pretty solid week and, therefore, another training update from me.

As with last week, I had taken the day off work and Lisa and I dropped the boys off at nursery / school. You may recall from my earlier blog that Tuesdays are the only day when the boys are both away for the full day meaning that Lisa, in particular, is a "little" more free to decide how to spend the time.

I must add the word "little" when emphasising how "free" Lisa is to decide what to do for a day since, clearly, a woman's work is never done!

That said, we both turned up, all bright and breezy, to go for our second run together and, after last week's success, we were feeling confident.

Lisa had specifically asked me to push us a little further than the 1.8 miles we did last week and so I planned a 3.5 mile route using an online programme. I did make the mistake of telling her as we set off how far the run was due to be... it turns out that this was more information than she wanted to have - preferring, instead, to just run... my bad!

We set off and, again, immediately felt pretty good. Our pace certainly wasn't blistering (the run took around 39 minutes) but it was steady and enjoyable.

I think I speak on Lisa's behalf too when I say that we both enjoyed it (although we might have different definitions of the word "enjoy"!).

I didn't start to tire during the run at all and felt that I could have kept running far beyond the point at which we stopped so the early signs of my foray into the "running world" are good.

What's more, at 3.5 miles (having, in the last few years, run only 3 miles on any one occasion during sprint triathlons), it is the furthest I have run for, probably, 15 years – since before my hip made it impossible for me to walk properly let alone run. So that is a huge win.

The next day, unlike last week, my legs had no remnants of having done any running at all despite the dramatic increase in relative distance.

I'm not ignorant enough to think that, as a result of those first couple of miles last week, my body has developed some kind of conditioning for running so I can only conclude that my running style must have been different.

I certainly felt like I was making more of a conscious effort to "bounce" into each step rather than "fall on my heels" as if landing from a great height.

It was a good job that my legs felt fresh when I got out of bed on Wednesday morning. It was the second day off work in a row and I had planned a bike ride with one of those "sporting friends that I have never actually met" as referred to in my last blog.

Sadly, he had to withdraw and so, as a last minute decision, I decided to go solo.

It was cold, it was foggy and it was a little breezy but I had a "day pass" from Lisa and I was going to use it to put in what is inevitably to be my last serious ride of the year.

There is a route that I have been meaning to do for some time and I had half-planned on suggesting it to my riding partner for the day.

He might have objected, of course, but, since I was alone and objecting to my own suggestion would be plain weird, I thought I might as well..... just do it (as a well-known sports manufacturer might say).

So, off I rode.

I tried to focus on making sure that I got my nutrition right and, every ten miles, I was reaching for food whether in solid or gel form. I was alternating between the two and, seemingly, felt pretty strong throughout so I must have done something right.

For those who aren't familiar with the town names in my part of the world, you can ignore the next bit, but for those who are; I went out of my home town and headed broadly south-west through Wells and Glastonbury. I turned west towards Bridgwater. From there, I basically headed north through Highbridge, Burnham-on-Sea, Weston-Super-Mare, Clevedon and Portishead before returning home.

In all, the ride was a smidgen over 100 miles and, in the first half, took me high up into the local hills before dropping back down to a broadly flat second half.

With the conditions as they were, I was never going to treat the day as a race but I did set my mind on maintaining an average overall pace of 15 miles per hour or more. I finished at an average of 15.5mph - and that included a number of occasions where I got stuck in traffic, crawling along for what seemed like an age with no safe way around it. I was satisfied.

I love riding with friends, as alluded to in my last blog, but riding solo can be equally rewarding can't it? I had just myself for company. I didn't feel like I was holding anyone else up for instance and I always knew that, if I felt like it, I could alter my route on a whim (I didn't.... but I could have!).

Basically, I was able to just... well... ride.

Having said that, I also had no-one to duck in behind on those sections where I seemed to be battling a headwind whichever way I turned... but even that just added to the challenge and made the whole experience even better.

My longest solo ride prior to Wednesday had been around 80 miles. I remember that day well. It had been a beautiful sunny, summer's day. So the extra distance, combined with the more challenging conditions, made this ride a bit of a step up but a thoroughly enjoyable one, I must say.

As seems to be a running theme in my blogs, I wasn't sufficiently tired so as to feel knocked out for the rest of the day and, coming into the Thursday morning, when I would ordinarily swim, I felt perfectly okay to hop on my commuter bike to the pool (and on to work) rather than chickening out and driving my car or, worse still, not swimming at all!

With a hundred miles completed on my bike, the hundred lengths of my local pool had a nice symmetry to it and I turned up at the pool on Thursday at my normal 6:30am ready to go.

With trust in my swimovate watch increasing at every use, I found myself not even counting for the first few lengths; something that I have still found myself doing, despite not having to, for the last couple of weeks. Up until Thursday, I have had to remind myself NOT to count but there was none of that this time.

I felt completely at ease with the whole "swimming" thing and it almost became like an "out of body" experience at times.

I actually got into such a trance at one point that I effectively fell asleep for maybe 40 lengths or so before needing to nudge myself, and my technique, back into something resembling "effort". That blip did show in the stopwatch as I registered a time that was around 2 minutes slower than the last few weeks for the same 2.5km swim but, you know, I really wasn't bothered.

The fact that I wasn't bothered shouldn't be interpreted as a lack of care, mind you.

No, I'm not bothered because I can immediately put my finger on what happened to make me slower. I certainly would be bothered if I couldn't, for the life of me, work out what had happened.

What pleases me, actually, is just how effortless those 40 lengths or so must have been for them to have just slipped past almost un-noticed... and at only a few percent slower than my normal pace too.

So, a run, a bike and a swim in three consecutive days. Perhaps I should think about entering some kind of event which incorporates all three! If only there was such an event!

Oh the weather outside is frightful... December 21st, 2013

Another training update from me as we head into this festive period.

Shortly after finishing my last training update blog, I had a text conversation with the mate who had kindly volunteered himself as my running partner – you know; the one who was going to get me pounding the streets on foot as opposed to two wheels – mentioned in an earlier blog.

Having put in a couple of runs with Lisa, I was feeling quietly confident and I was even considering taking him on the same route that Lisa and I had done – the 3.5 miler.

To put that into perspective, he is going at it from pretty much a standing start although, I should add, he is no stranger to cardio-vascular exercise being a regular in the cycling group with which I ride.

And so it was arranged. We were going to meet up on Saturday night and go for that run.

Saturday night came, the rain lashed down and the wind picked up.

When I say it "picked up", I mean it literally "picked up" – as in "picked up trees". It was pretty blustery to say the least.

As neither my mate nor I are big fans of running at the best of times, we agreed to postpone the attempt until the following evening. I am making that sound like a mutual agreement and, in fairness, it really was.

In true competitive spirit, though, I think I managed to manipulate the text message conversation to make it look like it was him postponing and me grudgingly agreeing not to run. (He reads this so my dastardly plan is now out in the open but... hey ho).

The following day came but the weather remained the same – as did my tactics of making the ensuing text message conversation look like it was my mate who was looking to postpone – not me. This time, though, he was on to me and actually challenged me about who was initiating the postponement. I accepted that, on that occasion, that it was a mutual agreement.

So – the training week didn't get off to the best start.

We had a couple of days of reasonable weather before Wednesday came around and, sure as eggs are eggs, the weather once again started to look as if the end of the world was nigh in time for our regular Wednesday night bike ride.

All we needed were four horsemen and we could have had our very own apocalypse.

Yet another carefully worded text message conversation with the de-facto leader of the cycling group (he was trying to beat me at my own game – I declare it a draw) and, before I knew it, the Wednesday night ride was being cancelled on the grounds of safety.

It turned out to be the right call, too – the evening that followed saw some pretty unsavoury weather – certainly not the kind of conditions that you would have wanted to be balancing on two rubber contact patches barely bigger than a special edition postage stamp – no matter how bright your lights or good your balance is!

Whilst I have no readily accessible alternative to running in the comfort of my own home, I do have an alternative to cycling and so out came the torture trainer…

Did I say "torture"?

I clearly meant "turbo".

I popped the back wheel in, pointed the bike at the television in my gym and hopped on.

I'm not going to lie to you, reader – I have promised myself that this would be an honest blog and indeed it will be.

My hour on that turbo trainer was tough.

I'm not sure if I was just feeling generally sluggish what with the increasing number of, err, Christmas snacks that have been gliding quite nicely down my throat this last week or so, or whether I had the Turbo's adjustment screw pushed up against the back wheel a bit too firmly, thus creating just that little bit more drag than normal.

Either way - the next hour was more "endured" than "enjoyed".

I can normally manage an hour at pretty high effort - endurance sort of stuff - (i.e a high resistance setting, in top gear, averaging around 23mph).

Not last night.

I got to the 10 mile mark in around 26 minutes. The TV programme on the television in front of me was boring me senseless but the remote was out of reach. In lieu of something good to watch, I was "clockwatching" – this might have been my biggest mistake.

As I painfully watched each tenth of a mile click by, on through the 10 mile mark, I recognised that I was finding the session hard and decided to drop down a gear for a mile or so, just to spin my legs with less resistance and recover a bit.

I brushed my iPhone with my hand as I pulled it away from the gear changer and, for some reason, the app that I was using to log the session stopped.

I want to say that the only reason I stopped pedalling was to sort out the iPhone app but, truth be told, the stop was very welcome.

After only 26 minutes, I was relieved to have an opportunity for a break!!!! More than disappointing. An hour at this kind of effort doesn't normally phase me in the least and yet here I was after 26 minute - grateful for a rest!!

Oh dear!

I sorted the app but, by then, my rhythm was broken.

I did get going again and completed my intended hour but, again in the interest of being open with you, the remaining 34 minutes was completed in chunks, with a couple of further stops when my legs felt like they were going to explode.

All in all, my one hour session saw me cover a smidgen over 22 miles of forward motion and get off feeling a little down-hearted that my session hadn't been in keeping with normality.

Strangely, the next morning, when the weather had abated a little bit, my cycle down to the pool for my Thursday morning swim saw me feeling a little more spritely and, actually, I felt pretty good despite battling a headwind all the way (albeit not the "hurricane-like" conditions that had caused us to call off the road-ride the night before!)

To top off a pretty disappointing training week, the pool building was in darkness as I rolled to a halt outside. Initially, I figured that I was just early (I get there as it opens) and locked my bike up as normal.

Then came the rather disappointing news from one of the pool's employees, who was also stood outside with the accumulating queue of early swimmers.

Apparently, his colleague (the one with the keys) had overslept and would not be in for an hour.

I can't wait an hour. I have work to go to and that would simply not leave me enough time to swim.

I went home... disappointed for the fourth time in the week! Even more so as, what with my plans over the Christmas period, that was my last realistic opportunity to swim until the 9th January.

As you will all know, though, I tend not to stay down-hearted about things for long.

I work on the basis of allowing yourself some time to be grumpy about things (for that is when you get to mentally run through what went wrong and work out whether you can do anything differently) but, fairly quickly, I tend to pick myself up and leave the negative thoughts behind me.

Consequently, I write this blog feeling pretty "chipper" (that'll be "upbeat" for those who don't know the word "chipper"!) despite it having been a tough week.

It wasn't all bad, though. I did eventually get to go out on that run with my mate, despite the rain, and a fun run it was too. This blog is already long enough so all I will say is that it was, again, very steady and I felt well within my own limits.

I suspect that this will be my last blog until after Christmas so I will just take this opportunity to thank everyone who reads this blog for your support over this last few months and to wish you all a very merry Christmas... and if you are of a culture / religion where you don't celebrate Christmas, make sure that you have a great week anyway, whatever you plan to do, and I will see you all on the other side!

Bring on 2014 – December 28th, 2013

Every now and then, when the mood takes me, I sit down to write a blog which isn't related specifically to any particular training period but, instead, is a bit more general.

You may have noticed.

I don't always publish them immediately though – I sometimes prefer to wait until I think would be a good time.

I sat down to write this blog in mid-December and, due to its very nature, knew that I wasn't going to actually publish it until… well… today.

My blogs tend to be an un-edited stream of consciousness (as you can probably tell!) so it only took me half an hour or so before it was finished. I read it through and, by my very modest standards, it was okay. I saved it in my "drafts" folder and went about my business.

BUT….

I read it through this morning, just before I clicked the button to "publish" it and, as far as I could see, it made me sound a bit angry… A bit like a grumpy old man having a rant.

I am not an "angry" man. I am not a "grumpy" man. I am not even an "old" man (okay… that may be a bit more subjective!). I think that I might have "liked" said blog, had it been written by someone else but, as a product of my own typing fingers, I was less keen.

So… instead of publishing it, let me give you a summary of its content.

The premise of the blog in question was to discuss the merits of making New Year's Resolutions and it essentially pitched people who do make resolutions against those that don't believe in doing so.

This became the basis for the angry / conflicting tone.

You see, I deliberately highlighted a divide in the general population and then set each side to war against each other… a war of words… and I was metaphorically fighting for both sides – a double agent if you like.

It went on to eloquently, if I say so myself, outline all of the very valid reasons NOT to believe in making New Year's Resolutions. All of these reasons, of course, boil down to the basic principles of "why wait until some arbitrary date to change?" and "why try to change your habits at one of the most difficult times of year to succeed?"

I then stated my own personal view that New Year's Resolutions are perfectly valid, despite not really making any of my own.

I reasoned that now is a pretty good time to say "out with the old and in with the new" and I was pretty convincing too… although you'll need to take my word for that being that the evidence is sitting in my "deleted" folder soon to be trashed forever!

So, in lieu of the blog itself, I will skip to the conclusion which was that; if you don't believe in making New Year's Resolutions – that is perfectly understandable and very logical… so don't make them. But please don't outwardly decry those that have made them for they are already having a tough enough time just trying to stick to them without you poking your nose in!

Similarly, if you are making New Year's Resolutions, don't be too bothered by those that are happy to share all of the very valid reasons for NOT making them. You are trying to make a change (presumably for the better) and that should be applauded – however arbitrary the date that you choose to start seems to be.

For my part, as I say, I won't be making any.

Not because I think that there is nothing that needs changing but because I probably fall into the category of people who constantly analyse what they are doing and adjust it as they go along. It doesn't always give positive results but it seems to be the way that works for me overall.

Having said that, I mustn't lose sight of the fact that my whole interest in fitness and training effectively started with a New Year's Resolution made ahead of January 2004 – but that is another story.

So, in the absence of a resolution, then, what will my 2014 hold?

Well, for sure, this will be the year that I complete the Swedish Ironman in August.

It feels pretty good just typing that.

Whilst confident, I know that it will be one of the most physically demanding challenges that I have ever faced or am ever likely to face. But I am up for it and I just know that it will be a great, if very emotional, day.

From a training perspective, the year will be largely focused on that day in August where it all needs to come together but I don't want to find myself willing my time away so I am going to make the most of the 8 months leading up to it.

I have already entered at least one "Ironman Distance or more" organised bike ride per month between now and then, with the crowning glory being a 250 mile one-day event in April. That should really help me to understand what my maximum one-day range is for sure!! In between times, of course, I will continue to cycle both with my regular cycling friends and alone and expect to end the year either around or above the 100 miles per week, on average, mark.

In terms of swimming, I will be stepping up my endurance and continuing to work on my technique. From a distance perspective, I am feeling comfortable at the 2.5km that I swim on a Thursday morning so may well start chucking increments of 200 metres or so on to that although my time in the morning is a bit limited by the fact that, of course, I need to go to work!

From a "swimming events" perspective, I am entering a 5,000 metre swim that will take place in March. I also need to step up my Open Water experience pretty dramatically so I will be looking for every opportunity to do that – especially as the temperatures start to improve.

Having not yet competed in an Open Water Swim Triathlon (or, for that matter, anything longer than a Sprint distance tri), I have entered the Bristol Triathlon. It is both Open Water AND an Olympic distance triathlon and takes place around 6 weeks before the Ironman so that will be a good experience as a warm up, I'm sure.

In short my wider training goals will be to get comfortable at exceeding the Ironman distances in both the swim and the bike so that, when I set off on that day in August, I am not going to be entering new territory during the event. If my tactics regarding the run are to work, I need to feel 100% comfortable with both the swim and the bike. I need to feel like neither are going to get close to distances that I have covered previously.

So – on to those running tactics.

I am pleased to have kicked off some kind of regime but, still, for reasons that regular readers of this blog know (see the preface if you don't), I have no intention of exceeding 6 miles in training... and even that won't be a regular thing.

Now – plenty of you will think that is mad given that I will need to cover more than 4 times that on the day of the Ironman and I do understand your view. Only time will tell how that will pan out but, trust me, I "think" I know what I am doing!

From a non-training perspective, I hope to achieve all of the above without overly compromising my family.

Sure, I know that I can't achieve all of my training expectations AND still be "present" with my family at all times.

I also know that Lisa and my boys will support me in this crazy Ironman challenge despite inevitable ups and downs in their reactions to me saying that I am "heading out for a session."

BUT... I certainly don't want to be an absent husband or daddy and will look to fit in as much training as possible during times which impact on them as little as possible. Either that or I will involve them as far as I can.

With any luck, my boys will actually take something positive from what I stand to achieve in 2014 and if my methods and results teach them that working hard towards a goal is a good thing, either for now or later in life, then I will be a VERY happy man.

To finish off what is inevitably my last blog of the year, may I take this opportunity to wish you all a very Happy New Year and may it bring everything that you want it to bring!

With a lot of work, support from family and friends (both online and offline), and a dash of luck (we all need luck, however prepared we think we are), I am sure that it will be a great year.

Rear-view mirror – January 4th, 2014

With my last blog having been a look at the year ahead I thought that, now we are in 2014 (wow... 2014... how did that happen?), it might be a good chance to look back on 2013.

Obviously, this blog will focus on my "training" year, rather than anything else. My wider life has been pretty exciting too but now is neither the time nor the place for that!

Fairly early in the year saw my first century ride. 100 miles on a saddle and a dogged affair it was too.

It was a cold and windy day in March – so cold that my arms picked up a dusting of frost going up one of the hills and so windy that, at times, I swear that I was almost "track-standing" into a headwind despite trying my hardest to move forwards.

That event, entered with a few members of my cycling group, was only ever going to give me 78 miles of the 100 I wanted that day so, bearing in mind what I have just said about the weather, it took a particular kind of motivation to deliberately add 22 more miles on the end just to break my target. But I did it. And it felt great.

Leading on from the above, the year also saw my first solo 100 mile ride – only a few weeks ago, actually.

Again, the weather was hardly conducive but, nonetheless, that was a very satisfying day indeed.

Continuing on the bike theme, 2013 saw me enter a ride which pushed me up to 190 miles in one day.

I say "me" but that word ignores the support that I got from one of my cycling buddies. I couldn't have done it without his companionship (and a well-timed bowl of chips with about 25 miles to go). I can genuinely say that getting to the end of a 190 mile ride and actually feeling pretty "alive" as I dismounted was one of the highlights of my training year.

In speed terms, I like to think that I am faster cyclist than I was at the start of 2013 and my improved times over similar routes to those which I was cycling in 2012 would seem to support that view.

So – moving on to swimming; I came into the year being able to cover a Sprint Distance Triathlon swim (400 metres – 16 lengths of a pool) but barely any further than that.

Even then, every one of those 16 lengths needed to be completed using the breast-stroke method given that I was a "head-up", "keep my face out of the water" swimmer for whom managing even 2 lengths in front crawl mode was considered an absolute triumph.

Now, I swim 100 lengths, once a week, in full front crawl, and I really have no idea as to how far I "could" go being that I tend to feel pretty fresh at the end of my weekly 2.5km session. My technique needs work, sure, but is starting to take shape.

Sticking with water but getting away from the pool, I am now the proud owner of a wetsuit and, yes, it has got wet!

On a bitterly cold day in November, I ventured, with two mates, into a local marine lake and experienced brain-freeze like I've never believed possible. I lost all feeling in my hands and my feet became so numb that I couldn't really stand on them.

That was one enjoyable day!

I actually haven't been open water swimming since; not for lack of trying, though – arrangements with others just haven't been easy to make and I won't go alone just in case anything went wrong.

Getting away from swimming, I have even started to run. Yep. You did read that correctly. I have even started to run.

Up until a month or so ago, I would only run on the day of a triathlon but I have now started a light running programme on non-triathlon days too!

We are not talking running marathons here, mind, but running nonetheless.

With both my wife and a friend I have run a few miles at steady pace and was surprisingly okay after my longest run thus far of 3.5 miles.

At 3.5 miles, I ought to add that that also makes it my longest run (Triathlons included) for 15 years or more.

As some of you will already know, very soon after the year 2000, my ability to run and, subsequently, even walk, deteriorated severely and, because of that "back-story", running is probably the thing that makes me most nervous.

I know that, medically speaking, I shouldn't make a habit of running but I'm being sensible.

Having said that, when I was told that I would be in a wheelchair for the rest of my life (for the second time), I would have given my right arm just to have been able to WALK normally again... so to have even imagined the idea that I would be running would have seen me fall over in shock!

Leading on from that, the concept of entering a Triathlon would have been most bizarre so to get to the end of 2013 having bumped my total "Triathlon count" up to 8 certainly gives me goose-bumps.

2013 has seen me continue to build and develop as a Spinning instructor as well. I now teach three per week.

I must be doing something right too; One of my classes successfully petitioned to keep me when it looked like the leisure centre where I teach was going to drop me from the schedule (for some completely unknown reason, I should add).

I was even presented with a really lovely Christmas present from two of my Spinning "students". A great big hard-back book about the history of the bike. It was entirely unexpected and I was touched, to say the least.

I had a look back over my data-logging for the year and was surprised to see that, in total, I have covered 5,715 miles of exercise in one form or another (on a bike, running, on a cross trainer, in the pool etc).

Of that figure, 4,372 has been done on a bike (around 500 of which were on a Turbo Trainer). I averaged 16.49mph and climbed 141,102 feet. What's more; based on the app that I used correctly interpreting my heart rate data (which it seems to do pretty well as far as I know), I burned 175,577 calories on my bike alone. That's 70 days' worth of food!!

For those of you who, like me, believe that the year should be measured by more than just the figures above, though, I can't talk about 2013 without mentioning the support that I have had.

The most important support, of course, comes in the shape of a sexy-wee Scottish lass called Lisa... my wife (clearly!). She enables me to be the person you read about in this blog.

Don't get me wrong, mind, it's not all roses — I overstep the mark that even Lisa can put up with on plenty of occasions and friction can certainly occur although, for the vast vast majority of the time, she is not just "passively tolerant" but, instead, is "actively supportive".

My boys, too, need a mention.

At 6 and 4 years old, they put up with a daddy who is a bit mad (even I acknowledge that from time to time)... I have even, on a number of occasions, managed to get them to help me clean my bike at 5:30am (their fault, mind, for "choosing" to wake up!!) with me having "scheduled it for that time of day" rather than trying to do it at times which would otherwise impact on the more conventional family time.

They're special kinds of boys who would put up with being taught about cleaning a rear cassette rather than watching children's TV.

As for friends, I have lost count of how many friendships have been started or developed this year both online and off. There are cycling friends, swimming friends, running friends and triathlete friends. There are a good number of non-sporting friends too who seem to be polite enough to listen to my one-track-mindedness and some of them even seem intrigued by my ways.

And whilst we are talking of friends, it would be wrong not to mention lost friends — of which there is mercifully only one.. but one is one too many.

Sadly, one of my cycling friends passed away this year and that did bring things into perspective a bit. He was a true gentleman, an "all-round" nice chap and a good cyclist to boot. I know that the cycling group with which I ride is poorer without him but richer for having known him.

I don't want to end the blog on a sombre note, though, so I asked myself.... Is there one thing can I take from 2013 that wraps it all up in a neat bow and summarises it all?

Well — I guess that "one thing" would be the fact that I have entered an Ironman.

I couldn't have done that without the confidence and support that I get from family and friends.

I couldn't have done it without knowing that my training in all three of the required disciplines was going in the right direction.

And, do you know what? I WOULDN'T have done it had I not understood what it feels like to face the very real prospect of losing the ability to complete physical tasks that most, understandably, take for granted.

Indeed, my appreciation for what I can do now, thanks to a genius surgeon with a scalpel and a lifetime of experience, having come so close to not being able to do it, makes me want to tick as many boxes as I can - The "Ironman" just happens to be the "daddy" of my to-do list.

Yes – it is safe to say that entering an Ironman is the one thing that almost "proves" the existence of everything else that happened in 2013 and in the years leading up to it.

Here is to an amazing 2014.

Cometh the hour... loseth the hour – January 9th, 2014

I was pottering around on the internet earlier in the week, as you do over lunch or in the evening when you are in between other tasks, and I came across the reason for this blog.

As any basic online search will tell you, Ironman events have a "strict time limit of 17 hours". I suspect that a good percentage of the regular readers of this blog already know this.

So, for the last few months (since I entered Ironman Sweden) I have been feverishly going through permutations in my mind regarding different scenarios. Most of the scenarios have involved me estimating my swim time, estimating my bike time and arriving at how much time I would therefore have to run the marathon bit at the end.

This "time to complete the marathon" is the key to my success on the day, with my reluctance to train too hard for the run.

Many a time, I have said to Lisa (and others) that I would start celebrating at the end of the ride section if I got off the bike with, say, 8 hours left of the available 17 as, in all fairness, I could probably walk a marathon in 8 hours.

Don't get me wrong, I had never intended to take 17 hours on the day but you may recall from an earlier blog that I refuse to set myself an overall time target.

I'm happy to set myself a time target for the swim and a time target for the bike.

Assuming that I hit those targets, I will be an ecstatically happy man just to cross the finish line, even if it takes me the rest of the available 17 hours to complete the run.

In other words, I don't want to go into the day with a strategy where I might need to put my hip under unnecessary pressure and if I have to walk during the "run section" so as not to risk damaging it, then I will walk.

So – all of my permutations leading up to a few days ago have been based on a 17 hour available timeframe.

All of them have involved extrapolating out various scenarios regarding my swim and bike times and calculating how long I would have to do the marathon.

This, in turn, has led me to understand how much time I would have, on average, to run each of the 26 miles to be covered. It has been a source of great comfort that, with even the most pessimistic estimates regarding the swim and the bike sections, the resulting "running speed" required to complete the event has always been, pretty much, a walking pace.

Can you imagine my surprise, then, when I read that the Ironman Sweden cut-off is 16 hours rather than 17?

I assumed that I had mis-read and promptly looked elsewhere for clarification.

The internet search that followed was very much akin to a scientist knowing what results he wants from his experiment and deliberately moulding the process to suit his theory.

I was "googling" (other search engines are available... but let's face it, they aren't really!) terms such as "Are all Ironman events 17 hours?" and "Ironman Sweden 17 hours". I so desperately wanted to read even one line, however unqualified it was, supporting my 17 hour calculations.

I couldn't find anything.

I should, of course, searched must less "loaded" phrases and, as soon as I did so, my concerns became reality.

16 hours it is.

Not 17.

I'd lost an hour.

Now, just as I never really intended to take 17 hours to complete the event, I'm not really sure I ever expected to take as long as 16 either so this new information really shouldn't have bothered me. But it did.

It bothered me enough to get a spreadsheet going (when in doubt, do a spreadsheet!). Spreadsheets are great, aren't they? They can either allay your fears or confirm them.

Either way, you end up better informed... which is always nice in itself.

Based on some fairly pessimistic timings for my swim and bike, timings that should be within my reach by the time the day comes, and including cautiously long transition splits, I am in "16 minute mile" territory to complete the marathon ahead of the 16 hour cut-off.

Now... I know that I CAN run at 8 minute mile pace, but I also know that I would not be able to keep that up for 26 miles.

And, after 2.4 miles of swimming and 112 miles of cycling, my ultimate running pace will be even more unattainable so it is not giving me any comfort when I think about applying it to a 26 mile slog.

What is giving me comfort, though, is that my running pace when I have been out with Lisa and a friend has been around the "ten and a half minute mile territory".

That pace, meaning no disrespect to either Lisa or my friend, leaves me feeling well within myself and I reckon that I could hold that speed for quite a while if it was demanded of me.

So, for every mile I do at that pace on the day, I push the pace that I need to maintain for the remainder of the run further and further beyond the 16 minute mile target that I could conceivably start with.

It seems logical, then, that there will come a point during the run section when I will "know" that I have finished... even if the finish line isn't in sight.

As you may have already spotted in previous blogs, I like to have a "point" - a "moral of the story" if you like - for these blogs which aren't specifically related to a training period. So what is the moral of this one?

Well, in the blink of an eye something material changed in my expectations of an event. At the same time, my perception was that something had affected my ability to succeed at said event.

To start with, I effectively tried to ignore the change by searching around for information which disagreed with the new information.

However, once I accepted that the change was simply a fact that I needed to get used to, I embraced it.

I got myself organised. I rationalised what the change REALLY meant to me and, pretty quickly, I realised that my initial reaction had been irrational.

I adjusted my mindset accordingly and, as a result, very little will change in terms of my preparation for August despite what, on the face of it, seemed like quite a big bit of "news".

Only by embracing change and obstacles can we possibly seek to overcome them.

And when we do embrace them, we might just find that they really weren't as bad as we thought they were – just as I did with this one.

Back on the horse... err.. bike... – January 12th, 2014

It has been quite some time since my last "training update" blog so I thought I would bring you all up to speed.

Don't panic though – I know I have a natural ability to ramble on and on but you're not about to be subjected to a blow by blow account of all of the training that I have done since before Christmas!

Christmas is a pretty good place to start though.

I went into the festive period determined to give my family some of the time that I normally take away from them in the quest for training hours and so I knew that the Christmas week, in particularly was always going to be light on miles.

Indeed it was.

In registering just 32 miles, it was my lightest week in the whole of 2013 and the first time that I hadn't broken 100 miles since March last year.

But that was fine. Not one part of me would have done it any differently.

To go off on a tangent for a moment; Lisa is from Scotland and we had planned on going up there as a family for New Year.

I had even managed to persuade her that me taking my bike was a good idea, and had got as far as planning a lovely route for me to do on my own whilst we were there, but very high winds made the thought of towing a caravan for 500 miles each way slightly too much to bear so we sadly aborted on the morning that we were due to set off, electing to stay at home instead.

Working around our adjusted plans, I did get on the Turbo Trainer a few times as well as enjoying a couple of road rides.

On one noteable occasion, though, when I was due to venture outdoors on the bike, I looked out of the window before setting off and the ice looked pretty severe.

I did start the ride nonethless but, with one of the group come off on the slippery roads within a couple of minutes of setting off, I aborted, inwardly comfortable with my decision to have turned back towards home within a few minutes of setting off.

Lisa was grateful that I had elected not to risk it, needless to say.

This last week or so has seen a return to the normal training regime, happily and I have even managed a run with Lisa, which is incredibly pleasing.

Don't get me wrong, I managed my break without feeling too much by way of withdrawal symptoms but it didn't feel quite right and by the time I got back on with it for real, I was starting to feel edgy!

So, let's jump straight to the regular Wednesday evening bike ride – 8th January.

All day, it was threatening to rain and the forecast for the evening really didn't look great. However, I am blessed to be part of a group who laugh in the face of rain and so I knew that I could rely on them to drag me around a route.

Having got home from work, then, I ate dinner and started on what has become my standard Wednesday evening ritual of converting my commuter bike into a winter training bike – this basically involves removing my panniers and getting rid of the superfluous stuff that clings to the frame for my journey to work – a bike lock etc.

By 7pm, I was heading off up the road and the first thing that struck me was that my old friend, the "headwind", was out to play. I knew the night would be tough.

I duly met up with the group at the corner of my road and we collectively decided that, with the weather forecast as it was, we'd stick to a straightforward flat route and off we went.

It did, indeed, start to rain very heavily and for a good portion of the 30km that we covered, I could barely see anything – what with the dark and the rain combined with the flashing red lights of those in front and spray from the road.

As always, though, the strange pleasure that I derive from that kind of adversity meant that I returned home with a broad grin on my face and a spring in my step. I'm not sure that Lisa would say the same, though, having been treated to the sights (and sounds) of me trying to peel my sodden cycling gear off in the living room!

The following day, I returned to the pool, as is my normal routine for a Thursday morning.

My last "attempt", you may recall, was a few weeks ago and that didn't go too well, ending with me riding off without even getting wet due to the pool manager not turning up to open the leisure centre on time.

This meant that it was some four weeks since I last swam and I have to say that, as I arrived at the pool this time around, I wasn't feeling too confident. I suspected that, even in those few short weeks, I would have become a little rusty in terms of swim fitness.

I had this mind-set right up until I pushed off from the side of the pool to start the first length but, even within a few short metres, I could feel that my reticence was misplaced. I was feeling strong.

The lady swimming next to me was marginally (and I mean VERY marginally) slower than me so after a few lengths, when we found ourselves alongside each other, I decided that I wouldn't glance down at my watch / length counter to check how many lengths I had swam until I had done an extra two lengths over her and, effectively, caught her up again.

It was a good game to play, as it turned out. I could pitch my speed against her relative position in the pool. It pushed me on, took my mind off of the distance completely and, because my "closing speed" was SO gradual, it took almost 50 lengths to catch her back up. As I did so, I congratulated myself on getting halfway towards my hundred length target without even thinking about counting lengths.

Then it hit me.

When I embarked on this Ironman adventure, I set my sights on stepping up my endurance a bit "in the new year".

Now – I don't know if you've noticed this but it IS the new year.

Suddenly, I had the choice between backing out on my earlier promise to myself OR revising my morning swim to go for a longer distance.

I knew that I had plenty of time so I knew that I wasn't under any pressure to get out of the pool.

I took a few lengths to ponder this conundrum and reached the only conclusion that I could.

Knowing that I really wouldn't be happy with myself if I stopped at 100 lengths having previously planned, months ago, to do more as soon as 2014 arrived, I revised my goal for the day to 120 lengths (3,000 metres) and mentally re-focussed on the longer distance.

I pressed through the 100 length mark and a cursory glance at my watch told me that I had surpassed that mark at close to my fastest ever pace, which was incredibly pleasing, and for the remaining 20 lengths, my speed didn't drop one iota.

What's more, the recurring theme that runs through all of my blogs of me "getting to the end without beginning to tire" was maintained and I proved this to myself by setting my fastest ever time to get from the pool to work on my bike shortly afterwards.

All in all – a great morning's training then!

Obviously, I have missed out an awful lot of activity in the interest of bringing this blog up to date but, to wrap it up: I have started my 2014 training year in the manner in which I intend to continue.

As at the date of writing, I've averaged in excess of 17 miles of training for each day of the year thus far and, whilst I know that it is way too early to start extrapolating that out over the whole year, I noticed that my average daily figure in 2013 was just over 15.5 miles (and that included the halcyon days of summer when conditions afforded me so much more by way of opportunities) so, considering these are the bleak and baron winter days, I'm a very happy "Ironman to be" indeed.

Is vanity really where it's at? – January 16th, 2014

It's ten years since a New Years resolution, made over a drink with a friend on New Years eve 2003, saw me commit to get fit in 2004.

Actually, that's a lie.

The New Years resolution was to lose weight. Fitness was relegated to being just a possible by-product of my resolution rather than the goal itself.

You see, I had put on a little bit of weight and my appearance was that of someone who was carrying more than their natural frame was designed to.

I kept the New Years resolution and it became a way of life. The same, sadly, cannot be said of my friend who dipped out within a few weeks.

But, this blog isn't about that particular journey. I have already referred to it in a previous blog (Procrastinate? Maybe tomorrow... – October 9th, 2013) so if you want to see the clichéd "before and after" photos, you'll need to flick back to that.

No, this blog is all about the motivation for exercise and, over the last couple of years, I have noticed a huge shift in that for me personally.

I was quite specific above when I said that my resolution was to lose weight rather than to get fit.

It was, to be really blunt, based on vanity.

I just wanted to look "better" (whatever that means) than I did and, modesty aside, I reckon that I achieved that goal fairly quickly, in terms of what MY understanding of "better" was, at any rate.

I think I allude to having "felt" better in that previous blog to which I have referred above and that may have been true but, if I really bare my soul for a moment, I was more concerned with how I looked.

It strikes me that social media is littered with fitness oriented accounts and that these can be divided between two very distinct categories.

There are those that are promoting what I would call "Vanity Fitness" and those that are promoting "Sport Fitness".

"Vanity fitness" accounts are there to thrust photos of conventionally beautiful people in front of us, encourage us to judge our appearance when compared with these physical specimens and offer us quick fixes as to how we, too, could look like that if we did this, that, or the other.

That approach would have appealed to me ten years ago, I can't lie, but now I see another side of the story.

Firstly, and this is fairly obvious, who is to say that the photos posted on these accounts represent everyone's view of what "beautiful" looks like? I can certainly say that some of the photos I've seen of so called "perfect bodies" certainly don't look perfect to me.

In fact, one of them that springs to mind looks like someone who needs help, if only to find the oven, such is the extent to which her skeleton is visible.

Far from demonstrating that "thin" meant "fit" or "healthy", this person looks like she wouldn't have the energy to run to the end of the road and like she may well snap if she tried.

So, the "Sport Fitness" accounts then. What do they do?

Well, they promote ideas that will help you go faster, last longer or achieve a better result at your chosen sport.

People following these ideas will end up looking like a typical participant of their sport of choice so, for instance, a cyclist will end up looking like a cyclist... a swimmer will end up looking like a swimmer... and a triathlete will end up looking like a triathlete... and so it goes on.

I'm not saying that there is no vanity here at all but what you end up looking like is a by-product, not the product itself.

It's not that I am critical, necessarily, of the people who train for "vanity" - after all, I was one of them - but I do think that they are missing a bit of a trick which would help them to hit their vanity goals almost by accident.

Let me try to explain.

If you are chasing that dream body from, let's be sensitive about this, a little way from the finish line, then seeing images of "perfection" is probably more de-motivational than motivational, especially if your genetic make up simply won't ever let you get there.

Plus, of course, your "after" picture is not as likely to be airbrushed nor is it likely to benefit from lighting designed to make you look more muscular or defined than you really are in quite the same way as it is in those images you see online.

And if, as a "complete beginner", you train for "vanity fitness", it might be weeks or even months before you see even a small result. It takes a special kind of motivation to carry on working out despite the absence of obvious results.

Through that whole period, you are a slave to the bathroom paraphernalia - the scales and the mirror - which, again, can be a little tough to deal with and, actually, a bit demeaning really.

On the other hand, if you adopt the "Sport fitness" style approach then, to be fair, it really doesn't matter where you are on the journey, whether you are a couch potato or an elite athlete, there are always improvements to be enjoyed.

In fact, it is almost the complete reverse of the "vanity fitness" approach where results are slow to come by at the beginning and speed up as you go along. With "physical fitness" as a focus, the complete beginners are likely to be the ones who see the biggest improvements early on which must be good for motivation, surely.

It's the elite athletes for whom the improvements are harder to come by but, of course, if you ever get *there*, you are so entrenched in your new life that you're not about to drop your search for incremental improvements anyway.

And, what's more, the "vanity fitness" approach implies some kind of "finish line"; the perfect body that you have always dreamed of.

But, as we all know, there IS no finish line.

Let's assume, for a moment, that a "vanity fitness" adoptee achieves the "look" that they want.

Then what?

Where do they go from there with their training? Do they plateau and feel a bit lost? Do they keep pushing and, if so, on to what, exactly? Or do they let it drop and then feel bad about themselves all over again?

They are left in the dark a bit with nothing but a body that they are happy to look in the mirror at. What have they really achieved?

It is not as if they can show their body off in all of its glory at work and, even when they are in an environment where it is more socially acceptable to display some flesh, the most that they might get will be a sideways glance from a passer by who'll have probably forgotten what they saw within a few seconds.

If, however, you opt for "sport fitness" then it is not so much about how others see you.

It becomes more about your own inward sense of satisfaction at having hit a new fitness goal - you've completed a particular challenge, for instance, that you wouldn't have been able to complete before. You feel less of a need to be validated by those around you - you become "self-validating" almost.

You become your own hero.

And what of this "finish line" that is implied in the "vanity fitness" approach. Well, the old cycling adage of "it never gets easier, you just get faster" must surely apply. i.e there IS no finish line.

AND - I say again – you get the physique that you deserve anyway, merely as a by-product of your efforts.

So - Sport fitness goes beyond looks, it becomes about performance and, in that context, motivation almost has a habit of breeding rather, than deteriorating, as you progress.

So, if you have set yourself a new year's resolution to lose weight with the goal being to "look better" then there is, let's be really blunt, a good chance that you are on the verge of falling off the wagon.

It is mid-January after all.

Instead of feeling low about it, try to switch your focus away from a vanity based target and on to a physical fitness based objective.

Get yourself entered into a sporting event of your choice – a triathlon or an organised bike ride, for example – and specifically train for it.

You'll start to see measurable improvements in your performance pretty quickly and the motivation you'll take from that will inadvertently take your mind off of the vanity side completely.

And with your mind elsewhere, you'll end up with a physical body which is designed to do what you have trained it to do, as far as your genetics will allow anyway, but you will have had so much more fun shaping it along the way!

Where are the brakes on this thing? – January 21st, 2014

Another training update from me.

Let's start where I always tend to start with these training update blogs – with the normal Wednesday evening bike ride.

All day, the weather was threatening rain of deluge style proportions but the fact that I so wanted to get out on my bike, couple with my much mooted bizarre enjoyment of such conditions, meant that I made sure to contact Spencer, the cycle group leader, to let him know that I was still up for an evening spin if he was.

I would have gone out alone but company is nice so, thankfully, he responded to say that he was also happy to go out and I set off at the normal time, around 6:50pm, to meet him a few miles away, for 7 o'clock.

Within seconds I was as wet as it is possible to be so, thereafter, the weather wasn't really an issue.

Despite the dark, wet and windy conditions, I was surprised to see that the group turnout wasn't limited to just Spencer and me. In fact, two other stalwarts had turned up and the mood was surprisingly chipper.

There have been quite a few of these Wednesday evenings now where we have been rained on quite heavily and, whilst we have still all been out there on our bikes regardless, the winter hasn't been completely without impact.

Our Wednesday evening rides, which got up to the around 30 miles on occasion in the glorious summer months are now struggling to break 20 miles in this dark, wet and cold winter.

Our Wednesday evening rides, which took in all kinds of ascents and descents in the glorious summer months are now, broadly, flat in this dark, wet and cold winter. (The funny thing that is now running through my mind now is that, in posting this blog on a Tuesday, you can bet your bottom dollar that Spencer will read this and plan a hilly route for tomorrow!)

The winter, then, has dulled my "summer sharpness", I suspect, but, you know, I am considerably more active this year than I was in January 2013 so I just know that, as the days lengthen and the sun becomes more of a regular cycling partner, I'll be straight back up there in a jiffy.

Anyway – it was a thoroughly enjoyable ride, covering 20 miles in a little over 1 hour and 10 minutes.

131

As sure as day turns to night, Wednesday night turns to Thursday morning and regular readers of this blog will know that that can only mean one thing – "swim session Thursday".

I arrived at the pool at 6:30am and, psychologically, was still buoyed by my successful swim last week when I stepped up my distance from 2,500 metres to 3,000 metres.

I was really looking forward to getting in to the water.

This time last year, swimming really wasn't something that I enjoyed – not least because I couldn't really do it.

These last few weeks, however, I have found myself waxing lyrical about it in much the same way as I do about cycling.

Don't fret, though, you cycling-fanatics out there, cycling will always be the closest to my heart of the two, but swimming now comes a very close second. (I should probably mention that my wife and kids come before either of them, shouldn't I?)

Those demons that I was plagued with last year – the sense of "drowning" within only a few lengths and the customary day long head-ache on leaving the pool – are now distant memories - Not by accident, mind, I worked hard to understand what caused them both and equally hard to take steps to rid myself of them.

Bizarrely, though, the only after effects of the swim now seem to be a propensity to sneeze a lot during the 12 hours afterwards but I am putting this down to a reaction to chlorine. If, of course, you know better then do let me know!

So, with this air of positivity about my swim, I set off on my way to repeating my 3,000 metre swim from last week.

I was immediately pleased to see that the lady who was swimming next to me last week was, again, alongside me.

If you read my earlier blog, you'll know that she is very marginally slower than me and, last week, my "game" of putting two laps over her before looking at how many lengths I'd swam had helped me to pass 50 lengths last week almost without realising.

This time, though, she was doing sets and her incessant stopping every couple of lengths made the game impossible.

Did she not know how much I was relying on her to race me? Honestly! Some people think only of themselves with little regard to other people's needs!

So, in the absence of the game that got me so far last week, I just pressed on at my own merry pace.

I'm not joking when I say that I had completed an estimated 45-50 lengths before I decided to glance at my swimovate watch to get a more accurate picture of how far I'd swam.

An estimated 45-50 lengths without the slightest thought regarding distance covered!

Well, I'm also not joking to say that, having estimated 45-50 lengths, I was more than a little surprised to see, when I did look at my watch, that I'd actually covered 88 lengths! 88 lengths without really noticing!

I kept swimming.

And I kept on swimming.

And I kept on swimming until I got to the pre-defined target of 120 lengths and, bizarrely, my fingers wouldn't hold on to the side of the pool long enough to haul me out before my legs were kicking me off of the side to start yet another length. It was as if I couldn't stop!

I went on to cover 130 lengths, 3,250 metres, and only stopped when I reminded myself that I had work to go to.

Pace-wise, my average "time per 100 metres" was (to the second) the same as it always is and, again, I didn't slow during the latter part of the swim. I may not be fast but I certainly seem to have consistency on my side!

All in all, then, I would say that the swim could be described as somewhere between surreal and serene. Not a bad combination!

Fast-forward to Saturday.

Lisa and I scheduled a run together with my parents offering to look after my boys and there was a window of opportunity, in what was otherwise poor weather, for us to get out at around 10am, which we duly did.

Lisa mentioned that she sometimes feels a bit guilty regarding how slow she runs compared to my ultimate pace, which I think was her being too hard on herself, and my response was one that I had co-incidentally pondered during the week.

As I've maintained throughout this blog, I have no intention of setting the world on fire in the run section of the Ironman.

I just want to protect my hip and finish – I'd be more than happy to walk the whole way if that is what it takes.

So, in training with Lisa, I have automatically been running at a quicker pace than I will be happy with on the day of the event itself and, as you may have already read on these pages, so there is no question that she has been holding me up!

We set off on the run at 12 minute mile pace and then, at some point along the way, stepped up the pace to just "sub-9 and a half minute mile" territory after a mile or so.

We covered 3.3 miles in 33 minutes.

That was a bit silly.

I don't need to run that fast and, straight away, I was in to a pace which, whilst pretty comfortable, I know that I couldn't maintain for a whole marathon distance without risking my hip unduly.

So why did I do that?

All I can say is that I don't know… but I won't do it again.

A bit like the swim, I guess, I didn't really know where my own brakes were.

But, unlike the swim, this particular lack of control could do me physical damage so I must not succumb to that temptation again.

I just have to keep reminding myself that the run is the one area that I need to keep free from my competitive spirit and that, as long as I cross the line and collect a medal, I'll be over the moon!.

Again, this training blog needs to be brought to a close without mentioning quite a bit of work that I got in during the week – I've limited it, as I always do, to the "highlights", if you like.

On reflection, t was another positive week out there and, all things being equal, the next training update should include details of my first 100 mile ride of 2014 so stay tuned for that!

If I need anything, I'll ask! – January 25th, 2014

This blog is not so much a blog as a series of questions in a blog format.

It struck me the other day that all I know about the Ironman event to which I am signed up is that, on the day, I will be swimming 2.4 miles, cycling 112 miles and then running 26.2 miles.

Aside from that, I know nothing at all!

In the past, I have found myself giving basic guidance to triathlon newbies relating to what they can expect from the day and I like to think that the guidance I have given has been well received and useful.

Having said that, all of that guidance has been for pool-swim / Sprint distance triathlons where, at most, there have been around 200 competitors and the whole event has been wrapped up in the space of a few hours.

I suspect that the similarities between the types of triathlons that I've done and an Ironman begin and end with the sporting disciplines involved and so it has hit me that I have very little idea what Ironman Sweden will have in store.

I am conscious that quite a few of my regular readers are already "Ironmen" or "Ironwomen" so, as you read through this blog, please feel free to answer any questions that it contains in the comments box to both help me and to help anyone else who might be wanting to do one.

What if you aren't thinking of entering an Ironman? Will you get anything from reading this blog or should you just stop reading now?

I'm not sure but I'd ask you to risk it.

What I am trying to do is get across the idea that you can commit yourself to something... anything really... based on principle alone.... despite a large degree of uncertainty... knowing that, when the time comes, you can reach out to others for guidance.

I'm also trying to get the message across that asking for help is a perfectly acceptable thing to do!

So - the first thing that I notice whenever I look at Ironman events on-line is that, far from being a "turn up in the morning and go home when you finish" sort of affair, it looks to me as if the whole occasion effectively takes place over a number of days with both pre and post-event "things" taking place.

I deliberately used the word "things" above as I have no idea what these "things" are – They seem to include gatherings, ceremonies, activities, procedural stuff and such-like but, really, I have no idea aside from the fact that "things" seem to exist.

So my question is; how do I know what these "things" are? Will I get a schedule of events from the organisers ahead of the day? By when would I expect to get this schedule (and, effectively, when should I start to chase if I've not received it?).

I then picture myself arriving at the start-line... gingerly wading into the water... full of nervous tension.

What happens then?

I reckon that there must be a couple of thousand people entered in Ironman Sweden and, with that many people swimming together, there must surely be a risk of a Tsunami the other side of the water!

Is there a starting pistol with everyone setting off at the same time or do you set of in waves (pun very much intended)?

I make no bones about the fact that the swim bit does make me nervous as, right now, I have so many uncertainties.

Some of these uncertainties (what it is like to swim in really choppy water, for instance) will no longer be an issue by the time the day comes around since I will train these uncertainties out of me.

Other uncertainties will remain though.

So, please, what does happen? How do I make sure that I am swimming in the general area of other swimmers who swim at a similar pace to me? Is it really the "washing machine" that I have heard people talking about and, if so, are there any useful tips to minimise this?

Thus far, I have only limited experience of extricating myself from my wetsuit. I reckon that I can do something about that – practice it more, of course.

No matter how practiced I get though, I doubt I will ever be able to remove it in a graceful way and I reckon that the whole process will involve physical contortions and sound effects to match – you know, a fair bit of huffing and puffing as I try to force it firstly down to the floor and then over my feet.

I was watching an Ironman event on the television, though, and I'm sure I saw a team of helpers effectively pulling people's wetsuits off! Is this normal? Did it happen at all or were my eyes deceiving me? It would certainly help to have someone there to do this but am I expecting too much?

Assuming that, one way or another, I manage to remove my wetsuit without doing myself an injury, my next focus will then be on my bike.

Phew.

Of the three disciplines, this one holds the least amount of fear.

But, paradoxically, it also holds the most amount fear – i.e this is the section which I might approach with complacency and I fear that that might cost me dear.

So – having swam 2.4 miles before I mount my bike, I reckon that, unless I take on some form of nutrition, I will have little chance of riding 112 miles without ending up in an ambulance.

I will be looking for food in my kit bag (which I THINK I've seen people carrying around transition areas on some of the online Ironman footage).

I'm also, clearly, going to need nutrition on the ride itself (and the run, for that matter).

Having previously done a non-stop solo ride of just short of Ironman distance, I know that I found a good balance in taking on fuel every 35 minutes or so. That meant that I loaded my bike up with as much as I was likely to need (and a bit more) before I set off.

BUT... watching these Ironman events on television, where, granted, the cameras tend to be trained on the "elites", I see that their bikes always seem to be devoid of anything that would weigh them down! What do they eat and where do keep it such that it seems invisible to the TV cameras?!! The same goes for the run!

Finally, by way of introducing the last question, for now anyway, I can't wait to cross the finish line and hear those "You are an Ironman" words that I've heard about.

I really can't wait.

I'm not sure if I've said this before but, as a family, we are making a 2 week holiday of the whole event with the Ironman itself sitting right in the middle. The main point here is that we are going to Sweden AS A FAMILY.

My wife and boys will, of course, watch the "grand-depart" and then, to state the obvious, they will have a whole day to kill (is there anything for them to do?) before I get to that finish line BUT I really want them to be AT the finish line when I am.

I might be able to give an educated guess as to when I am likely to be running, walking or crawling over the line but I can't be sure and I don't suppose that they will want to stand there for, say, a window of 2 or 3 hours just waiting.

I also don't suppose that there will be physical room for that to happen on the basis that there could be hundreds of other families all trying to do the same thing at the same time – waiting to welcome their loved one "home".

This is especially true at my end of the field – I'm pretty sure that I will be finishing with the other "one-off" / "occasional" Ironman Triathletes who will want their families there – unlike the "elites" / "regulars" finishing ahead of me and for whom it is just another day.

So, is there any way that we can remove some of the guess-work from this? Is there any way that we can plan to ensure that Lisa and the boys are at the finish line when I get there? (Please note that if there is no way, I'm going to create one so, if you're thinking of stealing my thunder on the creativity front.. hands-off… it's now on-record as MY idea!!)

In short, I fear that the whole euphoria of the achievement might be tainted if I can't share it with my family immediately – plus, I'm going to want a pretty big hug and it won't feel quite right to grab a random stranger!

I have so many more questions to ask and this may well be the first of a series of questions that I drip-feed on to the pages of this website over the coming months so please do keep coming back to help me out!

As I said, I wanted to get this blog out there - not just to help me or to help anyone else who might have the same questions about an Ironman event that they have entered but also to get across to everyone else that uncertainty is good.

Why is it good?

Well, firstly, it adds to the whole excitement, that's for sure.

More importantly, though, uncertainty creates the environment to make connections with others. I tend to find that, as a rule, people are kind and they are happy to help.

So, if you are uncertain about something that you have committed to do, I hope this blog gives you the nudge you need to ask for someone's help.

I would suggest that all of my questions are easy to answer... if you know the answer... just like any question... but that doesn't make it a stupid question for, as we all know.. there is no such thing as a stupid question.

The Jack and Grace Cotton Audax – 28th January, 2014

I want to make the focus of this blog the bike ride that I did on Saturday – kind of a "not so short" story, if you like – so I will completely ignore my other training, if that is okay with you!

Saturday, was the day of "The Jack and Grace Cotton Audax" bike ride – a fairly local annual event that I entered some while ago.

The route itself was 65 miles or so and, knowing that I want to get at least one "100 mile plus" ride in per month, I planned to ride out to the start which was around 18 miles away from home, just south of Bristol.

The additional 18 mile ride back home from the finish, then, would see me break the 100 mile mark.

I knew that quite a few of my regular cycling group were planning on doing the ride too so I was certain to see familiar faces as I arrived at the start.

What I didn't expect was for my mate, Tom, to ride out to the start with me... He actually CHOSE to leave home a little before 6am to cycle out to Bristol with me and, what makes that more remarkable is that he wasn't even going to do the ride itself.

He was going to start and then, 30 minutes in, turn around and go home so he could meet his own deadline of being back by mid-morning.

Anyway, Tom duly arrived at 6am and off we set at a leisurely effort towards, firstly, another cycling friend's (Adam) house where we were promised bacon rolls before a short hop from there to the start.

The trip to Adam's was straightforward and we arrived probably a little sooner than I had anticipated but Adam was ready for our arrival all the same.

Spencer, the leader of the cycle group with which I ride, plus two others from the same group (Pete and Tracy) arrived shortly after us, having elected to transport their bikes to Adam's by car.

We were all set for the off.

The first half of the Audax which, for me, made up miles 18 to 50 of the day's ride, was spent at ease, pleasingly

We elected to join the group departing at 8:30am despite the fact that it was around 8:35 before we actually set off.

This meant that, by the time we were cycling, the rest of the 8:30 bunch had a little head start on us.

Against that backdrop, we seemingly spent the next 32 miles catching groups of cyclists, drifting past them, before concentrating on reeling in the next group who were a bit further up the road.

Somewhere into that 32 miles, Spencer and Adam, who are much stronger cyclists than I am, dropped me and, unexpectedly, I pushed ahead of Pete and Tracy.

With Tom having duly turned back after 30 minutes, I found myself cycling alone.

It wasn't an issue though.

I had the benefit of a fairly kind following "breeze" and I got to 50 miles for the day averaging 17.5 miles per hour (not including stops, of course) which I was very pleased with, particularly given how relaxed I was feeling.

The first "control" point (that I stopped at, anyway – having missed the first one) was a pub and came at around the half-way point of my 100 mile target. Having already made sure to take on nutrition at 10 mile intervals, I had no need for any of the snacks that were on offer - I stopped only to, err, use the "facilities" before jumping back on the bike and pressing on.

Rather than a circular loop, the route for the day was more of an "out and back" affair and so I always knew that the breeze that had helped me on the way out was going to be less welcome in the second half.

What I didn't really prepare myself for, though, was the fact that the breeze was going to become more of a... well.... read on and you'll find out!

I made a couple of right turns and found myself pointing south having been facing north for a few hours. The pace slowed as I pushed into what I would now describe as less of a "breeze" and more of a "wind".

Regular readers of this blog will know that wind is not my friend!

Whilst I was contending with the ever building wind speeds, then, the next thing that hit me was that, despite a fairly flat "out" section, the remaining 30 miles or so of the Audax itself were decidedly "lumpy".

There were no big climbs to contend with, granted, but hardly any of it was just flat.

I was either descending or ascending and, as is often the case when the wind is already trying it's best to knock the stuffing out of you, it felt like there were more "up hills" than "down dales"!

I had not seen any of the rest of the group for quite a while now and so it was nice to get a text message from Spencer when I was around 10 miles from the end of the Audax (around 73 miles into my day's riding), saying that he and Adam were at the final control point, a café, and enquiring as to my whereabouts.

It turned out that I was literally a couple of hundred yards away from them

Incidentally, Spencer and Adam had arrived 15 to 20 minutes ahead of sending that text message to me – I don't want to give the impression that I was hot on the heels of those guys!

Meeting up with them and electing to enjoy a flapjack with a cup of tea, was welcome indeed and spirits were high.

The wind was really picking up now, though… so much so that it seemed to be the main topic of conversation amongst fellow cyclists at that café.

That said, the sun was out and the sky was pretty clear. We had a ten mile run in to the Audax finish and then, of course, I had an 18 mile ride back to my home. What could be simpler?

My legs screamed as I got back on the bike - cold muscles and strong head-winds joined forces in an attempt to dampen my spirits.

Adam and Spencer dropped me fairly easily in that 10 miles and, whilst they kindly "tried" to let me stay on their wheels, there was little point in pretending that I could ride at their pace so I let them go.

By now, the "wind" had become a "gale" and I was being blown all over the place.

At the finish, I reconvened with Spencer and Adam and we went back to Adam's house where Adam's hospitality meant that I promptly shovelled another cup of tea and piece of carrot-cake down my neck.

A glance out of the window showed dark clouds had gathered and it looked decidedly violent.

Such was my determination to get through the 100 mile mark, that I declined Spencer's offer to chuck my bike on his car roof for him to give me a lift home.

I also turned down a text message from Lisa, warning me of the weather closer to home and offering to come and pick me up.

I got back on my bike.

The ride home, through the centre of Bristol and out the other side, was a total disaster.

I was crawling along in stop-start traffic down the only descent I was going to get — where I'd rather hoped to get a couple of "free miles".

I was either having to lean into the strong crosswinds at an angle of attack that I don't think I've ever ridden at.... OR..... I was having to stand up on my pedals just to generate enough power to keep moving forwards into the wall-like head-wind.

The wind even managed to part me from my bike on one occasion. I was stopped at some traffic lights and even my best efforts at bracing myself weren't enough to save me from being blown over and landing in a heap on the floor!

Then the rain came. It was hurting my face!

Then the hailstones came. I was begging for the rain to return!

Then I picked up a slow puncture which I doggedly refused to fix properly as I just couldn't face standing in the gale force winds and hailstones to change an inner tube!

So, I found myself stopping every couple of miles just to pump my back tyre up.

Why did I do this to myself? I wanted my 100 miles and I was going to get it. But why?

With around 8 miles to go, and with regular text messages coming in from Lisa offering to pick me up (she was understandably concerned for my safety), I agreed that I wasn't going to make it home and asked her to come out to pick me and my bike up. I carried on riding whilst I "waited".

We effectively crossed paths when I had just 5 miles to go but, crucially for my state of mind, I had completed 100.2 miles.

Why did I give up?

Wind? Rain? Puncture? Exhaustion?

Any of these would have been good reasons but, the truth is, none of these came into it. I was as wet as I was likely to get and the puncture was manageable .My legs were still turning, despite the wind, and another 5 miles was well within my capability.

Safety, then? It had to be safety didn't it?

Nope. That would have been a sensible reason to stop, of course. It was certainly too dangerous to be riding, I reckon... but it wasn't what stopped me.

I was very grumpy at myself after the ride and I couldn't put my finger on why... until Sunday morning when, still feeling annoyed, I worked out my reason for having given up with a paltry 5 miles to go.

As I've said before in this blog, I will always try to be honest on these pages, however daft I might end up looking and this time is no different so here goes!

I stopped because my average speed was dipping dangerously close to sub 15 mph territory. I just didn't want to log a ride with a "14 point something" average speed.

My app in front of me, having been reflecting a healthy 17.5mph average earlier, was now showing 15.1mph average for the day and I knew that, in the next few miles, with gusts of winding slowing me to 11-12 mph in places, even on the flat, it would dip below that "15" mark before I got home.

So I stopped.

How mind-blowingly ridiculous is that? How frankly weird does that sound? What kind of a nutcase even cares about that when he's facing the other stuff that is going on?

This completely mad reasoning is why I was grumpy at myself for stopping.

I knew I'd been silly and I was cross.

It was completely irrational but I stopped for vanity... and, in the cold light of day, that did irk somewhat!

And, the thing that really stings is that, when I uploaded the ride to Strava - because of the different ways that Strava treats stopped time (at traffic lights, road junctions etc) - my average on there is shown at 14.5 mph anyway!

So my reason for stopping was irrelevant!

I feel a bit "ungrateful" for being disappointed with a training week that involved over 185 miles of exercise, including a 100 mile bike ride, but I am and I can't help that.

It's all character building stuff though - I'm over it now and have moved on! Less nonsense and madness in future, I promise!!

All in a week's work – February 4th, 2014

You know… it's not easy training for an Ironman.

I don't think that anyone will ever tell you it is.

It takes a lot of time for starters.

I suspect that many of the readers of this blog have an image of my family being "widowed" by my training – You might picture a forlorn looking wife and boys, longing for me to just give them a few of my valuable minutes.

It might even be that some of you would love to do something like an Ironman but are actually put off by this blog, with all of its talk of training hours, on the basis that you just don't feel that you want to spend SO much time away from your loved ones.

So, I thought I would just pen a blog to redress the balance a little and tell you how I fit it all in whilst trying not to put my family in a position where they see no other option but to "divorce" me!

First things first then… what family time do I get during my working week?

Well, I get to spend every morning of the working week with my boys and Lisa… from the time they get out of bed until around 8:15am, when I set off on my bike to work.

On Tuesdays, I don't ride to work and, instead, get to do the "school run".

So, every morning, I have plenty of time to give my boys breakfast, to play with them a little, to make Lisa her morning coffee and even to do a spot of housework – basic housework, I grant you, but housework nonetheless.

The only exception to this is that I am out of the house by 6:15am on a Thursday for my swim session… that is the one morning of the week when I don't see my family at all (if my tip-toeing around to avoid waking them up has been successful, anyway!)

I then spend three of the five evenings of the working week with Lisa and the boys. These are Tuesdays, Thursdays and Fridays.

All three of these evenings are completely free from training and, on a Friday, I even get to be an official parent-helper at Angus' Beavers sessions.

What about the weekends?

I am a "present" husband and daddy for pretty much the whole of Saturday.

I get to give the boys breakfast, play with them a bit as well as doing some of my own chores. Lisa gets a well-earned lie-in too.

Once we are all out of bed, Saturday is generally taken up with whatever we all want to do as a family.

This can vary from something as sedentary as a "stay at home day", watching films, right to the other end of the scale where we find ourselves out and about being active for the whole day... on our bikes, swimming, sight-seeing etc.

On a Sunday, I get to give the boys breakfast and play with them for a while. Lisa still gets a bit of a lie-in but, admittedly, I am then absent from around 9:15am until 11:30am.

Sunday afternoons and evenings are one hundred percent training free, as a rule, and I spend it all with Lisa and the boys.

The only exception to this weekend routine tends to occur when I have an endurance bike ride scheduled.

For 2014, I have one "100 miler or more" in the diary each month between now and the Ironman itself in August and they do tend to take me "out of commission" for the whole day.

Aside from to train, I rarely go out without my family.

I have no particular love of the pub or golf or football.

I've even stemmed my passion for motorsport these last few years which I would have never thought I could do.

So, hey, it sounds like I get to spend lots of time with Lisa and the boys doesn't it?

So when on earth DO I train?

Let's start with mornings.

I get up at 5am every day – around one and a half hours before anyone else in the house – and that extra time gives me the chance to do a resistance session or a Turbo Trainer session (depending on which I think I need the most) as well as my morning stretches, which I do every day without fail, and which are designed to strengthen and protect my hip.

So – as well as having time with Lisa and the boys for six out of every seven mornings, my determination to get up so much earlier than them also means that I can pretty much train for each of those mornings too.

On a Thursday, I am up even earlier - at 4:30am - to get out of the house by 6:15am for that weekly swim.

It's not easy dragging myself out at that time of day, I must confess, especially since I will have been cycling the night before, but it's a lot nicer than trying to take yet another evening of the week away from Lisa and the boys.

All of this, of course, is forgetting that, as a cycle commuter, I am putting miles in my legs just getting to and from work – which is all good!

As for the evenings…

Monday evenings, I leave my day-job and go straight to my "second job" as a Spinning instructor.

I teach two sessions on a Monday night, in two separate locations, riding between the two. The whole night, then, is spent training and I don't get home until 9:15pm.

On a Wednesday night, I get in from work, eat and, pretty much, head straight back out on my bike to join a group ride. I am out for up to 2 hours in the winter – sometimes longer in the summer.

That is it for evening training, then, until Saturday night when, once the boys are in bed, I either hop on the Turbo Trainer or I go out cycling on the road. Either way, Lisa doesn't see me for an hour or so of the evening.

When I run, I tend to do it on a Saturday morning, with Lisa – so I get to spend more time with her and the boys spend some time with my parents, their Grandparents.

I then finish off my training week with the third Spinning session on a Sunday morning… again, as the instructor. I cycle up to the leisure centre where I instruct just to get a few more miles under my belt.

I know that many Spinning / fitness instructors don't subscribe to the idea of pushing themselves as hard as the rest of the class but, believe me, I push myself HARDER than anyone in front of me… so it really does make up part of my training week as well as being a bona-fide job in its own right!

There is quite a bit of training in there, of course – I doubt there is a short cut to being an Ironman finisher, after all.

Saying that, I sometimes wonder whether I'm doing ENOUGH. I only do one bike ride of more than 20-25 miles per month, for example.

On top of all of that training, there is the ancillary stuff – the "cleaning my bike", for example. For this kind of thing, I tend to get up EVEN EARLIER just so that I can do it without impacting on Lisa and the boys.

And, lastly, there is writing this blog!

People seem to think that I must spend hours on these blogs but my writing method means that they tend to be unedited and just pour out of my fingers on to the keyboard before I click "post".

Consequently, I can easily rattle a new post off in my lunch hour at work – so I do – I am right now, in fact! It takes no time away from my family at all.

Whilst I undoubtedly dedicate more time than most to training, I also hope you can see that my schedule does have a fair amount of time when I get to enjoy the company of Lisa and my boys.

Sometimes, I think it is hard for even them to see that I'm not "always" training – I think it's easy for them to think that I'm never around and I'd be lying if I said that it didn't cause any conflict at all.

Let's be left in no doubt that Lisa does end up picking up an awful lot of the slack whilst I am training and, of course, at work.

Aside from the general tidying, emptying/stacking the dishwasher and general stuff that I can squeeze in first thing in the morning before I go to work, she does the comfortable majority of the housework.

She does all of the clothes washing, ironing, pretty much all of the cooking and, as a rule, all of the grocery shopping – most of which she has to fit in during her normal day when, let's not forget, she has her own agenda of things that she needs / likes to do as well as looking after my boys outside of school / nursery hours.

The things that us blokes tend not to notice – you know, the "picking the clothes up off the floor", the "replacing the toilet roll" and the "putting the shoes back in the cupboard" – these are all her domain as well... and I concede that! – but that's not so much a symptom of me training for an Ironman... that's just me being male.

All of Lisa's time, effort and support is especially appreciated but the main point of this blog is to let you, the reader, know that it IS possible to take on something like an Ironman without completely extricating yourself from family life.

I hope I've demonstrated that, whilst you do need your partner and family to be "on board"– as well as having a fairly healthy dollop of determination to do things at times of day that others may class as plain wrong – you CAN fit in training around your family life.

I do it.... just!

So, if you are thinking of getting into something that looks like too much of a demand on your time, rethink whether it really is possible or not.

It might just be... but you have to want it enough!

Determination is key – hence this picture that Lisa bought me and which is hung on my bedroom wall – it's the first thing I see as I get up every day.

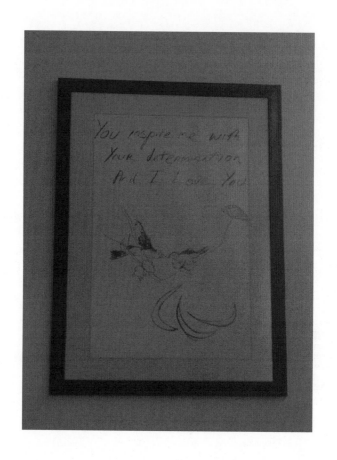

Getting your CV in order – February 8th, 2014

A couple of weeks have passed since my last training update blog and, when I wrote that last one, I made the conscious decision not to pen another until I had something new to say.

You see, I had managed to get myself into a pretty good routine of loving my bike-riding, enjoying my swimming, and finding running pleasurable. I was steadily consolidating my ability in each and was into a good routine.

But nothing particularly new was happening each week so I figured that you wouldn't want to just keep reading the same old same old every time you clicked on my page.

Now I've got you thinking, haven't I?

Why have I sat down to write a training update now then?

What has changed?

Well, I guess it all started a couple of weeks ago with "that" ride (the aborted Jack and Grace Cotton Audax which is the subject of an earlier blog) and a subsequent session on my Turbo Trainer.

I was doing a "Sufferfest" training video.

For those who don't know, Sufferfest is a company that produces videos to which you train on your Turbo Trainer. You set your iPad (or your own screen of choice) in front of your bike, press start, and start pedalling.

It tells you how much effort to put in at any given moment and is set against a backdrop of pumping music, motivational footage of pro-cyclists showing you how it should be done and mild abuse, in the form of subtitles, designed to drag yet more performance out of you.

Sufferfest have developed their own hard-core training acronyms including the catchy - IWBMATTKYT ("I will beat my ass today to kick yours tomorrow").

They like to attach phrases to effort levels too… for example, one of their definitions of how you should feel when you are pushing at 10/10 effort is: "Stick a fork in me, I'm done".

It's pretty tough stuff.

Turbo Training, for me, used to involve setting the resistance up to high, getting the chain onto the very smallest cog at the back and just peddling at nigh-on maximum effort for an hour.

I'd cover around 22 forward miles in a session and tended, as I tired, to progressively slow down as the hour went on.

Then, somewhere around the beginning of the year, I started to do these "Sufferfest" videos instead as I thought that I could do with shaking my training up a bit.

In the session that I am referring to, the screen in front of me told me to push on to just shy of maximum effort for a handful of minutes.

Bearing in mind that, before I discovered these "Sufferfest" videos, I was regularly sustaining that level of effort for up to an hour, you can imagine my surprise when the next few minutes were a struggle.

With my modest understanding of anatomy and physiology, I reasoned that the "interval" nature of the session that I was riding was bound to affect my ability to sustain high output and I didn't give it much more thought.

I then noticed over the following few days that my rides to work were becoming more and more of a struggle.

Even if I seemingly pushed myself, I couldn't get within 20% of the time that I was taking to cover those same 5 miles only a few weeks before Christmas. 20%!!

Again, I found an excuse – the head-wind was to blame. Of course it was.

My training routine carried on unabated.

Fast-forward to Thursday 30th January and I found myself in a swimming pool in Newport, South Wales, 30 miles away from home. I was due in a meeting over there and, rather than forego my Thursday swim session, I had sought out a pool closer to said meeting.

I got 2 lengths into that session without managing more than a few strokes in full front crawl!

I stopped to regroup, a little perturbed by my failure, and started again.

I did another two lengths – again failing to maintain front crawl for more than a few seconds at a time.

For context, if you are new to these pages, you are reading the blog of someone who normally has absolutely no trouble swimming in excess of 2 miles in full front crawl without tiring or faltering.

Again – I searched for an excuse. The water was colder. That was it.

The water was, indeed, much colder than the normal pool in which I swim and I suppose that this was one reason for this "hiccup" (my ability to breathe does seem to be affected by temperature and I am very conscious that I need to rectify this long before my Ironman in August).

But... I'd had a week of making excuses and there was something wider going on here.

Surely, I couldn't have suddenly gone from being physically fit enough to do this stuff, without batting an eyelid, to struggling... in a matter of a couple of weeks.

And then it hit me... it was my CV.

And I don't mean my Cardio Vascular fitness or, for that matter, my Curriculum Vitae either.

I am talking about complacency and vacancy.

I had become complacent that I could just do this stuff and, as a result, I was mentally vacant when training.

Back to that morning in Newport, then. I stopped at the end of my 4th unsuccessful length of the pool – this time for longer and with more purpose.

I stood still and gave myself a stern talking to (not out loud, you understand – that would have looked plain weird and I might well have been asked to leave!).

I inwardly told myself to stop taking it for granted and dragged my mind into the moment.

Once I had done with the self-awareness stuff, I pushed off the side of the pool with a renewed determination to get through any breathing problems that I was putting down to temperature.

I got straight into my typical rhythm very quickly and I think, as a by-product, I learned a valuable lesson in the process – the lesson being that once you have warmth in your body, the water temperature is, to an extent, irrelevant. I'll need to remember that for my next open-water swim!

155

I, complete with my adjusted mind-set, went on to swim that 3,250 metre session in a quicker time than ever before.

And not just a couple of seconds quicker... I was a few MINUTES quicker.

Furthermore, I was challenging myself to take as few strokes as possible per length and, sure enough, my Swimovate watch subsequently told me that I had beaten my previous record in that area too.

In all other areas of my training over the coming days, I found myself replacing complacency and vacancy... with focus.

A focus on ensuring that I was mentally present rather than just physically going through the motions.

It showed.

My riding was stronger, I felt better and, as a result, I recovered what I had seemingly started to lose.

I even got on the Turbo Trainer for an all-out, nigh on maximum effort, session... just to see whether I could maintain that output for a prolonged period of time, like I used to routinely do.

I managed it comfortably.

I even maintained a higher average speed than I used to and still felt lively at the end.

And it doesn't stop there.

On Wednesday night, our group road ride was cancelled due to dangerously high winds so the Turbo Trainer was once again called into action.

Never have I managed longer than an hour on the Turbo before stopping through a combination of boredom and "perceived" exhaustion (I say "perceived" as, clearly, I am not "really" exhausted – not once have I been unable to summon enough energy get off and walk away, for example).

Wednesday night was a chance to take the recognition of my own complacency and vacancy, and really channel it into something positive.

I loaded up the "Sufferfest" video called "ISLAGIATT" (Snappily titled but, to expand the acronym, means "It seemed like a good idea at the time").

What followed was 1 hour and 56 minutes of hard work.

More than half of the session is spent simulating the kind of effort that you might expend on a hill and what's left is spent in either stages of recovery, or flat out sprints.

It was the first Turbo Training session that I have ever done where I have taken on nutrition during the session itself – an energy gel at the halfway point. I even had electrolyte infused water in my bottle.

It was a "2 t-shirter"… i.e I needed two T-shirts to get through it.

Why 2 T-shirts?

Let me put this as politely as I can, I was "perspiring" sufficiently so as to make the first T-shirt unwearable by around 1 hour and 15 minutes.

I got to the end having covered nearly 36 forward miles at an average of 18.5mph and I was thoroughly delighted with myself – especially since I felt recovered within just a few short minutes.

As it turns out, then, the mental issues that had started to creep in don't seem to have detracted from my actual training - I am now doing things that I couldn't have done not so long ago.

When I consider the wins that I have had since my last training update, it seems that, somewhere amongst this complacency and vacancy, my body has found physiological improvements without me noticing.

Having said that, those same mental issues did give me a few uncomfortable moments where I felt like something was going wrong so I am grateful that I noticed them early and dealt with them.

As is so often applicable to life in general, then, training really is as much a mind game as it is physical process and this last couple of weeks has certainly reminded me of that.

Weather the weather, whatever the weather – February 13th, 2014

A few weeks ago, I was pondering the effects of winter on my cycling performance.

This has cropped up once or twice in my recent blogs and I have been bemoaning what has felt like a "winter slow down" as we have got deeper and deeper into the current season.

Off the back of one of my blogs which drew reference to this, a few weeks back, one of my twitter-buddies presented me with some "homework" and it got me thinking.

He suggested that there were 16 reasons as to why our cycling tends to slow down in the winter.

I sat, pondered and managed to come up with the following list before the cogs of my mind ground to a halt (perhaps the winter had got to them too):

• Wind – Winter tends to be windier and, since this is the bane of my cycling life, why not start here? It is, clearly, much harder to pedal into a headwind and, let's be clear, don't they all seem to be headwinds? As we all know, there is no such thing as a tailwind… if we are going quickly, it is because we are simply a fast cyclist… full stop!

• Cold – Winter is colder than summer… hold the front page! Cold muscles don't work to maximum efficiency and breathing is more laboured as our lungs struggle to deal with the colder air. Plus, a whole bunch of scientists have convinced me that the molecular resistance of cold-air is greater than warm-air. I don't pretend to understand the science, and I wonder how much real difference it makes, but, hey, it's an excuse and is, therefore, something I'm happy to blindly cling to!

• Extra clothing – An extra result of the cold is the clothing we wear. We spend all summer in figure hugging Lycra; punching through the air with the minimum of resistance – the air sliding off of our streamlined forms with seemingly no drag. By contrast, the winter is spent riding along with all sorts of additional fabric flapping around in the breeze as we dress ourselves in as much warm attire as we can lay our hands on. If Lycra gives us "marginal gains" then these extra bits of cloth must contribute towards "marginal losses".

• Winter bike – I am lucky enough to own a winter bike whilst my summer bike broadly relaxes, keeping itself both warm, dry and clean. My winter bike is a much heavier animal, especially with fully-laden panniers on my commute to work, and is much less mechanically sound. I can't select half of the gears (I really should fix that!) and the rear brakes are suspect to say the least. It's hardly surprising that I'm slower on it when compared to its fair-weather counterpart.

• Dark – Whilst the last few weeks have seen a very welcome lengthening of the days, it is still dark by the time I head out in the evening for Wednesday evening group rides. Despite my bike being fitted with lights that, apparently, make me look like an oncoming train to other road-users, I simply can't bring myself to push as hard into what is basically the unknown right up until only a few seconds before I ride through it.

• State of the roads – I don't know about you but, where I live, there is a sense that maintaining roads is low down on the local council's priority… certainly lower down than funding their own Christmas party anyway. As a result, I spend most of my time chattering over poorly maintained surfaces and the winter weather takes its toll on those even further. It's hard to maintain a good pace when you are doing an impression of a slalom skier weaving around rim-threatening potholes and gaping cracks in the tarmac.

• Hazards on the roads – Whilst we are lucky, in the part of the UK in which I live, to not have a particularly snowy climate (although, now I've said that, I bet we'll get loads of it just to teach me a lesson), it does rain a lot in winter and an abundance of water, when combined with all of the other things that we might encounter on our roads such as slippery leaves, for instance, makes cornering and descending at speed more… err… "interesting". I'm afraid that I have no longer got the "bottle" to push through those hazards like some of the people I ride with. I prefer the "tip-toe" approach on any surface which offers up anything less than 100% grip.

• Rain – Aside from the hazardous surface that it creates, it's simply harder to ride in rain. Your visibility suffers and your focus isn't wholly on turning your pedals. Instead, you are either distracted by how uncomfortable you are OR you are too full of your own self-satisfaction at how very "hard-core" you are being to maintain your concentration on forward motion.

• Diet – It's winter. It's cold. It's dark. What we all want is some of that homely food with steam pouring off of it. You know… the "sit heavy on your stomach, stodge-fest" that tends not to be found under the "great sports nutrition" section of your local library. Worse still, we throw all manner of food down our neck at Christmas and then wonder why our bodies are protesting the next time we get on the saddle.

• Mental – My last blog focussed a bit on the mental side of things and, clearly, this is a huge influencer of our performance. Our chances of success at any task are massively affected by how we approach it mentally. "Whether you think you can or think you can't… you are probably right". I can't remember who said that and, whilst I could "Google" the answer, it's not important so I shan't bother. The important bit is that it is true. The winter tends to make most of us feel a bit "lower" and that manifests itself in our performance. I tend to get told that I am fairly consistently positive in spirit (and I guess I am) but, for some, these winter months are tough on their morale and that is bound to impact on performance.

That is only 10 reasons why the winter makes us slower so I reached my limit some-way short of the target of 16 that I started with.

I might be missing some obvious ones or, equally, I might have covered more than one reason in the same bullet point. I don't know. Answers on a postcard if you can come up with more.

What I can be sure of, though, is that the combined effect of all of the above is bound to make winter miles slower than summer ones – each "reason" just nibbles away at our performance until, when combined, they positively bite a big ol' chunk out of it!

What we must remember, though, is that every mile we cover is a mile more than we would have covered if we had not got off of our backsides to begin with and, actually, training in the more arduous conditions might just result in bigger physiological gains than might be achieved through the comparatively much easier summer miles.

Fairly predictably, 7 of the 10 "reasons" are things that are outside of our control in that they relate directly to weather.

So – with so much being beyond our control, are we doomed to slow down over these months?

Outside of jetting off to spend your winters in warmer climates, then, yes, I suppose we are….

But there is one thing that might help you to reduce the impact of the winter.

It's certainly something that I am using and have mentioned it already in previous blogs.

I'm referring to a Turbo Trainer.

Over the last few weeks, as the weather where I live has turned increasingly nasty, quite a few people have asked me for details of the particular Turbo Trainer that I own.

I'm certainly no expert on Turbo Trainers... in fact, I reckon that what I know about them could be written down on a single page of a small pad of paper.

Having said that, I have been happy to share what little wisdom I have and have generally started by saying that mine certainly wasn't expensive. I only want to use it for a couple of months of the year (and, even then, as infrequently as possible) so why spend hundreds on a top quality "dust-gatherer"?

In my view, for the price of an average night out, you can get yourself a decent enough Turbo Trainer and immediately start rattling off miles in the comfort of your own home.

It isn't as enjoyable as riding on the road on a sunny day, clearly, and lacks the "hard-core points" that are there to be won by braving the winter elements... but when those elements make riding down-right dangerous, why chance it?

With the last two weeks' worth of Wednesday evening group rides having been rightly cancelled due to such high winds, I have spent longer on my Turbo Trainer and have developed something of a love for it which I never thought I would have.

Much of this love is down to the "Sufferfest" videos that I mentioned in my last blog.

Yesterday, for instance, as I watched the wind battering my office windows at work, knowing that the Wednesday evening group ride was a non-starter, I actually found myself looking forward to the 2 hours of hard "Turbo Trainer" effort that I was going to inflict on myself.

So – if all of those reasons why we slow down over winter are starting to get to you and you are running the real risk of stopping altogether, get yourself one of these fairly inexpensive pieces of equipment and make yourself feel good about training all over again.

Feeling good will lift your spirits now whilst the training itself will pay dividends on the roads in those glorious summer months.

It's one of this rare win / win situations.

Rough winds do shake the darling bike of February. February 17th, 2014

Another training update and today's instalment follows on very neatly from my last one which, you may recall, was about the effects of winter on our training.

Goodness, sometimes it's as if all of these ramblings are, in some way, joined up!

As I alluded to in said blog, my normal training routine has been subject to subtle amendments over the last couple of weeks due to the mad weather that Mother Nature seems to have been inflicting on us.

Don't get me wrong, I'm extremely grateful not to be living in other areas of the UK which have been turned into lakes.

In some cases, all that those poor souls can see are the roofs of their homes poking out above the surface of the water.

That said, the winds that have battered the area in which I live have brought their own particular brand of chaos.

Trees have been uprooted, walls and fences have been blown over and, speaking personally, we even had some random chunks of concrete appear by our back gate – the source of which is, as yet, unidentified!

In the face of wind speeds that will apparently break through concrete, then, the decision has been taken not to pedal around on a comparatively flimsy piece of equipment, balancing on two narrow strips of rubber!

This has affected both my commute to work (where I have mostly driven over the last couple of weeks), the Wednesday evening group ride and my rides to and from the leisure centres where I instruct Spinning.

But has it stopped me racking up the miles?

Seriously?

If you think for one moment that the answer is "yes", you clearly don't know me very well.

As you know... I have a Turbo Trainer and I am not afraid to use it!

Having posted, in an earlier blog, that I tried out the 2 hour "Sufferfest" Turbo session, ISLAGIATT (It Seemed Like A Good Idea At The Time) as a replacement to that particular week's Wednesday ride, I promptly did it again two days later, on the Friday.

And, before some of the more eagle-eyed amongst you point out that, according to another earlier blog, I don't train on a Friday night, I would point out that Lisa had a rare night out with friends and so, once I had got the boys to sleep, I did my Saturday night session on the Friday so I could get my time with my long suffering wife the next day!

Last Monday saw a brief break in the wind so I did opt to hop on my bike to work.

This was a stroke of luck as my car needed to be left in a nearby garage for a new tyre to be fitted so, short of taking Lisa's car and leaving her with no way of getting around, I really needed to cycle!

In fact, Monday turned out to be quite a day for training.

Leaving work at 5pm, I did my normal bike ride to the leisure centre where I teach my first Spinning class of the evening.

At this point, I would remind you that, even though I am the instructor, I do push myself hard on these sessions – Monday night was a "hill climbing" session so I worked especially hard.

A quick ride to the next leisure centre where I instruct my second Spinning class of the evening and, before I knew it, I was again pushing myself through the "hill climbing" profile that I had already put myself through once before.

This was followed by my final cycle of the evening – the one that gets me home.

Ordinarily, Monday's would stop there.

I'd get in and sit down.

But, on this particular Monday, I still had a car to collect so, at 9pm, I got home and immediately swapped cycling shoes for running shoes. I then ran the mile or so to the garage where my car was waiting outside.

Okay – it was ONLY just over a mile.

But it was a run tagged onto four pretty solid hours of training and, I have to say, I felt extremely lively.

163

As always, I didn't run quickly and had to restrain my pace to the 10 minute mile rhythm that I am trying to develop. I felt like I could have gone on forever.

Monday was, indeed, a great night.

Wednesday was equally great although there really isn't much I can write about it.

In lieu of the group road ride which was cancelled due to the continuing high winds, I decided to, once again, put myself through the 2 hour "Sufferfest" Turbo Training session that I referred to before.

What a solid two hours that was!!

I really wanted to make sure that I was exhausted by the end so I pushed harder at the beginning than I might normally.

By 90 minutes, the "final whistle" couldn't come soon enough and, for that last half hour, what might normally be, say, five out of ten effort, felt like nine out of ten effort.

Once I had stopped, and as soon as I had rid myself of sweaty clothes, I collapsed on the sofa with Lisa, particularly satisfied with the extent to which I had pushed.

On the basis that the Turbo session was done fairly late on Wednesday night, you'll understand when I say that, at 4:30am the following day (when my alarm went off on Thursday so that I could get up to go swimming), getting out of bed was a bit tougher than normal.

I rarely wake up with sore legs from training but this was one occasion when I did – It was a pleasing soreness – the kind of soreness which reassures you that you really were working as hard as you thought you were!

Against that backdrop, then, I suspected that the swim might be difficult.

It didn't start out as particularly difficult, though.

In fact, I went for the same strategy that I had the night before on the Turbo i.e push myself a bit harder at the beginning with the aim being to see just how tired I could make myself by the end.

Regular readers will know that I have never yet got to the end of a swim feeling tired and, as it happens, I wanted to challenge that norm last Thursday.

So I swam harder than I normally would and sustained that effort for longer.

I tried to increase the effort I put into each "pull" phase of my stroke and gauged my success at so doing by targeting as few strokes as possible per length — mentally chastising myself at the end of each length if I hadn't hit a specific target number of strokes.

As a result, then, the first 100 lengths were set at a pretty impressive pace (for me, anyway).

And then it hit.

I started to feel tired. It felt great!

I started to feel a bit nauseous. Bizarrely, that felt great too!

Each of those last thirty lengths felt a bit longer than the last and I reckon that, by the end, 25 metres felt like 50.

Before the very last length of my 130, I even paused momentarily to glance down the final 25 metres and gulped at how far it looked.

Despite the great pace for the first 100, then, my having slowed in the final 30 led to an overall time which was around 1 minute slower than I would ordinarily take to swim the 3,250 metres that I covered.

I was happy with that… it's what I aimed for.

Even getting out was a struggle!

Having nigh-on destroyed myself on the Turbo Trainer the night before and then doing that to myself in the swim just a matter of hours later, my body became a magnet for sugar.

Shortbread and sweet tea seemed to make a bee-line for my mouth and I wasn't in much of a state to stop it!

Yep, it's fair to say, that was one positive week's training.

I'm a team player – February 24th, 2014

This Ironman is incredibly important to me.

But – and I don't mean to question your support, dear reader – just how important is it to you?

When I'm done and this blog becomes nothing more than an online relic of some anonymous individual's mad-cap challenge, the very best I can hope for is that some of you will have been inspired along the way to do something that takes you closer to your limits than you might otherwise have gone.

Even then, I'm not nearly arrogant enough to think that this blog could inspire action if it weren't for you, the reader, being pretty much ready to "take the leap" anyway.

So… with that in mind, and once you take into account the effect that training has on my wife and boys, the whole Ironman thing is a pretty selfish act.

But… to make the whole thing seem a little less selfish, I will be using my Ironman event to raise funds for charity. This has always been my attention although I've not written about it before.

Crossing that finish line will seem a little more worthwhile if I do so in the knowledge that I have helped others. I will be achieving something more tangible than simply a sense of self satisfaction.

So… Why am I mentioning this now?

Read on!

I reckon that the basis of this blog occurred sometime in October 2013 but I can't be absolutely sure.

A chap called Matt Pixa dropped me an e-mail, all the way from California, USA.

That e-mail started a chain reaction of events which has, so far, led to barely more than you reading this although I hope that it will have much more exciting consequences over the coming months!

In his e-mail, Matt wrote that he had spotted a LinkedIn discussion that I had initiated. He had gone on to read about me on the pages of this blog.

As a result of what he had read, he was asking me to be part of a great new team of Ironman Triathletes and, with a very impressive back-story, Matt had the necessary passion to get this team well and truly off the ground!

If I was reading his approach e-mail correctly, I was learning that the concept of the team involved every member training and competing under a united banner – "Team MPG".

There would be a sense of identity and belonging... with team colours and all!

Most importantly, though, every member was also out there trying to raise funds for charities of their individual choosing.

Each member would have a central "team platform" from which to publicise their fund-raising efforts and this platform could be used to attract charitable donations the size of which, as lone individuals, we could only dream of.

The identity and profile that could be gained from the concept would create a "brand awareness" springboard, if you like.

In return, Team MPG would cost the team member.... well... nothing.

There would be no membership fees... nor would those at the organisational end of Team MPG be asking for a cut of the charitable donations made.

Every penny (or, should I say, cent) donated would end up with the intended charity which, again, is down to each individual's preference!

So... I was invited to be a member of a team which would give my fund raising efforts an enhanced profile and publicity as well as making me feel part of a community with the chance to mix it up with some truly amazing individuals. What's more, there was no downside!

All sounds pretty amazing doesn't it?

Now... I hope that, through these pages, I come across as generally positive... because I like to think that I am... BUT... I do have a cynical side and the level of benevolence that seemed to be inherent in this proposed team model made got me thinking.

I responded to Matt, almost apologising for my cynicism, pointing out, basically, that if something LOOKS too good to be true, it quite often IS too good to be true. I was asking him for the "catch".

To his credit, Matt took the request in good humour, acknowledging what I was saying, before convincing me that the concept was every bit as honourable as it appeared.

He went on to demonstrate that the project is genuinely about helping charities whilst, at the same time, creating a small community of team members, all working together to the common good.

Sure, Team MPG is formed off the back of a company that Matt founded and there would inevitably be good publicity for the business itself but, in essence, Team MPG was a "cost" to the company in the same way as a marketing budget might be, rather than an outright investment.

A few e-mails later and I was not only accepting the invite to be part of Team MPG... I was jumping at the chance.

What a complete honour and just how excited do you think I am?!?

Last week, those who follow me on Twitter and with whom I am friends on Facebook will have seen me post a picture... the picture below, in fact.

That is my team clothing. I am a team player! I am a Team MPG player!

That jersey and shorts combo will be darting around the English countryside at every opportunity – worn with pride.

There are only 10 of us in the team and I am the only one outside of the USA which, in a very real sense, makes my membership of the team even more of an honour.

Team MPG has gone on to be recognised as an official USA Triathlon club!

But I still haven't told you why I am blogging about this NOW...

Well, in receiving my team clothes, it now feels a bit more "real" so I felt that it's a great time to shout it from the rooftops!

A dedicated website will be up and running fairly soon, I hope.

It would be great if as many of you as possible could get behind this amazing project even if all you do is share this blog with others.

It will not have escaped your razor-sharp attention that I have managed to write this whole blog without mentioning the specific charity for which I will be raising funds.

I don't do that kind of thing by accident!

In the interest of maintaining suspense, though, that level of detail isn't quite ready to go live.

I'm afraid that you'll need to wait until another blog, which I will publish over the next week or so, for more information on that front!

Gospel Pass Audax – March 1st, 2014

Another move away from the norm with this update which will review the second ride of 2014 to take me through the "100 miles in 1 day" marker. Come to think of it, having done one in December, this will be the third calendar month running where I have done at least one 100 mile+ ride.

Before I even got on the bike, I had a decision to make.

Many of you will know that I have, in the last two weeks, taken delivery of a shiny new bike:

I had only done two 15 mile "feeler" rides on it before the day of the big ride but the weather was looking like it was going to be kind so… what do I do?

Do I rely on my guess-timates at setting the bike up and take it on a 100 mile ride – risking discomfort (or worse) if it turned out that I'd got it wrong?… or do I leave it in the garage and stick with my faithful older bike?

My head was telling me to stick to "familiar" but my heart was yearning to go "new".

My heart won.

The plan for the day was to drive to a location a few miles from the start of the Gospel Pass Audax event, due to set off from Chepstow (South Wales), and I was giving the leader of the group with which I cycle, Spencer, a lift - our bikes on the car's roof-rack.

We met Adam, another cycling buddy that I've mentioned in previous blogs, and the three of us had our very own Grand-Depart before arriving at the official start-line in good time.

The first few miles of the Audax itself were, basically, uphill so it was a really good opportunity to get a feel for the new bike and I have to say that I was immediately delighted with how it felt.

As we climbed away from the start, the legs were feeling good and the weather was being kind, albeit a little on the cold side.

By and large, the three of us spent much of the first hour drifting past other groups who'd started ahead of us.

Overtaking other groups makes you feel almost invincible doesn't it?!

Then came a reminder that I wasn't Chris Froome as another little group, all fresh-faced and spinny-legged, eased passed us, putting me firmly in my place! Adam seemed happy to let them go and we pedalled on at our own merry pace but Spencer was quite keen on going with them.

That burst of speed by Spencer meant that Adam and I didn't see him again for a few miles.

In fact, we didn't see him until shortly after a poorly maintained road gave him a puncture and, as Adam and I came charging down one of the few descents in the first 15-20 miles of the Audax, we saw Spencer's crouched over form, front wheel in one hand and inner tube in the other, by the side of the road.

No – before you even think it – we didn't breeze on past him!

We stopped.

We didn't help though... goodness no! – It was more of an opportunity to take photos than anything!

The one that follows is of Spencer and me (note the Team MPG shorts!)

The unscheduled stop was not too far from the first control point where we again took the opportunity for a quick photo. This one shows Adam and me "testing" the bench outside the pub – I'm pleased to say that it passed!

The route-sheet seemed to indicate that the next control point, at approximately the halfway mark of the ride, was only around 25 miles away.

As it turned out, it was around 31 miles away but hey-ho, what's 6 miles between friends.. even if pretty much all of it was spent going up-hill?

Over the course of those 31 miles, Adam and Spencer both pushed on ahead of me and I found myself in my own company – really just enjoying the new bike and the sound of my inner voice commenting on the surrounding countryside.

We'd had a bit of a strong cross-wind for the first 40 or so miles since leaving Chepstow but, for the final 10 miles before we got to the half-way control point, the general direction of travel turned into the wind, and that did make going a bit tougher.

Rather than bemoan the head-wind though, like I normally do, I decided to just accept that it was what it was.

After all, I was on my own, seemingly in the middle of nowhere and no amount of whinging was going to make it go away. The only thing that whinging would achieve would be to make the ride less enjoyable... and I was very much minded to enjoy every minute.

As I arrived in Hay on Wye, where the next control point was meant to be, I realised that I didn't actually know where I was going. I knew I was in the general vicinity though so I relied on a bit of guesswork.

The sight of hoards of bikes outside of a pub told me that my hunch-based, improvised, route had been on the button!

Having been easily dropped by them, I expected to see Spencer and Adam polishing off the final mouthfuls of cakes and teas but was pleasantly surprised to see that they were actually only a couple of people ahead of me in the queue to buy.

It seems that they had only arrived a few minutes before me... All three of us had, thankfully, arrived before the main "pack" were able to lengthen the queue such that it was out of the door and down the road!

I'd like to say that we all tucked into a very scientifically balanced, nutritionally perfect plate of food but, well, a picture paints a thousand words so I'll let Spencer's camera do the blogging!

As we set off, we all knew what was to come... the climb that gives the ride its name... The Gospel Pass.

If that name means nothing to you then don't panic. It meant nothing to me before Saturday either.

What a difference a day makes (24 little hours... brought the sun and the flowers... ahem... sorry... back to the blog)!

I now know that the Gospel Pass is the highest road pass in Wales... and Wales is pretty well known for having more than its fair share of hills so the title of "highest road pass" should help you to envisage what came next.

This is a picture that I have lifted from the internet but you only need to Google it to find more...

Now, I'm not necessarily saying that it was "Alpe D'Huez" (having ridden up that one in August 2012) but let's not make any mistake about this – with 54 miles in the legs and knowing that my legs still needed to ride another 50 or so to the finish, it was a tough climb.

The sense of reward at the top was amazing.

And I'm not talking about the view... nor am I referring to the seemingly endless descent that followed – although both of those were wonderful.

No – I'm talking about the reward that I got simply from having ridden up it.

The satisfaction that came from knowing that my legs kept turning at a decent rate, despite both the gradient and the winds that tend to come when you are in such open territory on the top of a mountain!

The climb split up our group of three such that, by the time I got to the top, Adam was out of sight in front (unsurprisingly) and Spencer was out of sight behind (surprisingly).

Surprised or not... I was riding on my own once again.

It wasn't unpleasant, though. My bike was still feeling comfortable and I was generally feeling strong. The long descent from the top of the Gospel Pass gave me a chance to get some speedy-thrills and to rest my legs.

I grabbed the opportunity to do both.

Adam couldn't wait for us at the final control point, 25 miles from the finish – he had been a bit pressed for time so had had to push on – but I took the opportunity to "regroup" with Spencer.

We readied ourselves for the final 25 mile hop to the finish of the Audax, which included another big climb, and, fueled by some of Spencer's Jelly Babies, the run in to the end was fairly uneventful.

Again, we took in some lovely scenery and the general feeling of the day led us to stop briefly for another photo opportunity:

From the Audax finish line, we just needed to pedal the final few miles to where we had parked the car and the day was done.

It really was a great ride and, from a personal perspective, I felt like I had life left in my legs as we pulled up to the car (I'm thinking along the lines of whether I could have completed a marathon immediately afterwards – I'll need to in the Ironman, after all!!).

I reckon that I got my nutrition about right and I was pleased to find that my new bike was comfortable over that kind of distance.

In all, we covered around 110 miles and climbed around 7,500 feet.

Just for fun, and to use a new toy that I found the other day, the image below is a "3D" elevation profile just to give you a feel for the route.

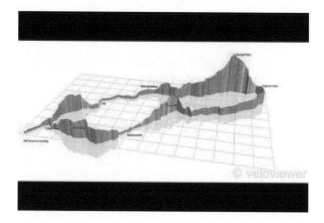

Would I do that event again? – You bet... It was a great day out with friends, the route itself was beautiful and it felt great to just ride... What's not to repeat?

The BIG announcement – March 9th, 2014

A couple of weeks ago, I blogged about my involvement with Team MPG (Titled – "I'm a team player") and I promised then that this blog would follow soon so... here it is.

The preface to this book gives you my backstory but, in short, it involves cancer, two occasions of being told that I wouldn't walk again and a total hip replacement operation.

Said hip operation a few years ago was carried out by one genius of a man.

Truly.

And I don't use the word "genius" lightly.

When another expert in the same field had told me that all was lost and that I might want to start preparing for life in a wheelchair, Evert (for that is his name!) saw me, I think, as something of a project.

I still remember him looking at me the first time we met, contorted in the chair in which I was "trying" to sit, saying that he thought he could make a difference.

I still remember him looking at me, led in the hospital bed the day after he'd operated on me, saying that the operation had gone well.

I still remember him watching me lowering myself into a chair like a "normal" person might, knowing that what he had done was successful.

I also remember the fantastic physiotherapy that I had and the expert guidance that I was lucky to receive. The advice I received then is the reason that I still, to this day, do the daily leg and hip exercises I was taught right at the beginning.

Lastly, I remember (and still benefit from) the support that I got from Lisa.

The first weeks after my operation called on Lisa to do things which would ordinarily be done for people who are a little longer in the tooth, shall we say – fetching things, shifting specially designed chairs around the house every time I wanted to sit somewhere different and even putting my socks on for me.

Lisa is the sort of person who likes to "understand" things. If she doesn't know much about a subject, she sets about exhausting Google with her constant searching until she is something of an expert on the subject. As a result, she knew exactly what I could and could not do.. even before I did!... and this helped me no end.

In short, I was exceptionally lucky to benefit from a really great process from the start. It all joined together well; from the optimistic and quite brilliant surgeon, through the exceptional physiotherapist and on to the magnificent support from my wife and boys.

That process catapulted me into the person who now finds himself writing a blog about competing in an Ironman Triathlon... it's all a bit surreal really!

Evert has become a family friend since my operation and, one evening, a long time ago, I found myself at his house, discussing his charity.

The initial thought was for me to work with his charity... but the meeting took an unexpected turn part-way through.

Evert was quite clear that not everyone is as fortunate as I was and, as a result, the majority of people tend not to recover from where I was to go on and enjoy the new-lease of life that I have.

Many... the majority even... struggle with lack of support, lack of good physiotherapy and lack of information about a whole host of things ranging from what they can do "pre-operation" to help their subsequent recovery... to what their employer needs to know about their capabilities on their return to work.

It is hardly any wonder that these people see a hip-replacement operation as the beginning of the end rather than the beginning of a beginning... as it should be.

A few cups of tea and a cheeseboard later, and I was talking with Evert about Lisa and me setting up our own charity, working alongside his own, but entirely separate.

Our charity would aim to become a vehicle for offering both emotional and tangible support to those in need... people who find themselves where I did... but without the lucky bits!

It would also offer assistance to third parties... by which I mean that, sometimes, it is not only the person facing the life-changing operation that needs support but, also, those around that person might need help or guidance too.

A few more cups of tea, and perhaps another cheeseboard later, and we had the basis of a whole new charity for Lisa and I to set up and run.

Now... my hip issue can be tracked back to the cancer I had as a child, as you may have read in the preface.

A charity dedicated to supporting people with bone and joint conditions brought on by cancer is quite specific, I reckon.

Specific is fine... there is nothing wrong with specific.

But we want to help a less "niche" portion of the population and it dawned on us that a whole host of other conditions (or even accidents) can lead to bone and joint issues, all of which can ultimately put people in a similar position to that in which I found myself.

That makes things much broader and all of those people, as well as their families and friends, need support which, currently, they are most likely not getting.

A check online revealed that, unbelievably, there aren't any other charities out there doing quite what we wanted to do so, in a nutshell, this is what Lisa and I have set up a charity to achieve (our official charity objects):

1. To promote the education of employers in the needs of employees with joint / bone related health issues

2. To promote advancements in the physical preparation of individuals ahead of joint / bone related surgery

3. To promote advancements in the physical rehabilitation of individuals following joint / bone related surgery

4. To advance and / or promote the emotional and educational support to individuals / groups of individuals / carers of individuals living with, or recovering from, conditions affecting their joints / bones.

5. To promote the benefits of lifestyle choices geared towards reducing the likelihood of future surgery as a result of conditions affecting joints / bones.

Yep... we have set up a charity!!!

The name of the charity was inspired by my two sons, Angus and Evert (yes, we named little Evert after big Evert because, quite simply, without one, the other wouldn't exist).

One day, they were saying that they thought our joints moved so freely because they had honey in them.

And there you have it – "Honeybones". Our charity is called "Honeybones".

Evert, the surgeon rather than my son, has kindly agreed to be a Patron of the charity as has multiple Olympian, Oli Beckinsale who has a very impressive story to tell of overcoming a serious back injury before going on to return to world class competition.

Initially, the charity is online-only.

Our website is to be found at www.honeybones.org and we have a discussion forum at www.honeybones.boards.net.

Please do take a look!

Initially, we see the forum as the heart and soul of the charity.

We want people to contribute to the forum from anywhere in the world – offering each other support and information as well as just a general chat for those who are stuck in the house and for whom day-time TV has lost its shine.

The forum needs to become a way of reaching out to other people in similar boats whether or not they want to discuss the thing that has brought them there in the first place.

Once it is up and running and we have raised some awareness of our presence, sponsored events will follow and, beyond that, we can start funding more tangible help – physiotherapy, support groups etc

All of it is geared towards educating, supporting and inspiring an improved quality of life for people who have conditions affecting their bones and joints – hence our strapline.

It goes without saying, then, that Honeybones will be the charity of choice for my Ironman.

Don't worry, though, this blog will not change – it won't suddenly become a platform for blatent "sponsor me" plugs so please don't be put off of coming back to read about my Ironman journey... I will undoubtedly mention it, of course, but only when context allows!

If the bike fits – March 14th, 2014

What with reviews of single events, and announcement re Honeybones, it seems like a long time since I put a training update on here so now to make amends!

Let's start with swimming.

It has been a great few weeks and since my last big bike ride, my main mental focus has been on a 5k swim that I am entered in and which takes place in a little over 1 week's time.

As long-time readers of this blog might recall, it was my intention to steadily up the distances that I swim the further into 2014 we get and so, for yesterday's regular Thursday morning swim, I decided to do just that.

My intention was to go beyond my usual 3,250 metres and on to 3,500 metres – just an extra 10 lengths.

As I swam closer to the 3,500 mark, though, I found myself thinking that only another 15 lengths would get me to Ironman distance and it would seem such a shame to stop short of that having come so close, especially since I was still feeling quite fresh…. so I pushed on.

I got to 3,900 metres which, as many of you will know, is a smidgen over the distance required of me in the Ironman and, pleasingly, the time on my stopwatch showed that I was a couple of minutes quicker than my personal target for the event itself.

I normally have a cup of tea and a sit down after finishing my Thursday morning swims... but yesterday was different.

Because I swam for longer, I had less time on exiting the pool before I needed to be at work so I pretty much needed to simulate a triathlon transition before getting on my bike.

During the improvised "transition", I took on nutrition and plenty of fluid (having come prepared with both) and, actually, felt ready to roll as soon as my backside hit the saddle. That was extremely encouraging.

Despite feeling so great about my swimming at the moment, it dawned on me the other day that it is the only source of "reservation" that I have about the Ironman.

I know that I can swim the distance required and that I can do it within the cut-off time I will be given.

I know that I can ride the distance required and that I can do it within the cut-off time I will be given.

For some bizarre reason, I have no concerns about my ability to get myself around the marathon run bit either.

Lastly, I'm not particularly worried about stringing the three together in succession.

The only "obstacle" that I can see is the fact that I am used to swimming in a pool rather than the open-water.

If I was sitting here typing this now as an acclimatised open-water swimmer, this part of the blog wouldn't exist – I would be totally relaxed about my ability to at least finish the event.

I'm not an acclimatised open-water swimmer, though.

My last, and so far only, attempt at open-water swimming was good fun... but it hardly proved to me that I was a natural and, since that day, the water temperature over the winter has kept me away.

Now, I don't know about where you live but the weather is a little more "spring-like" here now so... this coming Saturday, barring a total logistics disaster (i.e no-one being able to come with me, since I don't want to go alone!), I will be donning my wetsuit once again and, hopefully, taking one step towards overcoming this uncertainty before it eats away at my general confidence.

Where, on my last attempt at venturing into open-water, my success-ometer was geared simply towards getting in and getting wet, this time I will only be satisfied if I get some proper swimming in.

So watch this space!

That brings you up to speed with my swimming training so what about cycling.

Well, the 110 mile ride in February certainly was throwing myself in at the deep end when it came to getting used to a brand new bike and, since then, I have done quite a few smaller rides which have still counted, in my mind, as "learning how it feels" sorties.

And it feels great.

I've managed some pretty decent average speeds (for me anyway!) and even managed to absolutely smash my personal best up over a relatively short but sharp climb a week or so ago – I even stuck with Spencer (just) all the way to the top – bear in mind that he is normally stopped somewhere up the road waiting for me to catch up.

The one thing that jumps out at me about my new bike, though, is how much better it fits my body geometry. I was always aware that my previous bike was too big for me (as is my commuter bike) but I don't suppose I was ever aware as to what effect that had on overall performance.

I'm no expert, of course, but I am not sure that a better fitted bike has necessarily made me quicker over any section of a given route (aside from the hill-climbing performance that I have mentioned) but, string them all together and I seem to have been able to maintain my pace more consistently which has meant that my overall average speed per ride has improved.

I also think that all of that winter training has made me a stronger cyclist even though it didn't feel like it at the time.

I guess one of the more pronounced examples of having found some performance from somewhere came the other morning when I got on my Turbo Trainer (using my commuter bike).

I was feeling restless on what otherwise should have been a rest-day and, at 5am, I couldn't resist a quick spin before the rest of the house woke up. I wasn't expecting a great deal in terms of performance as I loaded up a "Sufferfest" 35 minute time-trial style session.

I delivered a 35 minute average of 24 and a half miles an hour. It's normally quite an effort to break a 23mph average.

There was no discernible difference, in terms of level of resistance acting on the rear wheel, from how I normally set up the bike so, to all intents and purposes, it was an "honest" performance.

Now, I wasn't wearing my heart rate monitor but I didn't FEEL like I was about to have a coronary attack at any point so the result wasn't any harder to come by than the norm.

Was this just one of those bizarre one-offs?

I'm not sure… maybe… maybe not – but the fact of the matter is that it showed I CAN do it, and I seem to remember that, when I bought the Turbo Trainer, a year and a half or so ago, anything upwards of a 18mph average on like for like resistance settings was deemed an absolute triumph.

The Wednesday night ride of a couple of days ago did nothing to dampen my sense of feeling stronger either – we set out on the group ride at the normal time and the pace was fairly swift by my standards particularly given the fact that it was a cold, dark and foggy night (not windy, though.. mercifully!) AND when we take into account the few climbs that we tackled en-route.

Okay, so the scores on the doors (namely; the average speed for the ride) didn't exactly set the world on fire.

Furthermore, I didn't get a whole string of "personal bests Strava segment times" either (which, I need to remember, were mainly set in the glorious summer we enjoyed in the UK last year) but then again, I wasn't really chasing "maximum pace" or "personal bests" either.

The key thing, though, was that I felt more consistently strong and, actually, I was closer to hitting "Strava segment PBs" towards the end of the ride than I was at the beginning which seems to support the notion that I seem to be able to better sustain my effort for the whole of the ride.

I am putting this down to how much more comfortable and well fitted my bike is but, who knows, it could equally be psychological.

Either way, if it is working, I won't knock it.

How did I feel as I got back through the front door – 1 hour 34 minutes and 25 miles after having set off?… Pretty fresh.

So a really great few weeks' training where, at times, I have felt almost invincible.

Now, I just need to make that feeling last another 5 months and Ironman Sweden will be nailed!

Come out from the cold – March 19th, 2014

Saturday was open water swim day – as I predicted in my last blog.

Let's go straight for the jugular here shall we?

Did I manage some "good technique" swimming? No

If, on Friday, you had told me how Saturday would pan out, would I have been happy? No

Am I happy? Yes

Why am I happy? Read on but, in a nutshell, it's all about hindsight and perspective.

The weather was beautiful. The sun was out and it was actually quite warm for the time of year.

Lisa and the boys were going to watch me in what was only my second open water swim. We were meeting up with two friends, Della and Adam, at the lake in North Bristol and they were also going to be getting wet with me.

The facility where the swim was going to take place is a real hidden gem – the local triathlon team train there and there is ample space for parking and a bike transition area. The owner has even mapped out a 40k bike route which sets off and finishes at the lake. Furthermore, he reliably informed us that the path which encompasses the lake is around 1k if you fancy running a few laps.

The lake itself is marked out with a 600 metre loop and, clearly, you can do as many laps as you wish.

It's perfect.

In fact, it came as a huge surprise when the owner told me that he doesn't hold events there – it's all to do with being too busy just keeping it up together. He really doesn't have the scope to add the job of organising a competition to his task-list.

Anyway, I digress.

When I swam in the local marine lake in November, an online search had indicated that the water temperature had been about 13 degrees Celsius and, I'm not embarrassed to say that I had found that to be very cold!! What I am going to say now may make me sound like a bit of a wimp to you hardened open water swimmers but I'm going to say it anyway:

I'm not sure I ever wanted to get into colder water than that!

When you consider the fact that the air temperature, at least, is a little warmer now than it was in November, you'll forgive me for expecting the lake where I was due to swim on Saturday to be a little warmer than 13 degrees Celsius and, based on that expectation, I stated in my last blog that I would only be satisfied on Saturday if I swam some proper strokes.

I know nothing about how open water temperatures work, it seems.

On arrival at the lake, the owner told all three of us hapless swimmers that the water temperature was around 8 degrees Celsius.

8 degrees!

I'm no expert in this but that sounded colder than 13 degrees!

It was.

Della was already neck deep before Adam and I even got to the edge of the lake. She is obviously quicker at donning a wetsuit than we are!!

She did shout back to the shore that it was, indeed, very cold and, actually, she has since implied that the sight of us two about to join her was what stopped her getting straight back out.

To her credit, though, she swam off whilst Adam and I were still lowering ourselves in.

As the cold sensation crept up my body, I started to have serious doubts about how clever this whole idea had been!

And I'm not joking... I mean actual serious doubts!

I shivered... a lot.

My breathing became a little erratic and almost immediately I was ready to get back out. I think I was so surprised to find myself immersed in colder water than I had encountered in my November attempt that my mindset was completely thrown.

That sense of "I can't do this" started to dominate.

In just a few short seconds, I was already annoyed and disappointed in myself... in equal measures.

I meandered out a couple of metres - to where the water was a little too deep for me to be able to stand - but I then deliberately started to drift back towards the little jetty from which I had got in... I was telling onlookers that I was getting out.

Lisa (who was standing with my boys watching) and Adam (who was with me in the water and seemingly coping much better than I was) were both discouraging me from giving up... as was the owner of the lake and he is a "shoot from the hip" kind of guy so I'll let you guess as to the nature of the "motivation" that he was dispensing!

Lisa suggested a revised target – swim the 10 metres or so to a particular yellow buoy... and then swim back to the shore. Only then would she be happy for me to get out! (she's a tough taskmaster, is Lisa!)

Gingerly, then, I embarked on a slow, "head out of the water" breast stroke swim to that buoy, fully intending to do the bare minimum!

I could feel some warmth getting into my body as I moved and, actually, the only bits of me that were properly cold by the time I got there were the bits that the wet-suit weren't covering – my hands and feet.

I went PAST the yellow buoy – still with Adam encouraging me to carry on and the next marker became my new target. This time, I added a bit of extra pressure in terms of challenging myself to try a bit of front crawl.

Not full on "head under" front crawl mind, but the kind of front crawl technique that you might develop if you've been told that your face would melt on contact with water!

I spent the next 500 metres or so alternating between the two swimming strokes, taking it deliberately easy, comparing notes with Adam and trying to work out whether my feet were still attached to my body (I was experiencing the same lack of feeling in my hands but, to be fair, I could "see" that they were still attached).

With about 100 metres to go of the 600 metre course, I decided that I would now see the day as a success if I completed the loop (which I really had no choice but to do) AND if I got my face fully under for a few strokes, just to see how it felt... I didn't apply any pressure on myself to do any proper breathing (as had been my intention before the day)... I just wanted to swim 4 proper front crawl strokes in full flight.

I did it.

Getting back out at the end of the 600 metres actually felt ok – I allowed myself a moment of reflection on the jetty before standing up and re-grouping with Della and Adam who had both done so well themselves.

We even managed a photo-shoot (below - that'll be me in the middle) before the owner treated us all cups of tea and some very welcome compliments for having got in to the water at all!

As I was getting out of my wetsuit, I mentally compared the three of us and concluded that Della and Adam had done SO much better than I had.

BUT... I have no idea how they were feeling or what was going through their minds, and so, for that reason, I have deliberately stopped myself pursuing the comparison route any further.

I'm too self-critical for comparison to be productive in this instance.

Instead, I have focussed on what I think I got done... just me... no-one else.

With the benefit of hindsight, the objective of getting some proper swimming done was a tough ask... the hurdle of swimming in even colder water than I had experienced in November was just too big to overcome in one outing.

But... I am immensely happy at having overcome that initial wobble (read; BIG wobble!) and continued.

I am also immensely happy at having swam 600 metres.

I am planning to go again within the next couple of weeks and, this time, rather than set myself what turns out to be an unrealistic target, I want to come away having got in, not faltered and swam a loop. I also intend to time myself around the 600 metre course to see where I currently am relative to my pool speed - that way, I'll be able to measure my improvements more effectively as I get more and more used to it.

I hope you can see why I am happy with Saturday despite not achieving my initial target. A revision of what "success" looked like was necessary from the start... I see that now... and I achieved that re-defined measure of success.

Confidence knocked?... not a bit... it's more buoyant than ever (pun intended).

It's nice to go a'travelling – March 27th, 2014

It's nice to go a'travelling…

… but it's oh so nice to come home.

Over the last few training update blogs, you may have noticed a surge in the regularity with which I mention my ever increasing love of swimming.

I believe that I have even felt the need, on occasion, to reassure all of you cyclists (and to reassure myself) that the pool will never replace the bike, for me, in the "enjoyable" stakes!

With that in mind, and remembering that I was unable to swim more than a length or two of full front crawl at the beginning of 2013, it was a bizarrely satisfying feeling to arrive at the pool for a proper, organised, swimming event on Saturday.

A pure swimming event.

No cycling.

No running.

Just swimming.

It was the first event that I have done which didn't involve either multiple-sports (Triathlon) or purely cycling.

I had set my sights on the Sport Relief Swimathon ages ago as forming part of my Ironman training.

There were a number of options that I could have signed up for: A 1.5km swim, a 2.5km swim, a 5k solo swim or a relay event if I fancied getting a team up together.

I could see little point in putting my name down for anything other than the 5km solo swim and so, on Saturday, I turned up at the pool (which happened to be the same venue that I train at regularly) to swim 200 of its lengths.

And what a great event it was too.

I had no idea what to expect before the day.

Lisa and the boys came to support me but I had no idea whether there was even going to be an area for them to sit as spectators. Furthermore, I had no idea how many other "swimathoners" there were going to be – for all I knew, I was going to be a lone swimmer in a closed lane whilst the rest of the pool carried on as normal.

I started to get a feel for the event as soon as I arrived… the presence of a whole pile of signing in sheets told me that they were expecting a big turnout and I suspect that there were in excess of thirty swimming-costume clad people standing at the side of the pool before the start.

The whole pool was "laned", which I don't think I've ever seen at that venue, and, what's more, the lanes themselves seemed narrower than normal. Despite being a regular face there, then, the whole venue had a wholly unfamiliar feel.

The walls surrounding the pool were decorated with "Swimathon" banners and there was Sport Relief paraphernalia everywhere.

They had put together a makeshift seating area for friends and families to cheer us swimmers on… a mini-grandstand, if you like.

I was also struck at how many non-swimmers there were – spectators and pool staff alike. There were people everywhere!

It even sounded different – where normally you can only hear the movement of bodies through water, this was drowned out (yep.. a water pun… I shan't apologise!) by loud, motivational, beat-heavy music and the whole place sounded more like a nightclub than a swimming pool.

It was all designed to create hype.

Hype is good. Hype is fun.

But hype can create nerves.

I needed to let all of this hype just wash over me (yep.. another water pun.. still no apology from me though!). This was just another swim and the last thing I needed was nervousness. Why would I be nervous, anyway? It was just another swim after all!

As I was stood by the side of the pool with a few minutes to go, after having chatted with a couple of the other swimmers, I did something that I have not done for a long long time… over 12 years, in fact.

Something I used to use in my motorsport days.

Back then, for the final minutes before a race, I nestle my backside into my race seat, helmet on, visor down, shoulders relaxed, and just blank out the rest of the world – disappearing into myself and calming down… almost as if everything else had stopped.

Now – the side of a swimming pool is a very different environment to the pit area of a motor-racing track but, at the same time, it is very similar…. lots of "stuff" going on but very little of it of any real importance to the task in hand.

As we all hopped into the swimming pool to acclimatise to the water temperature, most of us, me included, did a slow and steady two lengths just to warm the muscles up.

Between standing on the side of the pool, throughout my warm up lengths, and right up until the starting whistle was blown, I can genuinely say that I was only vaguely conscious of what was going on outside of my own head.

And, for that reason, by the time the whistle was blown for me to start, I was as calm as I am at the start of any normal swimming session.

And that was what it became… a normal swimming session.

The other 3 people in my lane were entered for the 2.5k distance so I knew that I was going to have the lane to myself for around half of my swim.

The deliberate and considered effort to quash any nerves before the start really paid dividends during the event itself – I was broadly aware of the music and shouting going on around me but, to all intents and purposes, I was swimming on my own, in a quiet and serene world.. one where there was no music, no spectators and no hype.

Consequently, it felt like no more of an "event" than any normal swimming session.

The only difference was that where, until now, the longest distance I have covered has been 3,900 metres, I was now targeting 5,000 metres – an extra 44 lengths.

I spent the first 2,500 metres or so dealing with the other swimmers in my lane – overtaking when I was faster and being overtaken when I was slower. I was also trying to experience and understand the effect of "drafting", being that Saturday was the first time I have ever really done that.

For the whole swim, though, I mainly concentrated on remaining detached from the hype of the event itself - maintaining my rhythm and composure as normal.

192

Almost before I knew it, I heard the chap who was counting my lengths shout "150 lengths done" – just 50 to go… that came as a surprise. I hadn't been looking at my lap-counting watch and, if asked, I would have estimated around 75 lengths to go.

And then, seemingly in the blink of a be-goggled eye, I heard the shout; "2 to go"!

I'm not sure what happened to those 48 lengths! They just disappeared.

I finished the 5,000 metres in 2 hours dead, which was quicker than I had expected.

I know that I am a fairly slow and steady swimmer, with my typical time over 100 lengths being around 1 hour 2 minutes. So, allowing for a steadier approach from the start, I wasn't expecting to even get close to the 2 hour mark.

What's more, my time meant that my 5k effort also saw me beat my "average time per 100 metres" previous best! I was incredibly pleased with that.

So how does this translate to the Ironman?

Well, it took me 2 hours to swim 5k when I know that, on the day of the big event, my cut-off time for 3.9k will be 2 hours and 20 minutes. So – to ensure that I clear the first hurdle at least, I will have considerably more time to swim a considerably shorter distance. Sounds good to me!

Aside from the "yet to be conquered" hurdle of doing it all in the open-water, you can see why Saturday's swim did my confidence no harm at all.

As to how I felt after the swim.

I felt fine.

There's not much more that I can say than that.

I took on some fluids and solids whilst getting dressed and, by the time I was out of the changing room, back with Lisa and the boys, I was feeling…. well… fine.

I haven't suffered any aches or pains since either.

So, back to the very start of this blog where I talked all that cryptic stuff about "going a'travelling", "coming home" and "loving swimming"

The morning after the swim saw me getting back on the bike and heading off to instruct my regular Sunday morning Spinning class.

I loved Saturday's swim, I really did, but I realised on that short, 6 mile, ride up a hill to the leisure centre that, if home really is where the heart is then, in training terms at least, my home looks more like a saddle than it does a swimming pool.

To continue the analogy, though, I remain surprised at how much I am enjoying my metaphorical "holiday cottage" that is swimming... particularly given how much I used to hate it!

Roll on my next open-water session when I do really need to start converting confidence into performance!

You bustin' ma baws? – April 2nd, 2014

Well, what a weekend I find myself writing about now!!

Saturday morning was due to be my third attempt at open-water swimming and I was actually feeling quietly confident as I turned up at the lake.

As you know, I will always be honest through this blog and I'm not about to change that approach... but I will be deliberately economical when telling you about how Saturday went... not because I want to deceive you in any way but more because it really didn't go well and I can't bring myself to relive it by typing it out in black and white!

In short: the negatives that I got from Saturday were that I STILL didn't manage any full on front crawl AND I found out that my hatred of wind on the bike transfers to the water too.

The wind made the water fairly choppy and it came as a real shock.

I'm fairly sure that Sweden, being a sea swim, will be even choppier so that has left me feeling a little bit worried.

Trying to see the positives, though, it was, again, very cold but, despite that, I had no "initial wobble" where I felt like I wanted to get straight back out (like I had last time). Instead, I was straight into swimming with little thought to temperature, albeit with my head above the water-line.

And that is where I am going to finish my account of the swim.

With any luck, more detail of the attempt will come out in later blogs – you know, along the lines of "Now that I am so good, I don't mind revealing that my earlier attempts involved... blah blah blah" – but for now, I'll leave it there!

Moving swiftly on to Sunday and it was the day of the LVIS Audax.

A 214km bike ride which they called the "Ball Buster".

You know that a ride is going to be tough when it weighs in at 214km.

You know that it is going to be even tougher when they call it the "Ball Buster".

I did a shorter version of the same ride this time last year and I remember that day well... It was insanely cold... very hilly... and I was feeling ill (I was actually sick just a few minutes before the start).

It was tough.

That day was the first day that I broke the 100 mile mark in one day on my bike, though, so I have bizarrely fond memories of it.

By contrast, Sunday was forecast to be warm, dry and sunny with only a fairly steady wind to trouble us.

As a group, we were going to ride to the start, around 7 miles away from home, and we met up at 7.15am to do just that.

I went into the day feeling really very organised indeed – my saddle bag was sorted a full 24 hours before it needed to be and contained all of the tools, auxiliary power (for those gadgets.. gotta love those gadgets) and nutrition that I was going to need.

On the morning of the event, then, it was a very relaxed Phil that headed off into the morning and I think that helped get the day off on a really good note.

Generally speaking, everyone had opted against full winter apparel, such was the lovely weather and spirits were high as we slurped our final cup of tea before the start.

The ride to the first control point took us through Bristol, across the famous Clifton Suspension Bridge, down 40mph hills and up steep climbs.

It also took us out into the glorious countryside before, eventually, we ended up in a little place called Hill where we all paused and enjoyed some home-made cake!

Our mini-group were three strong for the ride with Spencer taking up his normal position out in front, me somewhere in the middle and Pete a couple of minutes further down the road.

I'm not convinced that any one of us three "needed" to stop at the control points (I certainly won't be able to during the Ironman, I know!!) but they do give us a chance to regroup before pressing on again.

The stint between the first and the second control point was a bit of a slog but I managed, broadly, to stick with Spencer.

That stint included a hill which, for added context, beat me last year.

I remember having to stop half-way up to recover before pressing on.

I'm a year fitter now and there was no way that it was going to win this time.

Nope – this year, I showed it who was boss and enjoyed a wry smile as I got to the top without any real drama. It actually felt pretty average, as hills go, so either they've flattened it out a bit or I am a lot stronger than I was a year ago.

All the way to the next control point, Spencer and I were yo-yoing into and out of "riding side by side" so I wasn't ALWAYS in touch with him but just the fact that I was never dropping too far behind him was a real boost and, as we reached the second control at around 60 miles, life was feeling pretty good.

I was taking on nutrition well and, before the ride, I had decided to make a change to my routine for this.

Up until now, my longer rides had seen me taking on nutrition every 10 miles – alternating between solids and gels. It had dawned on me that the "10 mile rule" might be a little misguided as 10 hilly miles were always going to be harder than 10 flat miles meaning that I wasn't matching my nutrition to my effort.

So I changed my routine to one based on "time elapsed". I would take on nutrition every 30 minutes. It really worked and I wasn't feeling any of that sense of exhaustion that sometimes starts to creep in.

Once we had all regrouped at the second control point, Pete, Spencer and I pressed on into the third stint. This time we were aiming for Glastonbury and, once again, that stint included a particularly nasty little hill as well as lots of "lumps and bumps".

Pete dropped off the back a little bit but I found myself generally riding with Spencer.

I'm going to take some of the credit for sticking with Spencer but, at the same time, I know that he was deliberately taking it easier than he no doubt could have - he had made the conscious effort to pace himself through for the day.

Nonetheless, the fact remains that we were still riding together after 80 or so miles and that doesn't happen too often for me so I'll grab the kudos while I can, thank you very much!

Glastonbury was the third control point and we had around 50 miles to go (44 more of the route itself and then the ride home from the finish).

I like to break things up in my mind and I very much see 50 miles as two times around a typical "Wednesday evening bike ride" route.

Wednesday evening bike rides never seem like far so, really, with just two of them to do, we were almost home! That's my logic and I'm sticking to it!

Unbelievably, I actually dropped Spencer and Pete on a short and sharp climb not long after leaving Glastonbury and I was alone and out of sight until Spencer caught me around 15-20 miles later.

I managed over 15 miles of solo riding "out front" (okay, so it's not a race but, come on, let me have my moment!).

Just as I thought I was going to be waiting for both Spencer and Pete at the final control point (around 15 miles from the end), I heard Spencer's voice behind me saying "I've been trying to catch you since Wedmore!") – I can't pretend that I wasn't a little bit disappointed that he'd succeeded!

The pace over the next few miles was really strong and Strava even shows me logging a couple of personal records over some of the segments.

Here's a pic of Pete at the final control point!

The final control point allowed us to regroup for the final push which, thanks to yet another hill, did have a sting in its tail but we were all up to it and rolled into the finish together, with no drama.

We averaged around 16 mph riding pace which, knowing how hilly it was, bodes very well for my prudent estimates for my Ironman ride time.

Fast-forward to me arriving home and I was feeling so strong after 147 miles of hilly riding that I charged in, changed my cycling shoes for running shoes, and went straight back out for a run! (Isn't Lisa, my wife, a lucky lucky lady?).

I really wanted to see how wobbly my legs felt on a run after a 150 mile (as good as makes no difference) bike ride and I only intended on doing somewhere between 1 and 2 miles.

I can happily report that the next 1 and a half miles saw me comfortably running at 10 minute mile pace and, what's more, I woke up on Monday feeling ready to go (which is lucky since I instruct back to back Spinning sessions on a Monday evening after work!)

So... not a perfect weekend's training, what with that swim and all, but brushing that to one side, it was pretty amazing.

Mind, body and splashing in puddles – April 7th, 2014

A few of my blogs now have focussed on one specific event, being that I have deemed it, in some way, notable enough to have a blog to itself... and this one will be no different.

Having said that, the longer the events get, in terms of "time elapsed", the less able I am to give you a blow by blow account... and the event which I am writing about today was almost certainly longer than any event that I have ever, or will ever, do – yep, even longer than the Ironman itself... by quite a margin.

So, rather than subject you to a novel all about the trials and tribulations of the 265 mile bike ride (yes.. you did read that right... 265 mile bike ride) that Spencer, Adam and I did on Saturday, I'll look at it from a different angle to the norm.

I don't always "learn" something from the events that I do... I suspect that learning from everything is a bit over-rated and sometimes it can be quite nice to just enjoy the moment... but I did learn quite a few things from Saturday's mammoth ride.

<u>The world is big!</u>

I've learned that 265 miles is a long long long way.

This, in turn, taught me that we live in this amazing world where cars (other automobiles are available) make journeys feel so much shorter than they really are.

Sure, 265 miles would even constitute a long drive, I guess, but we'd do it without too much drama and barely even notice that we've covered that mileage.

Isn't that remarkable?

That you have the option to get from where you are now to just about anywhere without breaking a sweat, covering many many miles every hour, is simply stunning.

This learning point would be useful if I could make some money out of marketing the automobile, as a concept, but, since I think it is already pretty popular, I sense that I'm leaning against an open door a bit.

Potholes

I've learned that road surfaces in the south of England tend to improve as you travel east.

This might surprise a few of you who live over there in Buckinghamshire and who bemoan your own road quality but, believe me, an hour chattering along even the most "main" of roads here in North Somerset would have you clamouring to be back home!

It really was very clear that, the further east we got, the better the road quality became.... even the single track roads over there are more "ride-able" than the A-roads of the south west... staggering.

This learning point would only be useful if I was planning on moving house and hadn't yet decided where to go.

I'm not moving house.

Not useful then.

24 hour between sleeps

I've learned what it is like to be awake for, as good as makes no difference, 24 hours straight, spending the vast majority of it riding a bike.

I had taken the caravan over to Cardiff so that Spencer, Adam and I had somewhere to sleep which was only around 4 miles from the start line of the ride that we had entered.

We all got up at 4.15am to give ourselves enough time to eat breakfast, put the finishing touches to our bikes, in terms of prep, and to ride to the hotel from which the Buckingham Blinder Audax was to start, in time for the Grand Depart.

At the start, we were still "early" enough in the morning to observe a rather "worse for wear" party girl falling out of a taxi on her way back from a clearly exuberant night out... that is the time of day we're talking about here!

We might very well have seen the same girl when we got back to the same hotel for the finish some 21 hours later.

We didn't... but we might have.

That is the amount of time that elapsed between starting and finishing the ride.

By the time we got back to the caravan, packed our bikes away, and got into bed, it was around 4am. 15 minutes short of 24 hours since our alarms had gone off the day before.

Of the 23 hours and 45 minutes that had passed, we'd cycled for a little over 17.

17 hours of pedalling at an average of around 15 and a half miles per hour.

That's hard work.

Towards the end of the ride (and I'm talking the last 60 miles or so... it seems odd to think that the last 60 miles was deemed as the "end" of the ride when, in reality, that is quite a ride in itself), the silences between Adam, Spencer and myself were more pronounced.

Gone were the light-hearted discussions that we had been holding for much of the ride.

Gone were the more serious chats about making sure our nutrition was correct and that our level of power output wasn't such that we were going to exhaust ourselves before the end.

Gone too were any mentions of whether we were still "keeping to the correct route" – all of us just blindly following a course displayed by our gps units on our handlebars.

All of these were replaced with, generally, either silence or suggestions to stop in order to spend 30 seconds throwing yet another energy bar or gel down our throats. Speaking for myself, I had even gone past being able to do this whilst riding, as would be the norm.

The mind starts to change a little bit after that amount of time, I think, and you tend to retreat into yourself a little... especially when the black of night, combined with sporadic torrential rain, demands every ounce of concentration you can still muster.

I was also tired.

I don't mean "my legs won't move – tired", I mean "I need to sleep - tired".

A couple of times, and I think Adam experienced the same, my eyes started to droop as we got into the last hour and I needed to wake myself up!

I even took to riding directly behind Spencer for periods so that, as he went through puddles, the water that his back wheel flicked up at my face would keep me alert! Almost comical really.

In all fairness, my legs didn't actually give up the fight – they were still turning at the end and, at the point of writing this blog on Monday morning, I can happily report that they are recovered and I've got one eye on a Loch Lomond bike ride that I'm hoping to squeeze in over the next few of days whilst I am up there on a family holiday.

So... where those other learning points were of little use, having discovered what my mind and body does when it's pushed almost to the breaking point of its ability to endure will be massively valuable in the Ironman, I suspect.

Importantly, I now know what to expect from my body, and that can't be a bad thing to be carrying in my metaphorical tool-box on the day.

I'll hold on to Saturday's experience for as long as my memory allows!

Big belly

To lighten the mood, I've learned what it is like to have a big belly.

I don't normally have a big belly.

But... I felt like a right old "chubster" by the end of the ride such was the sheer amount of food, energy gel and electrolyte infused fluid I'd shovelled into myself in the preceding 24 hours... and it showed in the straining zip of my cycling top.

In fact... having the big belly was part and parcel of me getting through the ride.

My Garmin data estimates that I burned 11,719 calories (to be precise!).

I'd loaded my bike saddle bag and Tri-bag with nutrition and, taking into account the food I was taking in at the control point stops, I was eating every half an hour for the most part... dropping to every hour or so towards the end, simply because my body wouldn't accept any more food... and without that constant stream of calories, I would have ran out of fuel

I'm pleased to report, though, that the whole big-belly thing was only temporary though... phew!

To wrap up

The ride was amazing beyond words and I learned a lot more than what I've written about here... but you'll need to take my word for that!

And I've not even mentioned how great it was to ride with two other equally mad individuals whose company enabled me to complete it – I'd have had little chance of doing it solo, I think.

Having said that, finishing such an extremely "endurance focused" event with an understanding of what it takes from my mind and body was the most useful bit, in Ironman training terms and, weirdly, I hadn't even thought of that as a potential end benefit before I started to cycle on Saturday morning.

A picture paints a thousand words – April 15th, 2014

Last week, shortly after that 265 mile bike ride, I was luck enough to head off to Loch Lomond for a week's holiday with Lisa and the boys.

I was even luckier to be able to take my bike and, on the Thursday, I ventured off in the general direction of the Highlands with the intention of riding for two hours, turning around and riding the two hours back to where we were staying.

I can't even put into words how beautiful the scenery was so, in an unusual twist to my normal blogs, I won't even try.

And, I'm sorry, but it would just be wrong not to include the following (for all of you Strava users out there!)

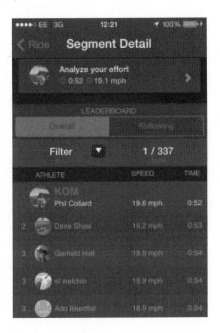

In all, I rode around 65 miles in 3 hours and 56 minutes... but the scores on the doors, whilst pleasing enough, were much less relevant than the scenery – a beautiful morning out indeed!

And now for something completely different – April 18th, 2014

The main body of this blog has nothing specifically to do with Ironman... or Triathlon.

It has nothing to do with swimming, cycling or running as stand-alone sports either.

In fact, it doesn't have any real place being here if "here" is a blog page about my training experiences for an Ironman Triathlon.

But... this blog page is about a whole lot more than that (or at least I think it is).

It's as much about the mind as it is the body and, despite the fact that today's subject matter is off-piste, I hope to bring it all back to a very relevant point or two towards the end... so wish me luck with that and read on!

As you may know, I used to be heavily involved in motorsport and even won a National Championship at my peak although, in recent years, I have turned my back on four wheels in favour of two wheels, swimming trunks or the soles of running shoes.

I have turned my back on a highly-strung race-tuned engine in favour of the most complicated engine of all... the human body.

I have turned my back on cleaning oil and grease off of expensive machinery in favour of... err... cleaning oil and grease off of expensive machinery.

Motorsport has never been too far from my heart, though, so Monday was an emotional day indeed.

It was the day when my oldest son, Angus, had his first drive in a proper racing kart, as an early 7th birthday present.

A friend and racing team owner had sourced the right genre of kart for Angus' size/age.

Despite being a lot slower than their adult equivalents, these karts are still pretty rapid and I was fully expecting it to give him one of the most exhilarating experiences of his life so far.

I think I was more excited than he was!

That is not to say that he wasn't excited, though – what 6 year old boy wouldn't be positively "cock-a-hoop" at having the opportunity to drive something capable of 50mph, with his backside only an inch away from the tarmac?

We arrived at the circuit and the first priority was to get Angus kitted out for the day:

Then we needed to get him to the kart itself:

Whilst, as a competitive Dad who rather likes to throw his boys in at the deep-end, I would love for him to have just gone out on the track on his own and just push as hard as he could from the start (like he would have done "in my day"), today's health and safety rules dictated that, as a beginner, he needed to stay behind an adult driver who would limit his speed to what looked like barely faster than a running speed.

Over the course of Angus' first session, the "guide-driver" drove progressively faster but it was hardly a "white-knuckle" pace by the time they were shown the chequered flag.

I can't pretend not to have been a bit disappointed – not in Angus' performance (which was flawless) - but more because I could sense how Angus was feeling... he wanted to be "let off the leash".

Over the other two sessions that he took part in, he still wasn't allowed to fully "open it up" but during the debrief afterwards, he was talking of having "slid the back-end of the kart"... so he was clearly being given more of a free rein than he had been at the start.

Here are some more photos of the day (starting with one of Evert, who at least got to sit in one) - you'll note that I am also in my old racing overalls...

I even managed to get myself some track-time and, although I was pretty rusty, I was pleased with my pace.

All in all, it was a great day.

The weather was perfect.

The whole family got to watch Angus gaining his confidence and, certainly by the end, really getting to grips with it all.

He really did seem to just… well… "get it"… and what, to him, must have felt like pretty brutal acceleration and aggressive handling characteristics didn't seem to phase him one bit.

In short, he did amazingly and watching him left me with an ear-to-ear grin that lasted hours!

But what has all of this got to do with the main topic of this website?… Triathlons? Cycling? Swimming? Running?

Well… I guess that there are a couple of answers to that, even if I ignore the almost endless list of literal parallels between all of the sports.

Firstly, there is the notion that, for a whole day, my attention, from a sporting perspective, was no longer on swimming, cycling or running.

I was immediately sucked back into the four-wheeled, petrol infused and noisy world that is motorsport.

For just a few hours, I focussed on things that used to "get me going" over ten years ago rather than those that make me buzz today.

This served not only to remind me how much I love motorsport but, actually, the feeling I got when I returned home and saw my bike in the gym of our house, through refreshed eyes, served to underline how much I also love cycling, and triathlon in general.

To be reminded that there are other things out there that "float your boat" is great and it is equally energising to gain reinforcement as to just how much you enjoy your "regular" activities.

Secondly, it reminded me as to how you can take just as much satisfaction at someone else's achievements as you can your own.

For the whole evening after the day's events, I didn't give much of a thought to my own performance but, instead, I was recalling Angus' adventure, so proud I was of what he had achieved.

I was scrolling through the endless photos that had been taken of him during the day, thoroughly enjoying the process of selecting those which I deemed worthy of publishing to my various online profiles.

I was recalling every little thing he'd said about how the kart felt to him and, I admit, embellishing it in my mind to the extent that you'd have thought Lewis Hamilton had just given me a full debrief following a Formula One test session. (That's not to say that Angus' own words weren't impressive, mind – he actually gave me a pretty decent description of what it felt like to drive on "opposite lock")

And you know what?

It actually felt fantastic to be enjoying someone else's success.

And there were plenty of other instances of enjoying other people's achievements over the weekend too, with the London Marathon having taken place.

Countless people I know (either through Twitter or in "real-life") were taking part and I was truly delighted at every single message / tweet I saw in which they were announcing their finishing time.

I think that, sometimes, it is easy to fall into the trap of not wanting to lavish too much praise on others in the subconscious belief that, in some way, it means detracting from our own achievements - I certainly know people who succumb to that and I dare say that I have been guilty as charged on occasion too.

The reality, though, is that joining someone else in the celebration of their own success is incredibly fulfilling in its own right... the psychological benefits to both the receiver AND the giver of praise are pretty immense.

So, if you take anything away from this blog, it should be the importance of remembering to do something other than your "normal" sport to clear your mind once in a while...

AND don't forget to give the achievements of others the recognition you would like to receive yourself... if you're one of those that find it hard to praise others then, trust me, you are missing out just as much as they are.

It makes me sick, it does – April 23rd, 2014

It's been a few weeks since I sat down and wrote a basic training update so I thought now might be a good time.

The last four weeks or so have been a bit different to the norm with a number of events (a 5k swim, a 150 mile bike ride, a 265 mile bike ride and a holiday) to contend with and, coming off the back of a Bank Holiday weekend, I'm still not back to my regular routine yet.

Last week, however, did see my normal Wednesday night bike ride and, aside from the fact that it was a beautiful evening, riding in the setting sun, with a couple of hills thrown in, there is little to tell, really, so I'll just limit myself to saying that we rode circa 25 miles in 1 hour and 30 minutes.

I deliberately didn't want to spend too much time talking about that ride so that I could give myself more words for the rest.

I'll use most of those words to tell you about my swimming session on Thursday morning.

Despite the fact that I hadn't swam a great deal since the 5k almost a month before, I actually went into the session with quite a bit of confidence. So much so that I made the conscious decision to try to conquer a particular demon that has been gnawing away at me for some time.

Until now, I have only ever breathed to one side (my left) every four strokes… but the awful open water swim from a few weeks ago – the one that I am still not ready to give you a full debrief on – taught me that I need to learn how to breathe to both sides.

So, on Thursday, I planned to swim the first 10 to 15 lengths as normal… just until I was warmed up… and then start to breathe bilaterally and see how it went.

The only pressure I was going to put on myself was to make sure I did it.

I wasn't bothered about whether it slowed me down or made my stroke less efficient. I figure that those things would come back to me given time.

It did slow me down and it did make my stroke less efficient. It didn't bother me.

But… it also made me feel really quite nauseous. That did bother me.

It is the same kind of nausea I get if I go on a child's roundabout (with my boys, I should add... I don't make a habit of hanging around children's roundabouts as a rule).

It's the same kind of nausea I get if I do a forward roll (again, whilst playing with my boys... it's not something I tend to do a lot at work, for instance!).

I can only assume that it is an inner ear thing that, in swimming terms, is brought on by switching my head from side to side.

By the way, I am now hoping that this is not going to be one of those examples you read about in papers where a chance comment leads to a medical professional remotely diagnosing some bizarre and life threatening condition!

No, potential for life-threatening condition aside, I think it's quite likely that I was moving my head too "aggressively" and that I need to make the whole motion smoother.

Anyway, I got around 70 lengths of full-on bilateral breathing done before the nausea just got too much and I made the decision to revert to unilateral breathing for the remaining 50 lengths of my target 3,250 metres.

I suppose I was hoping that reverting to my normal technique would "reset" the nausea and that I would start to feel okay again.

It didn't work.

The damage had been done.

I struggled on - having to stop sporadically until, at the end of the 113th length (2,825 metres), the giddiness and sickly feeling was just too overwhelming.

So overwhelming, in fact, that I hauled myself out at the deep-end of the pool (the opposite end of the pool from the changing rooms) rather than finish the swim session at the shallow end as would be the norm... I really didn't think that attempting another 25 metres was a good idea.

I had a dizzy walk of shame along the side of the pool, fighting the urge to be sick (which I didn't think would be particularly pleasant for the other swimmers). In fact, the only reason I wasn't sick in the changing room toilets was a self-consciousness thing since there were quite a few people around.

I only lost that horrible nauseous feeling whilst I was getting dressed some 10 minutes later.

Despite the obvious down-sides of the swimming session, I am in two minds as to how I feel about it.

The negatives to come from it are plain to see and don't need repeating.

The positives, whilst less obvious, are certainly there, if I look hard enough.

For starters, I now know that I "can" swim bi-laterally, if I need to – I managed 70 lengths without faltering, which is 70 more than I have ever managed before and that is something to celebrate indeed.

Plus… I can take some comfort that I have discovered the negatives with four months to go until the Ironman itself, whilst there is still time to overcome them… which I know I need to… so it's better to know now than discover them when it's too late.

In general, I think that it is important to acknowledge negatives and work on them BUT only to carry positives forwards so, next week, I'll try again and I WILL take a step towards cracking it.

Beyond that, I have a coached open-water session in the diary so no-one can accuse me of not doing everything I can!!

Moving back to cycling, then, and since the weekend was a "four-dayer", what with Easter and all that, I managed to convince Lisa that my taking Saturday morning to get out on the bike was a good idea.

Naturally, it ended up being a fairly relaxed definition of the words "Saturday morning" being that I didn't get home until around 2.15pm – The lack of any objection to this as I walked back into the house at the end served, again, to underline how understanding Lisa is!

It was the first ride for a while where I have joined my cycling group at the weekend for one of their "normal" ride out/stop for cake/ride back mornings so, needless to say, I had been looking forward to it.

We set off at 8am and, since I had never done either of the routes that were "on the table" for the day, I was happy to go with whichever the others preferred.

As it was, we decided to head up to a café north of Chepstow.

From a training perspective, there is little to report – I felt strong (for me, that is) throughout the 68 mile ride even though a headwind for the first half did its best to knock the stuffing out of me and I found myself in the rare position of being the wind-break to another group member rather than sucking someone else's wheel for shelter.. it felt quite nice, actually – almost like I was being complimented!

I tried to keep my focus on not pushing myself too hard, despite the fact that half of the group were notably quicker than me – I allowed them to drift away from me without feeling disappointed in myself, knowing that the group tends to stop every half dozen miles or so to regroup and, actually, I am never as far behind them as I think I am anyway - rarely more than a handful of seconds.

It is becoming increasingly obvious to me that trying to keep up with people who are, plain and simple, quicker than me is counter-productive... it saps both my physical strength and my morale.

Instead, and as a neat addition to my last blog, I'm happy to be openly impressed at their pace whilst, at the same time, keeping one eye on mine.

I try to improve to their level, sure, but I don't kill myself in the process.

Instead of worrying about my speed relative to others, I am mindful of how my average pace will position me during the Ironman against my own targets.

As long as I am pedalling along at a pace which I would be happy with on the day, the world seems a nice place and, so far, I am very much within my comfort zone in terms of how long I reckon the 112 mile bike section will take.

From a social perspective, the ride reminded me just how great cycling can be.

We were a small group of friends out for a ride.

And a cup of tea.

And a cake (there might have been a bacon roll in there too – protein, you see?).

We all enjoyed a nice chat both on and off the bike and there was generally a very relaxed and "at ease" atmosphere to the whole ride.

I shan't wax-lyrical any more than that in case you are eating – I wouldn't want to make anyone sick – but suffice to say that I thoroughly enjoyed the ride, covering 68 miles in a riding time of around 4 and a quarter hours.

Some positives and negatives to take from the week – just like life in general, though, I'll try to just hang on to the positives if that's okay with you!

World in slow motion – April 28th, 2014

Another training updated from me… let's start with swimming.

In my last training blog, I promised you that I would take a step towards cracking the problems that I was having with the old "switching to bilateral breathing" thing.

For those that didn't read my last blog (why not?) – I tried it the week before last, having ALWAYS only breathed to my left, and made myself feel genuinely sick in the process!

I like to keep my promises!

My written assertion to overcome the challenge didn't do a great deal to ease my apprehension, though, as I hopped into the pool for my Thursday swim, last week.

All I could think of was how my last visit had ended with me walking back to the changing rooms desperately trying to stop myself actually being sick.

Plenty of thinking in the week after that session led me to conclude that the nausea I experienced on my first attempt at breathing bilaterally had been brought on by moving my head too violently from side to side and that I had succumbed to, basically, motion sickness.

Assuming that I was right, I came up with the conclusion that I needed to make my head movement less aggressive and I resolved to try again the next time I was in the pool.

So, on Thursday, I found myself going for attempt number 2 at bilateral breathing.

I allowed myself 400 metres of "warming up", breathing only to my left as usual, just to get my confidence back and then, at the start of the 401st metre, I started to breathe every three strokes… i.e to both sides.

As planned, I deliberately slowed down the movement of my head, lengthening my stroke as much as I realistically could.

And when I say "slowed down" – I really do mean "slowed down".

I'm sure it didn't look as odd as it seemed but, I felt like I was swimming in slow motion – it actually felt "laugh out loud" funny.

A non-physical change that I also made involved my focus of attention.

In pure "mind over matter" tradition, I tried to think about other things – much like I normally do – rather than concentrating on "whether that sickness feeling was going to return"

I figured that, if I focussed my attention on whether I was going to feel sick, I was much more likely to... well.. feel sick... so, instead, I reverted to playing my normal games. This included "racing" the chap in the lane next to me (without him knowing), closing my eyes for a few strokes at a time to see how straight I could swim without any reference points and thinking about the day ahead.

I also, periodically, reminded myself that I COULD do this.

All the while, I was trying to ensure that my head movement was smooth and steady.

Almost in the blink of an eye, I had swam 107 lengths (to be precise!) and, crucially, the nausea hadn't made an appearance.

I swam on and got to my normal 130 lengths (3,250 metres) with no drama at all – all but the first 16 lengths of it were swam in the slow motion, full bilateral breathing, technique that I had committed to do.

But what effect had the "slow-motion" technique had on my swim time over that distance?

I was a minute slower than normal.

A minute.

That is all.

So... comparatively speaking at least, it was "not so slow-motion" after all.

Oddly, rather than feeling at all nauseous, I actually felt BETTER than I normally would expect to as I climbed out of the pool and I glanced back at the water from the changing rooms with a wry grin on my face... the kind of wry grin that the underdog in a boxing match might throw in the direction of the undisputed champion that he has just beaten.

It was a kind of "You weren't expecting me to beat you, were you?... but I beat you anyway" grin.

It reflected how I felt.

I even felt better for the rest of the day than I normally would.

That's not to say that I normally feel rough or anything, but going into a fairly warm and stuffy office environment after my Thursday morning swim does tend to leave me feeling that I am not "too far" away from getting a bit of a headache. It never develops into one but it always feels like there's one waiting just "around the corner".

But, on Thursday, there was no hint of that!

I'm putting that down to the fact that, by going from breathing every 4 strokes to every 3, I was taking in more oxygen which set me up better for the hours that followed. That might be complete nonsense, though – I just don't know!

Have I really cracked the whole bilateral breathing thing?

My head knows that it is a bit premature to say for sure... I don't want to get carried away after just one positive session any more than I would want to get too despondent after just one bad session.

Having said that, my heart is screaming "yes, you've cracked it" so, who knows, I might just have!

Moving away from swimming, then, I had a good training week on the bike too.

Having previously mentioned that a number of things over the last four or five weeks had rather got in the way of my regular schedule, I can report that I am back to normal now and, being something of a routine-junky, that pleases me greatly.

Wednesday night, then, was bike night and it was great to see that the group with which I ride continues to grow in numbers.

I think that there were 8 people out on Wednesday night, maybe more, and two of them were new faces which was nice.

The ride itself was great fun, as they always are – we took in a fairly flat profile with one big ol' hill thrown in around three quarters of the way around just for fun.

We maintained a fairly good average speed for the ride as a whole and I didn't really feel that I was pushing myself too hard – we rode just over 22 miles in around 1 hour 20 minutes.

What made the ride a bit more satisfying than normal is that, at 5am that morning, I had done a bit of a mini-brick session so to feel so comfortable at a decent pace that same evening was a bit of a win.

The background behind the brick session was that I had resolved to start doing a bit of running as soon as I got back into my normal routine and, since that happened this week, I really gave myself no choice but to get on with it.

Now, it would have been quite straightforward for me to get up at 5am and just "go for a run" as planned but, for added enjoyment, I thought it might make life a little tougher if I did a short Turbo Trainer session first.

I only did around 10 minutes on the Turbo, granted, but it was enough to fire the legs up and I pushed quite hard so that I had a bit of a burn going on as I got off the bike and put my running shoes on.

Out of the door I went and, mindful that I am targeting 10 minute mile pace in the run section of the Ironman, I deliberately didn't try to run any faster than that – In reality, keeping "one foot on the brakes" was harder than normal and I ended up at around the 9 minute 45 pace for the 2 and a quarter miles that I covered... but I'm not too concerned.

I'm happy just to have done it... and pleased not only with how lively I felt but also with how little it seemed to impact on me for the rest of the day (cycle-commute to work and evening bike ride included).

I'd like to think I'll make a habit of doing this morning "brick" routine but I'm going to be realistic and say that my reluctance to run too much might get in the way – so let's just wait and see, shall we?!

All in all, it was a really great week and a comment was made by a friend that, after being informed of my positive swim session, their faith in me being able to overcome any obstacle had been restored.

It was a light-hearted, tongue-in-cheek comment, of course, but, actually, it sort of reflected how I was feeling... I felt like I was "back" on form.

And that felt good.

It's not all about the winning – May 3rd, 2014

I spotted a tweet the other day which was promoting a link to an article by Ironman World Champion, Tim De Boom.

The tweet claimed that the article was all about what it takes to be a winner but, actually, it turned out to be less about "what it takes to win" and more about "how much he wanted to win" so, in a sense, the tweet inspired this blog more than the article did.

Irrespective of the article's content, I began to think about what had made me click on the link in the first place.

In those few seconds whilst I was waiting for my browser to present me with said article, remembering that I expected it to be about what it takes to win an Ironman World Championship, I concluded that I was going to be reading it purely as a "voyeur" rather than a "student"... in the same way that someone might read a car magazine article all about the latest Ferrari, despite the fact that they'll never realistically be able to afford one.

In other words – I was expecting the article to be interesting to me, sure, but was I really expecting it to be useful?

I didn't expect to read it and think: "Right... if I act on what I've learnt, then I too can win an Ironman World Championship".

I didn't even think: "Right... if I act on what I've learnt, then I can win a locally organised Sprint Triathlon".

With the best will in the world, I'll never climb on to a triathlon podium (without subsequently being booted off by the race officials, anyway!).

It's not that I don't "want" to win, it's just that I am perfectly comfortable to accept that I am not out there to win... it's just not realistic. My only competition is with myself.

So I didn't expect to find the blog "useful" then.

What about "motivational"?

Nope.

I didn't expect to be motivated by it either.

To me, external motivation can only really come from something or someone to which you can relate and, therefore, I didn't expect to be able to relate to this chap, given how very different our lives, goals and abilities are.

In fact, as opposed to it being motivational, I can easily see how a blog about "how to win" might have the opposite effect on someone who is considering dipping their toe into the triathlon world, or any other world for that matter.

Such a blog could easily leave the reader with a sense of: "Well, given that winning is beyond me, why should I even bother?"

A conversation with a friend the other day served to add more weight to this idea that, sometimes, a world in which "winning" is automatically deemed as being everyone's goal might drive away those that just want to enjoy an activity and notch up their own personal achievements.

The friend in question was asking me whether they would be quick enough on a bike to join the cycling group with which I ride on a Wednesday night and, occasionally, at weekends.

This friend had been told by someone else that they were simply too slow to join a cycling group and that they shouldn't even try!

In defence of the nay-sayer, they were probably trying to spare our mutual friend from a demoralising episode in which they spend the first few minutes of the ride watching the pack disappearing into the distance and the rest of it cycling alone.

The type of group that the third-party was likely referring to would have been a full-on, bona-fide, competitive cycling group, full of pro-wannabes – all kitted out with massively expensive equipment, fantastic athletic ability and egos to match.

At the risk of offending my friend – the advice that was dispensed, whilst blunt, was probably correct assuming that was, indeed, the type of cycling group that was being talked about.

So... it was "tough love"... but "love" nonetheless.

But the less formal group with which I ride fosters a much more inclusive culture where the capabilities of its members varies quite a bit.

If someone is a little slower then... well... it doesn't matter one jot. Everyone stops from time to time to re-group and, actually, I don't think that even the fastest members need to stop for any more than a couple of minutes before everyone has caught up.

Now, I'm not suggesting that a complete beginner could join the group I ride with... on a shopper-bike complete with a basket and frilly tassels on the handlebars, for example... but I wouldn't dissuade such a person from joining a cycling group, assuming they wanted to, either.

I would just tell them to join a different group... one which was more suitable to them.

And if a more suitable group didn't exist – I'd tell them to set one up... chances are that they are not alone in their desire to ride along at a particular pace.

The point I am making is that, whilst I genuinely think competition is a great thing (I'm inherently a competitive soul, certainly) and that articles about what it takes to win might well be interesting, we should never lose sight of what we, as individuals, are trying to get out of any given activity.

If "winning" isn't our goal, for whatever reason, then that's fine... there is no shame in admitting that.

Once we do admit it, to ourselves as much as to others, we'll likely find that our actual raison d'être is not unique.

And the more people realise that they are not alone with their own goals, the more new groups will start to form... full of like-minded people, of similar ability - each doing its own thing for the physical and mental well-being of its members.

That's when those who aren't blessed with the opportunity and/or ability to chase medals can start to appreciate that "not winning" doesn't have to mean the same thing as "losing".

And... breathe! – May 7th, 2014

I'm all for listening to other people's advice... As long as it is the same advice that I would dish out myself.

I know best.

I won't be told.

That is the sort of person I am, I suppose... I do, at least, acknowledge as much.

At the same time, I was getting to the point that my three unsuccessful attempts at open water swimming to date were becoming more than just a worry.

I was having serious concerns and, genuinely, even my Ironman entry was starting to look doubtful.

So... I set my natural urge to do my own thing to one side and booked a coaching session with a chap called John who runs his own company called "Tri-Coaching".

I put an awful lot of pressure on myself on the morning of the session and, as regular readers will know, my biggest single issue has been that, on previous attempts, I just haven't been able to breathe out with my head under cold water... no matter how hard I try.

That makes swimming outdoors a bit difficult, to say the least, and it has stopped me translating my hours and hours spent in a pool into anything useful in terms of the Ironman itself.

I have been doing the "cold bath" thing to help myself acclimatise and, specifically, I've been putting my head under the water to practice breathing out.

The one thing that my time in the bath has taught me is that, after half a dozen or so "facial submerges" (for want of a better phrase!), my body starts to allow me to breathe out, so a small part of me was feeling confident as I edged towards the lake.

It was only a very small part, though.

The rest of me, almost all of me, to be truthful, was terrified.

And that seems to be a good place to be a little more open about my last attempt at the lake – regular readers will know that I haven't yet let anyone know how it REALLY went – I've just limited myself to saying; "It didn't go well"!

I am not exaggerating one iota when I say that, the last time I was bobbing around in that body of water, I genuinely thought I was going to drown and I got to the point where I was actually trying to shout for help as I floundered around, desperately trying to keep my head above water.

I'd taken in more than a mouthful of water in choppy conditions and had gone in to full-on panic mode, the like of which I've not experienced before... ever.

The panic was probably brought on less by what was physically happening to me and more by the negative mind-set that my breathing issues had led to.

Whatever the reason, though, the panicking was leaving me wondering whether I was going to "get out of this one"... and that just made it worse.

On that day, I managed, somehow, to get myself across the 25 metres or so between me and safety and grabbed hold of some brickwork on the bank of the lake, by my finger-tips, at which point Lisa, who had run to the same spot, started to calm me down.

I hauled myself out of the water there and then and the journey home was not a pleasant one.

I was combining shock and relief with disappointment and a complete lack of understanding as to how I can go from being able to swim 200 lengths without tiring in a pool, to being a virtual non-swimmer in a lake.

Now you have context, you'll no doubt be able to imagine how anxious I was feeling on Saturday and how much I desperately wanted to drive home with a smile on my face.

John was great – the first thing he did was just to get me sitting on the edge for a minute or two with my feet dangling in the lake.

Slowly but surely, I got more and more "into" the water until I was up to my neck.

I felt comfortable so far... but that didn't do too much for my confidence since I'd felt comfortable to that point before.

Then came the moment when I was being told to get progressively lower until, eventually, my face was fully submerged.

At this point, I was told to breathe out.

As before – my ability to expel air deserted me as soon as my face got wet... but I thought back to my "practice" sessions in the bath and kept reminding myself that with each "dunking", I get one step closer to my body allowing it.

John confirmed what I think I had realised in one of those bath sessions – that I should focus on pushing air out with my core muscles rather than breathing with my mouth or nose.

And I did it.

With John's confident instruction, and my perseverance, I reckon that the whole "I can't put my head under and breathe out" issue was just a bad memory within around 15 minutes of the coaching session starting!

Unbelievable joy!

Having expected to spend the whole session just trying to get to THAT point, I was amazed to find myself actually doing swimming drills for the majority of the session!

John talked me through some really great techniques too... and identified some key points that I can now go away and work on to become more efficient in the water.

I would recommend John to ANYONE, however good they may already be – his manner was great and what impressed me most was the fact that he had clearly done his homework (mainly by reading this blog).

He knew things about me that he simply wouldn't have known had he not done plenty of prep – that inspired confidence and also meant that I didn't need to spend any of my time (or money) telling him about myself or my goals.

At the end of the session, he did say that I could either get out of the water there and then, or go for a single lap, 600 metre, swim.

I chose to get out.

Not because I was unsure as to whether I could have swam 600 metres but, conversely, because I felt SO confident that I could do it, that I just didn't feel the need.

Before the day, I would have been over the moon to have thought I would come away having even made a dent in the whole breathing issue… so to have not only got over it completely but also to have got some really great ideas as to how I can improve my technique was a HUGE win.

It was so huge and left me with such a great feeling that this blog won't even touch on my other training for the week.

And I hope you get some idea about how happy I am with that swimming session from the fact that, in excluding my other training for the week, I am passing up the opportunity to tell you all about a great 124 mile bike ride AND a brick session which saw me smash all of my running pace records straight after a tough tough tough 10 miles on a Turbo Trainer.

Happy…. and relieved…. indeed!

Tell Lisa; "I love her" – May 16th, 2014

My Ironman journey is full of "tick-box" moments.

Not in a boring, monotonous, robot-like manner, you understand... More in a "I've always wanted to do that and, WOW, now I have" kind of way.

So far, the path to August 2014 has been amazing.

It's seen me ride 265 miles in one day and manage to get to 6 straight months (and counting) of riding at least one hundred mile event per month, having only done my very first century ride a little over one year ago.

It's seen me swim in a 5,000 metre event having only really started to swim properly part-way through 2013. I even feel confident that I've broken the back of my open-water swimming issues despite genuinely feeling I was going to drown just trying, only a few short weeks ago.

I've also met, either in person or online, countless amazing people, training for and completing challenges that I can hardly even imagine being able to do. Inspirational stuff.

Friday gave me a chance to put a tick in another box when I, along with a group of six or seven others, including two who were already friends, went to Newport Velodrome.

I'd only ever seen a Velodrome on television... never "in the flesh".

I was the first to arrive and the lady behind the counter, having told me as much, invited me to go to the viewing area and take a look at the track itself.

Those of you who have been to a Velodrome will understand what I am going to say next and, if you haven't, you will "think" you understand but, believe me, you probably don't – that is not to come across as condescending... it's just that you really do need to see it to believe it!

I'm referring to how steep the banking is.

I had heard it was steep but my first impression was that either the laws of physics would need to be distorted for a couple of hours or I was likely to be going home in an ambulance.

My view didn't really change a great deal between then and the moment I actually sat on the bike... the fixed wheel bike... with no brakes... the one that I was about to ride around this track of certain doom!

It just didn't LOOK possible and I took some comfort in the fact that another member of the group was having similar apprehensions.

Thankfully, I took an equal amount of comfort in the fact that one of the group had done this before and, since he'd apparently survived intact, I reckoned that I had at least a 50/50 chance of seeing my wife and boys again.

The coach that was included in the price of the 2 hour venue hire that we had paid for, was superb.

He was a "shoot from the hip" kind of chap and I liked that... I think I needed it.

We started off just circulating on the flat concrete area inside the track just to get used to the bikes and the fact that our legs were our only brakes.

This wasn't as easy as it might sound as our head-strong coach had made it quite clear that the painted surface was slippery and that we "shouldn't lean too much nor go too fast" or we'd fall off.

What does "lean too much" mean?

What does "go too fast" mean?

I wasn't going to find out through experience, that's for sure, so I pootled around at a very steady pace indeed, as we all did.

Fairly soon, the time came for us all to get the bikes on to the track itself and, again, the coach was very reassuring with his instruction.

I think the most heartening thing that he told us was that the angle of the banking on the bends was a constant 42 degrees... however high up you went i.e. if you can ride around at the bottom, you can ride around at the top – the difference is only really in the mind.

So we started to pedal again, picked up sufficient pace (apparently, you need to be doing at least 20mph to get 'round) and took to the wooden surface of the track itself.

I had that little anxious moment that you get when you are about to do something that you are unsure of.

236

It was... well... easy.

Within a few moments, I realised that the text I'd sent to Lisa, telling her how much I love her and giving her the details of my life assurance policies and secret offshore bank account, was probably premature... and that I might even manage to escape any broken bones!

We were doing various different exercises fairly quickly into the session... involving drafting and chasing each other down... and the one thing that sticks out in my mind about this was just how great it felt to go high on the bank and then use the steep downward-gradient to catapult yourself into the next straight.

Not frightening at all... just great fun.

Once or twice, I was reminded of my angle of lean relative to the ground when going round the bends a little too slowly – my back wheel slipping an inch or two down the track thus making me feel a little bit more awake than I had been before!

Otherwise, though, the lack of incident meant that I could just enjoy the two hour experience that Newport Velodrome gave me.

It was all finished off by a timed single lap sprint which pitted us all against each other and resulted in a cast-iron way of placing our group in order from fastest to slowest track-cyclist.

Here are some photos:

Now, a couple of weeks ago, I blogged about how "not winning" does not necessarily mean "losing" and I stand by that.

I thoroughly enjoyed myself and the result of the "timed" session at the end did not impact on that either way.

So.. I "won" when it came to enjoyment.

But I "lost" when it came to the stopwatch.

And not just by a little bit… I lost by quite a margin.

I really want to use my medical history as an excuse as to why my legs don't have much power.

I want to tell you that radiotherapy as a child, coupled with the lack of muscle usage that went with the years of deteriorating mobility in my legs have made it difficult to build strength in my thighs.

That's what I WANT to tell you... but the truth is, I just feel like I would be making feeble excuses.

The fact remains that there I was, a regular cyclist... capable of endurance which, let's not be modest about this, is probably beyond most people.... and I had no answer to the rest of the group, which included a variety of abilities, in an out and out test of power.

I'm not saying I expected to win... that would be extremely arrogant – particularly given the fact that I already knew two of the others and know that they are fit guys, certainly... but to come last?

I didn't expect that.

It did get me to thinking, though, about my wider cycling.

I tend to struggle more than those with which I ride when facing a headwind.... Lack of power?

I am strong enough on steep hills, relative, again, to the group with which I cycle, but that is probably more down to my light frame. If you put me on a "steady" incline, the same riders that I pass with ease up the steeper bits take their opportunity to drift back past me... That's a lack of outright power.

I can't really "explode" from a squat to a standing position, either, in the same way that others seem to be able to.

So, what am I going to do about it?

Well, I need to understand whether I do actually have the basic ability to build leg strength or whether those explanations that I groped around for before can become more permanent fixtures in my "excuses toolbox".

So... I'll go in search of strength by incorporating, into my general regime, some pretty focussed resistance work for my legs.

I've already started, actually.

I did a "power building" session on my Turbo Trainer, and that'll be a regular fixture.

239

I've taken to using the gym where I instruct my Spinning classes for half an hour, before my session, to do some proper leg weights.

Even my Spinning sessions won't escape this latest mini-project... I've taken to pushing a higher resistance than those who I'm instructing just to see what my legs are capable of and to build on it.

If "feeling different" is any gauge of progress, the early signs are encouraging... I've made my legs ache in ways that they haven't before so I'm seeing that as a good thing.

One thing that I need to be careful of, though, is that I don't compromise my Ironman training and, unless you fancy telling me otherwise, I've come to the conclusion that having a bit more power isn't going to hurt.

So... stay tuned to find out if my legs will stay more like those belonging to the last chicken in the shop, or whether Mark Cavendish will soon be shaking in his boots at the very thought of me challenging him to a head-to-head sprint.

And then it hit me – May 22nd, 2014

Sometimes, things just "click", don't they?

It happened to me around 15 months ago with pool-swimming when I went from being unable to swim any more than a length in full front crawl to not having any problem with... well... just keeping going until the time I had available to me ran out.

Without any degree of over-exaggeration, that transition was an overnight thing.

Something just clicked.

Since then, any performance improvements have been incremental in nature and I would say that my "eureka moment" in the pool was the last time when something suddenly clicked into place... until last weekend, that is.

We all know the saying... you wait all day for a bus and then two come along at once.

It seems that the same applies to "clicks".

Two came along on Saturday... and they did my confidence no harm at all as we get into the final three months before my Ironman in August.

Regular readers will know that my last trip to the lake was a success (thanks, in no small part, to John of Tri-Coaching) and Saturday was going to be my time to find out whether I could carry the things I learnt with John into a session on my own.

By "things I learnt", I mainly refer to the acclimatisation routine that John took me through and which led to me conquering my whole "breathing in the colder open water" issue.

On Saturday, then, I deliberately went through the same process that I had with John.

I sat, firstly, with my legs hanging in the water.

I then got in to the lake up to my midriff.

Then up to my upper chest.

Then put my face under.

The fact that I actually expected not to be able to breathe out comfortably to start with meant that, when my experience matched my expectations, I wasn't disheartened… I was able to stay positive.

And THAT is key.

The eyes of complete strangers were on me but I didn't let that stop me repeatedly going through the same routine: head under, force air out, head up, head under, force air out, head up – all done whilst standing only a metre or so from where I'd got into the lake.

Each time my head went under, the process of forcing air out became easier and, when I felt ready to start swimming, I turned to face the first buoy and away I went… with the clear expectation of doing the 600 metre lap with no difficulty.

If the path to success were easy, it wouldn't feel like you'd achieved as much.

That mantra came in handy when, within a couple of hundred metres, I was back to struggling with my breathing – reverting to swimming without putting my head under at all.

This lasted for a few hundred metres.

Finding myself in that same spiral of disappointment at my own lack of ability hadn't been on the agenda and yet, there I was, having a waking nightmare once again.

As I made the final turn back towards where I'd started, I told myself (actually out-loud) that I just was NOT going to accept this.

And then it came.

"Click" moment number one.

I forced myself to dip my head under and to go into full front crawl… I forced myself to breathe out… I forced myself to slow my stroke down so that my head was above water for longer, allowing me more time to breathe in (rather than gasping).

Before I knew it, I was back to where Lisa and my boys were waiting – at the end of lap one… 600 metres in the bag.

By the time I got to the end of the lap, my front crawl stroke was every bit as normal as I would expect it to be in a pool and I was feeling over the moon.

The "click" had resulted in me going from failure (again) to wondering what all the fuss had been about... it was THAT huge... and it all happened in a few short metres.

I went on to swim another three laps of the lake bringing my total for the morning to 2,400 metres and, except for that wobble at the beginning, it all felt so serene.

I was calm and relaxed.

My stroke was steady and controlled.

I wasn't getting out of breath and the continual swimming experience that you get in open-water, compared to stopping every 25 metres to change direction as in a pool, was actually a welcome factor, rather than one which I struggled to adjust to.

That "click" meant that the hours and hours of work I have put in in a swimming pool were, for the first time, translated into open water success... and it felt great.

The buoyancy of the wetsuit made me faster, too – much faster.

One of my tweets, last week, suggested that, one day, I might actually prefer swimming in the open-water to swimming in a pool.

That time has come!

Let's leave that "click" alone and move on to the second one, then, shall we?

Before I'd set off for the lake, I'd adorned my bike with my Tri-bars being that it was my full intention to get out on a time-trial style ride on Saturday night to try them out.

For the benefit of those that don't read this blog regularly (and to remind those that do), my bike is only a few months old. I had not yet ridden it with the Tri-bars and with my first Triathlon of 2014 coming up next week, I thought it best that I give it a go.

Saturday evening, then, as the sun was losing some of its warmth and a little breeze had started to spring up, I kitted up and went out on an 18 mile route that I've ridden a few times before.

The fact that I've ridden the route before is important – it means that I know what a "good ride" looks like, from a stop-watch perspective, and what a "not-so-good ride" looks like.

I'm always a bit nervous of my ability to get into a full tuck on Tri-bars since the flexibility in my right hip stops my leg coming right up to my chest. This, in turn, means that riding with a flat back is not really on the cards for me. So, in short, Tri-bars call on me to adopt a riding position that I have typically found difficult to maintain for any distance.

In fact, as I went into Saturday's ride, I don't think I had ever managed longer than a mile or so in a tuck position without having to revert to the hoods just to allow my legs / hips chance to recover.

Cue "click" moment number two.

I managed pretty much the whole of the 18 mile route in a full tuck... aside from the moments where, at junctions for example, I needed to slow down and stand on my pedals to accelerate back up to speed.

I'm not sure quite what happened but just as it had in the pool last year, and just as it had in the lake earlier the same day, something just changed.

It felt great.

Feeling great is one thing... in time-trial terms, though, only the stopwatch can tell you whether it actually WAS great.

It was.

I have trawled through my Strava records for the last time I rode that route, so desperate I was to be able to evidence what I am about to tell you but, alas, I log so many rides that it's like looking for a needle in a haystack and I have given up trying.

You'll just have to believe me when I say that the last time I did that same route, I finished at an average speed of around 18mph... and I remember feeling happy with that.

Saturday, saw me get through the first 10 miles at a smidgen over a 20 mph average (the very first time I've covered 10 miles on the road in under 30 minutes) and I finished the ride with an average of 19.6 mph.

18.3 miles in a little under 56 minutes.

Now, the readership of this blog will be split between those that see a 19.6mph average as "slow", those that see it as "about right" and those that see it as "fast" but, listen, I am distinctly chuffed with that result so there!

As a quick bolt on, Sunday saw me doing a big legs session in the gym in my bid to increase my overall power. It was time well spent and my legs definitely felt like I'd pushed them hard later that day.

All in all, the last week has seen me gain confidence so I'd be quite happy to have a few more of those over the next three months, thank you very much!

Quantifiable progress – May 29th, 2014

On Thursday, I put it out there that I was going open water swimming in the evening and there will be people reading this who expect me to regale them with every intricate detail... they'll know who they are because they teased me about the fact that I was likely to do so.

I normally don't like to disappoint but, on this occasion, I just might.

It was a great swim... a REALLY great swim.

But just because something is "great", that doesn't mean to say that it is eventful enough to write about.

I managed an Ironman distance swim (3,870 metres), give or take a few metres, in a faster than expected 1 hour and 16 minutes but, aside from it having rained for the first 1,200 metres, it really was uneventful.

And in a funny kind of way, that was what made it great.

The fact that I got into the water, acclimatised, swam for 6 laps without tiring, stopping or having any problems of note, and got back out without any incident worthy of blog space is amazing to me in itself.

I even had a practice "mass start", complete with choppy water and all, but that didn't really phase me a great deal either (although, I would add, my use of the word "mass" is perhaps a bit of a stretch given the fact that the rain had kept most people away and there were only half a dozen of us).

Anyway... that was that, really, so I'll move on!

Monday morning was to see my first triathlon of the year – a sprint triathlon in the beautiful setting of a town called Westonbirt, not far from where I live.

The distances were a 400 metre pool swim, a 22.5km bike and a 5km run.

They ran the same event, at the same location, in August of last year and so Monday was a genuine opportunity to measure my progress if, indeed, any progress had been made.

Last year, the event had taken me 1 hour and 32 minutes.

My hopes for a faster time in the swim leg were high – last year took me 10 minutes 30 seconds – but that was before I really started to up my game in that discipline.

My hopes for a faster time in the bike leg were less high – I've done lots of endurance work since then, of course, but I doubted my ability to go any quicker over such a short distance.

My hopes for a faster run were nil. That's not meant to sound defeatist – it's just that I have probably only run a cumulative total of 25 miles since that day in August, for very good reason, as regular readers of this blog will know.

Before my allotted start time, I glanced into the pool and remarked to Lisa that, with waves of 20 swimmers at a time, being split between 4 very narrow lanes, the water was decidedly choppy as pool swims go.

That started to play on my mind a bit... but then I reminded myself that I was now well used to swimming in much harsher conditions and, after all, this was going to last just 16 lengths.

The last time I had done a triathlon, 16 lengths had pretty much been as far as I had ever swam in one go, and so it had still felt like a long way.

Nowadays, 16 lengths is the funny little bit at the beginning of a swim that I spend warming up.

It's the funny little bit at the end of the swim when I'm already mentally getting dressed, having a quick cup of tea and riding to work.

16 lengths on its own, in that context, isn't even really a "swim" anymore.

It's with that uber-confident mentality that I got into the pool, threw a little grin back at my family who were watching from the viewing gallery, and got ready to start.

We'd all been asked to estimate our swim time on our entry forms so that the organisers could group swimmers of similar ability together, thus reducing the risk of participants holding each other up or being intimated by much more capable competitors.

I had registered an overly-cautious 10 minutes.

Within the first length of the swim, I was regretting my prudence.

I was catching people mid-length and having to revert to breast stroke, just to slow down to their pace, before passing them at the end of the length. I also got embroiled in a bit of a race with another chap who, I reckon, was a lot slower than I was but who, when the opportunity presented itself to him, would draft along behind me, tap my heel before I had the chance to get a good lead on him (tapping the heel of the person in front is the signal for them to allow you past at the end of the length), go past me and then proceed to hold me up for the next length before we could swap positions again.

If that paragraph is a bit of a linguistic mess then... well... good – it's meant to be... it reflects the way I felt in the swim.

A "mess".

But not a "weak mess", I should add.

Despite the general disarray, I actually felt really strong and the 9 minute 29 second swim that I put in was the first sub 10 minute, 400 metre, triathlon swim that I have ever done... I reckon I could have been at least 30 seconds quicker, maybe a minute, had those external influencers been a little kinder.

Given that result, then, you can imagine that I had a smile on my face as I got out of the pool and headed for the bike.

The run to transition must have been around a third of a mile in itself, genuinely, and I broadly paced myself alongside other people who'd got out of the pool at the same time as me.

The bike leg was a bit of a game of two halves.

I went out quite hard and, at the half way point, had managed an average of over 20 mph, which I was delighted with.

Coming in to the second half, though, I think that I started to pay the price for my over exuberance and my average slowed.

Having said that, my spirits were high given how essentially strong my swim had been and I pressed through a bit of a "legs-on-fire" period, getting to the end of the bike course a full 3 minutes quicker than I had managed in August.

3 minutes!

That was quite a result.

Now I needed to park my bike and get going on the run.

If I had any criticism of the organisers of the day at all, it would be that the method for identifying everyone's place in transition was "woolly" at best – the stickers on which the race numbers were displayed were too small and old "number stickers", presumably used for previous triathlon events, were still visible, making matters even more confusing.

I don't know if anyone else experienced the same but I ended up running up and down the transition area with my bike for what seemed like an eternity, searching for the my allotted space – I just couldn't see where I was supposed to be and a marshall ended up having to assist me in looking!

That cost me time and I was pretty grumpy… but I resolved to move on and just get over it as quickly as I could.

Before the event, I promised Lisa that I was going to give more of myself to the run section than I normally would.

So I did.

Out of transition I went, wearing my Garmin so that I could monitor my pace, and, to start with, I was running sub-8 minute miles. I was feeling comfortable at that pace – albeit knowing that I was leaving little in reserve.

Over the 5k, the average pace slowed a little owing, at least in part, to the undulating nature of the course.

Throughout the run, though, my mind was frantically calculating how fast I needed to run to beat that 1 hour and 32 minute target time that I'd set last year at the same event in August.

It was fairly clear to me that I was going to beat it, unless something really went wrong over the last 5k.

So my attention was mainly given to beating 1 hour 30 minutes and, for most of the run, that was the time I was targeting.

As I came around the last corner and saw the finishing line, I glanced at my Garmin – I had around 4 minutes to run a distance that I could cover in 2, even at walking speed.

And so it was – I crossed the line in around 1 hour and 27 minutes – some 5 minutes quicker than the same event last year, despite the longer transition times.

I was faster in each leg of the triathlon – by quite a margin – and that felt good.

My only disappointment (if that is the right word) was that, whilst Monday's time would have been good enough to have finished ahead of a fair few of my friends that were also competing with me in August... had I actually delivered it in August... they too made similar improvements on Monday, thus going quicker than me once again.

I can't deny having felt a little frustrated by that.

BUT – I need to focus on the reality of this.

I was faster... much faster... than I was in August.

I had a lot of fun too and that is the main thing, surely.

Plus, of course, my strength doesn't lie in an event which rewards out and out speed over short distances.

My strength lies in the ability to just keep going, which is lucky, really, given that my A-race for 2014 is widely considered as one of the ultimate tests of endurance.

What's in a name? – June 6th, 2014

I was in the gym, the other day, doing some of those leg weights exercises that I promised to do a while back, in the quest for more power.

In those moments when I find myself demonstrating to all and sundry how pitifully weak my legs are, in terms of out and out strength, my mind often wanders to a much happier place – where I set about answering life's important questions (although I probably ask more than I answer!)

This particular day was no different and, whilst my thighs were doing one thing, I allowed my mind to do something else.

It all started with an observation of the guy next to me.

He was squatting with so much weight resting on his shoulders that I swear he was breaking wind, just a little bit, at the very bottom of each repetition, such was the extent of his effort, and, what's more, I was trying to figure out just how he'd managed to build biceps that were so big that sleeves were probably no longer an option – I reckon he could have filled a pair of trousers with each arm!

So, in a very real sense, you have a man-mountain with a flatulence problem to thank for what you are about to read... and those aren't words you'll read very often!

The fact of the matter was that this chap next to me was as wide as he was tall and I labelled him, in my mind, a "weight-lifter".

Despite the fact that I was lifting weights, I clearly can't apply the same tag to myself, and that got me wondering what label I might be prepared to accept.

So... what do I do?

I ride a bike... I swim... I run (whenever there is the finish line of an event that needs to be crossed, anyway).

I instruct Spinning classes... I work-out with weights in the gym.

I guess I could fashion a tag around any one of those activities but doing so would mean failing to acknowledge the rest.

Having said that, for this year at least, all of my training has been focused on one day in August and this prompted me to consider a tag with which I was wholly uncomfortable.

251

As someone who has completed quite a few triathlons now… as someone who considers triathlon to be amongst my hobbies… and as someone who is just a couple of months away from doing the daddy of the triathlon discipline, do I consider myself to be a "triathlete"?

It certainly pulls together all of the activities that I've mentioned already, since they are all focused on helping me complete triathlons.

But, before you say "yes, of course you should consider yourself a triathlete", I need you to think about the make-up of that word; "tri…athlete".

If I label myself as one, I am, by nature, calling myself an "athlete" which, quite aside from sounding a little arrogant, is definitely not a label I would associate with myself.

Looking around the gym that day, I suddenly started to consider whether, in their own words, I was surrounded by "athletes", "weightlifters" and "body-builders"… or whether the gym was simply full of people who… well… just like to go to the gym?

So… what tag would you give yourself?

And, before you say: "It doesn't matter" – I would stress that I already know that… but, let's be realistic, this blog doesn't really matter either but you've still read this far!!

So, humour me… if push came to shove, what would you call yourself?

Let's take the example of someone who rides a bike.

They could simply say that they are someone who enjoys riding their bike.

They could call themselves a cyclist.

They could call themselves an athlete.

There are countless other ways to describe someone who engages in the hobby of pushing two pedals round and round with a view to moving forwards but, in the deliberate order I have listed the three options above, each one tends to imply a more serious approach, and perhaps more individual ability, than the one before it.

So, perhaps the tag you choose to apply to yourself betrays a little about the level at which you see yourself as taking part.

But… and here comes a spanner in the works, it isn't necessarily contingent on ability… it can be as much about perception as it is about results or performance.

For example, someone I ride with has been known to point out that he sees me as a "sports-person" (there's another tag for you) whereas he sees himself as a "recreational cyclist" (and another one!!)… this despite the fact that over any distance I could think of, he'd comfortably beat me to the finish line.

It's all very confusing and I would love to hear your thoughts.

Personally, I think you are what others see you to be and, for the time being, let's assume I'm right… I tend to be right as my understanding wife, Lisa, would gladly confirm, I'm sure!

On that basis, then, I suppose that you don't need to ponder the question as to what your own label might be… since it isn't really your choice.

So, remember, if you catch me referring to myself as an athlete anywhere on these pages, it won't be because I think I am one… it'll be because someone else does!

Call me Colin Jackson – June 10th, 2014

When I was just a teenager, I remember marvelling at the use of words in an advert that I saw in a local newspaper. It was selling a solar powered torch on the basis that "1 hour's charging gives a full 60 minutes of usage".

The intention, clearly, was to manipulate people's minds into thinking that 60 minutes was longer than 1 hour.

With that in mind then, I dipped below the "10 weeks to go until the Ironman" marker on Saturday.

10 weeks doesn't sound like long... but 70 days does.

How I feel about these two figures tends to change with my mood and inner confidence.

I sometimes feel comfortable enough to talk in "weeks"... I'm quite happy to see the Ironman as "just around the corner" such is my confidence that I am ready to take it on.

On other occasions, when my confidence is not so high, I find myself referring to the number of "days" remaining. In those instances, I want that psychological comfort blanket convincing me that I've got ages in which to conquer the plethora of challenges that stand between me and the starting line!

Sunday, for your reference, was a "69 days remaining" day... that was how I was feeling.

It was the day of my first sea swim.

I've happily conquered pool swimming now.

I've happily conquered lake swimming now.

But Ironman Sweden is a sea swim... a "highly likely to be choppy" sea swim.

Everything I have read online has suggested that the leap from lake to sea is more challenging than the leap from pool to lake and I would remind regular readers that, when I first got into the lake, I went from competent swimmer to non-swimmer in a matter of seconds.

Success in a lake was only achieved after what I would deem as 3 failed attempts... and, before you question my use of the word "failed", I would remind you that, on the third occasion, I genuinely thought I was going to drown... and if that isn't a failure, I'm not sure what is!

So, given all of that – you can imagine that I wasn't exactly relishing the idea of doing what I knew I needed to do, sooner rather than later.

Within 5 miles of our home, we are lucky to have the coast – a little town called Clevedon.

As sea swimming goes, it probably doesn't get much tougher than Clevedon – it has the 2nd highest tidal range in the world and an undercurrent to match.

Temperatures are a "hardly balmy" 13-14 degrees Celsius at this time of year too.

It's not exactly your local swimming baths, put it that way.

Despite that, there is a bunch of nutters who swim there daily – whenever there is a high tide – and I'd picked up the phone to enquire about joining them on Sunday.

They were very welcoming.

Lisa and the boys came with me and, until 1 hour before high tide, the weather was glorious – the conditions were perfect for my first proper sea swim attempt (aside from holiday paddles, of course).

That was 1 hour before the swim.

I'm not sure what happened but, in that hour, black clouds filled the sky, rain fell with a vengeance and the wind whipped up – the water became decidedly choppy and conditions went from good to... well... poor!

Add to that the fact that, only that morning, I had been feeling rough – so much so that Lisa had even suggested a visit to an "out of hours" doctor as I fell through the door on getting home from my morning Spinning class.

I managed to whine so much that Lisa, in her bid to get to the bottom of just how ill I was REALLY feeling, suggested that we were either going to go to a doctor OR I was going to go sea-swimming – there was no in between (she's supportive, sure, but she also challenges me more than most of you will ever know!)

Trust me... with the combination of poor conditions, my morning illness and memories of my first attempts at lake swimming fresh in the mind... wading into the sea wasn't too appealing.

Just to get out of the car, I had to put my legs on auto-pilot – they dragged my unwilling body down to the area where the other swimmers were getting ready.

My auto-pilot then went to work in terms of making me put my wetsuit on.

All the while, my mind was protesting wildly... but I was ignoring it.

As I gingerly made my way across the pebbles towards the water's edge, looking at the waves as I did so, I can't deny having felt more than a little bit afraid... the word "terrified" springs to mind.

But – I was surrounded by a whole group of others – all of whom seemed just SO calm about it... I told myself that I'm not that much of a wimp and that I would just need to suck it up and get on with it.

And that is what I did.

As I walked in to the water, I started to think about going through my normal acclimatisation routine... the standing still, putting my head under, forcing air out, pulling my head above the water routine that John taught me in my coached session – the routine that I have employed each time since and which has served me well.

Too late.

No-one else was waiting around.

I didn't want to swim "alone", for my own safety, so, to stick with the group, I had no choice but to just ignore my routine and swim.

That change to routine further disturbed my mental state somewhat!

It didn't happen immediately – the temperature of the water certainly made it difficult to go into full front crawl from the start BUT... it did happen.

By "it", of course, I mean "swimming".

Proper, bona-fide, swimming.

Within a hundred metres or so, it became altogether more comfortable to get my head under water and I even found myself perfectly at ease with the considerable waves, although some of that was due to the fact that they were broadly "pushing" me along.

We swam quite a distance in one direction and I was having to keep reverting to "head-up" breast-stroke... not because full front crawl was tough, though – it was because I kept catching and passing the chap who was leading us around the route for the swim.

Since I had no idea what route we were taking, I couldn't very well "take the lead" so I needed to slow from time to time in order to stick behind him.

As we got to what transpired to be the turnaround point, he told me as much (for I was the closest to him) and suggested that we now swim back.

We'd gone under the famous Clevedon Pier on our way out and he told me that, to swim back, we would aim for the "third arch" and, from there, turn sharp left back on to the pebble-beach.

Being that I now knew the route back, I didn't need to "wait" for the chap that I'd been swimming behind... so I just dipped my head into a full front-crawl mode and went.

With such a big target as the "third arch of a Victorian Pier" to aim for, sighting was easy enough and I made amazing progress.

My swimming felt strong even though, having turned around, I was now swimming into the oncoming waves.

The very noticeable rising and falling of my body, with the waves, didn't seem to put me off my stroke... nor did the taste of the sea-water that I inevitably took in on occasion when my breathing-in coincided with one of the said waves.

Almost before I knew it, I was back at the shore.

My boys and Lisa were enthusing about how strong I'd looked.

My boys were applauding my bravery at swimming in killer-shark infested waters... I didn't correct them.

The fact the conditions were difficult was, obviously, a huge bonus, retrospectively speaking, given that it forced me to do something with which I was most uncomfortable indeed, but which I will almost certainly face on the day of the event itself.

And, you know what, I really can't wait to do it again.

With the strong current and huge tidal flow, though, I won't be tempted to do it alone and, sadly, the group of sea-swimmers that I joined don't really swim the distances that I need them to swim, nor do they do it "in earnest enough", to make it sufficient in its own right as Ironman training, so I know that I will need to continue with lake and pool swimming for a fully rounded regime.

Having said that, they are a nutty bunch and to know that I can rely on a group to be there… every day, without fail, to allow me to indulge this new-found, and most unexpected, love for sea swimming whenever the mood takes me, is a great feeling.

If you had caught me in the right frame of mind, before Sunday, I might have told you that sea-swimming (in tough conditions, to boot) was the last big hurdle which stood between me and getting to the end of the Ironman.

Having cleared that hurdle with all of the finesse of Colin Jackson at his best, you'll understand me, I'm sure, when I say that Sunday night was mainly spent grinning from ear to ear.

I just want to be alone – June 27th, 2014

If you had lived in our house for the last 7 months or so, you'd have heard the following exchange at least once every four weeks:

"Hi, honey, I'm home!! Another bike ride in excess of Iron-distance in the bag" – I cheerily say as I walk through the door at the end of the day following the completion of another long distance cycling event.

"But, Phil, you've been gone all day" – Lisa points out

"I thought I told you that I was going to be out all day." – I reply,... with a slightly defensive tone, believing that Lisa is referring to a longer than promised absence from the family.

"That's not what I meant" – Lisa begins... "You've done a long ride, sure, but it has taken you since first thing this morning and you are only just finishing now – it's early evening! There is no way you'll make the Ironman cut-off at that pace" – she continues.

"Ah... but today's time includes stops. My actual riding average was amply quick enough to make the cut-off" I try to reassure Lisa!

"But could you have kept up that average without the rests along the way?" Lisa probes!

"Oh yeah, no problem" I say, trying to convince myself as well as Lisa. "Well... I think so" I add!

And then I change the subject!

"I think so" is not really good enough, is it?

And so, on Sunday, I decided to put my assertion to the test with an Iron-distance ride where I focussed on total elapsed time.

I was going to be completely solo.

I was going to be completely "unsupported".

Focussing on total elapsed time meant that I COULD stop, if I wanted to, but doing so would damage my performance... just like in the Ironman itself.

Going solo would mean that I could not benefit from either the drafting of, or encouragement from, any fellow riders... just like in the Ironman itself.

Being unsupported meant that I needed to carry everything that I planned to eat and drink from the very start... no stopping at cafes or shops to stuff my face with cake or buy drinks. In actual fact, this made it harder than the Ironman itself which will have re-fill stations along the route. I was starting out with a much heavier bike than I will need on the day of the event itself. (see picture below... how many bottles?!?!)

Oh... and lastly, I was going to ride with the mind-set that I needed to have enough left in the tank to run a marathon at the end – again, just like the Ironman itself.

Yep – it was a full Ironman simulation bike ride... but slightly harder since I would carry more weight and less adrenaline that you get simply by being in an event.

Now... Ironman Sweden is pretty flat... but very windy (apparently).

I was unlikely to get the same amount of wind on Sunday so, to offset this, I threw in a couple of climbs in the first 1/3rd of the ride just to slow me down and drain some energy out of my legs... I figured that that would be broadly equivalent to having a windy but flat bike ride to contend with on the day.

And off I set – at around 6:30am on Sunday at a steady pace.

The weight of the bike was pretty noticeable – with all of that fluid alone, I had added almost 4kg of ballast (yes.. I had weighed each bottle of fluid before setting off... I'm that anal!)... Add to that all of the food I had in my pockets and my top-tube tri-bag and it was bound to make a difference!

I had been asked before my ride what overall time I was hoping for and I had replied that I would be disappointed not to go sub-7.5 hours.

Throughout the ride, I stuck to my normal nutrition plan of taking in food every half an hour – alternating between gels and energy bars.

I was resisting the temptation to push myself beyond the pace that I was trying to stick to even when other cyclists came into view ahead – It's tough not to up the effort to try to catch them but I restrained myself!

I wasn't wearing a heart rate monitor, and I have no power meter, so I was riding on "feel" and was trying to keep myself in my "comfort zone".

The first third of the ride, 38 miles, flew by, but then I had one of my "dark periods".

I get at least one of these "dark periods" on every long ride I do – a spell of a dozen or so miles where the whole enormity of the distance is the only thing that I can think of and, in those moments, I just want to stop, make a call to Lisa, and get a lift home!

BUT... I know to expect these "dark periods" now and so managing them is actually much more straightforward than it sounds... I almost embrace them. This particular "dark period" was no different and I rode through it, as I knew I would.

Up until the half-way point, I had been focussing on this notional 7.5 hour elapsed time target and, as I clicked through the 56 mile marker, I calculated that, unless something really rotten happened, I was on to beat it fairly comfortably.

If I had any reason to criticise my performance at all, it happened at around 80 miles.

As I got to within 30 or so miles from the end, I realised that my target of 7.5 hours was, by now, guaranteed (mechanical failures aside).

I also realised that a sub-7hr ride was on the cards if I just upped my effort just a little bit.

That was a mistake.

Why that was a mistake will be made clear later.

As I got to the end of the ride, 112.3 miles having been covered since I started, my total "elapsed time" was just under 6 hrs and 53 minutes. – Comfortably under both my initial 7.5 hour target and the revised target of 7 hours.

What's more, my subsequent Strava upload reliably informs me that, of that total elapsed time, I was stopped for no more than a few minutes – all but of a minute or so of that was not of my choosing – traffic lights etc … The one time that I did willingly stop was in order to "inhale" a banana – I can take on gels, energy bars and liquids on the move… but not bananas.

Overall, I was really pleased with what was a wholly uneventful, effectively non-stop, bike ride.

I got my nutrition right.

I got my fluid right too on what was a very hot day – even with all of those bottles, I sipped the last dribble as I came around the final bend before home.

And now back to that "mistake".

It's funny, isn't it, how £6.99 "feels" more palatable than £7.00? – It's irrational but advertisements rely on our irrational side when presenting us with the price of products, of course – and we must still fall for it or they'd stop doing it.

I succumbed to the same thing when I started to push for a sub 7hr time.

A deliberately slow ride that I did with two friends the other week, where we just wanted to pootle and chat, reminded me that, actually, the difference between "pushing yourself to within an inch of your life" and "taking it easy with loads left in the tank" is really VERY small in terms of average speed and yet, in the chase for that totally arbitrary "sub 7hr" finishing time, I fancied that I got the wrong side of that "line", pushing myself a bit harder than I had intended to over the last 30 miles.

The short 4k run that I did immediately afterwards (I simulated a triathlon transition in terms of getting my running shoes on) was, if I am being completely open with you, a struggle and I can be certain that I couldn't have managed a whole marathon!

I reckon that if I'd just allowed myself an extra 10 or even 20 minutes on the bike to get to the end, my overall exertion would have been SO much lower and it wouldn't have been anywhere near as hard to run afterwards.

OK, so I wouldn't have gone sub 7hrs on the ride but, really, what does it matter if it is for the greater good?

So, whilst it was a "mistake", it was also a learning point – I shall have to remember not to get carried away on the day and to ride to a plan.

It needs flexibility, of course, but, by and large, I need to keep my legs as fresh as possible and I shouldn't get sucked in to pushing too hard, and getting ahead of the plan, purely for the purposes of vanity alone.

I want to end this blog on a positive, though, and that is pretty easily done.

Sunday saw me simulate an Iron-distance ride with self-imposed conditions that would have made it harder than I'll face on the day... and it saw me do it in a quicker total elapsed time than I had expected.

What's more, I still ran at the end of it... it was a struggle, sure... but I ran.

With only just over 7 weeks to go, that sounds pretty good to me.

He shoots... he scores. – July 2ⁿᵈ, 2014

Until Sunday, my triathlon "career" had extended only as far as Sprint distance... and had never ventured into open-water for the swim leg.

Not even I thought that it would be a good idea to go from pool-based Sprint Triathlons straight to a sea-swim Ironman with nothing "in between" and so I had the Bristol Standard Triathlon in my diary for the end of June as, effectively, my warm up event ahead of Sweden in August.

The Bristol Standard Distance Triathlon involves a 1,500 metre swim in the harbour, a 40km mile ride - mainly along the banks of the River Avon, under the iconic Clifton Suspension Bridge - followed by a 10km run.

Let me tell you what my goals for the day were.

To get into a good rhythm in the swim. To learn what an open-water, mass start felt like. To swim the 1,500 metres in under 35 minutes.

To ride a decent pace in the bike without killing myself. I was going to be happy with anything under 1 hour 23 minutes (sounds specific but was calculated based on an average speed of 18mph)

To go sub 1 hour 5 minutes in the run. To not walk any of it. To run at a pace which I could keep up for MUCH longer – as I will need to on the day of the Ironman itself, of course.

What with transitions to contend with and all the rest of it, I reckoned I'd be happy with a 3 hour 10 minute finishing time.

On the subject of that run – it dawned on me that, what with all of the hip issues that shaped my life for SO long, I hadn't run more than 5.5k in one go since 1999 and, even then, I can probably count on one hand how many times I've done so in my whole life!

Yep – a 10k run was certainly new territory for me – as will the 42k run be in Sweden!! (Sounds like a big jump, doesn't it?!)

Being that it was my first Standard Distance Triathlon, my first open-water mass-start, my first run longer than 5.5k for 15 years, my first "closed roads" event AND the event that I was classing as a barometer for my ability to complete an Ironman, I did feel a little anxious during the morning of the event.

I'll concede that my tension spilled out a little... and that was to the detriment of Lisa and the boys, who'd come to cheer me on, but I couldn't really help it... so admitting as much in this blog is my way of apologising!

My nerves were placated a little just ahead of the "pre-race briefing", whilst putting my wetsuit on in transition, when I met a good twitter friend, Ian, for the first time.

Just having a chat with a more level and experienced head calmed my nerves and, before I knew it, we were in the water.

Unlike any other open-water that I have been in, there was no opportunity to wade in further and further, allowing the water to creep up your body for gradual acclimatisation – No, the "jump in" immediately saw me fully submersed, momentarily, and well out of my depth before having to tread water ahead of the start.

That did throw me a little but the temperature was fine so, to be fair, it wasn't too much of a drama.

I had heard all sorts of horror stories about mass-starts – the "washing machine" sensation springs to mind – so I positioned myself towards the back of the large pack... and out to one side. I didn't want to be right in the middle as it got nasty!

When the starting whistle went, it was mayhem, sure, but not nearly as bad as I had expected.

As it happened, the worst thing was the realisation that, having started towards the back, I was surrounded by people who were swimming much slower than I wanted to.

This meant that, for the first few hundred metres, I was switching between front crawl and head-up breast stroke as I tried to battle my way around (and, in some cases, over) the others.

I did get swum over, myself... once... by someone who presumably had also decided to start at the back and who was now realising, like I had, that he was too quick to have done so – that was an interesting experience... being largely underwater while someone effectively went over the top of me!

As that initial flurry died down, though, it all became much clearer.

Sighting was easier than I thought it would be – I was mainly using the group ahead of me as my sat-nav – I figured that they couldn't ALL be going the wrong way so, as long as I was still behind a good number of other swim-caps, I must still be on track!

Surprisingly, I spent most of the swim catching and overtaking people and was amazed when I got out of the water after what, my rough calculations told me, was less than 30 minutes – officially, my time was 27 minutes 41 seconds.

Needless to say, I was overjoyed with that.

The bike leg was an "out and back" route, repeated 4 times.

I set off quite hard but not so much so that I was going to destroy myself before the run…. Someone said to me after last week's long bike/short run session that the bike leg of a triathlon is all about who can "whisper the loudest" and that made sense to me.

With that in mind, I "whispered" as loud as I could.

There was a light head-wind on the way "out" and, as always seems to be the case, the expected tail-wind on the way "back" never did seem to offset it.

Despite that, with my 1 hour 23 minute target in mind, I was pleased to get off the bike in a shade under 1 hour 20 – a 30.7 kmh average pace.

Again, then, I found myself with a big ol' smile on my face.

My legs felt good as I got into my stride on the run.

Like the ride, it was a broadly "out and back" route which we were to repeat twice to get to 10k.

I deliberately kept my speed under control.

Firstly, I knew that just under half of the run would be in completely unchartered territory for me… I didn't want to run a strong first 5k only to crash in the second.

Secondly, as a warm up for the Ironman, I needed to feel as if the pace I was setting could carry me through a marathon.

As I got to within 2 km of the finish, I realised that a sub 3 hr finishing time was on… if I just kept my head and maintained my pace.

Up a couple of particularly steep ramps, I found myself saying out loud; "DO NOT STOP RUNNING" – a small number of others around me HAD succumbed and WERE walking, which made it harder to maintain my own focus... but I did it.

I rounded the final bend and estimated that, to finish in under 3 hours, I had just under two minutes to run what looked to be no more than 100 metres.

My run time was 34 seconds under my target of 1 hour and 5 minutes.

My overall time – 2 hrs 58 minutes and 41 seconds... a sub 3hr race!!

I'd smashed my targets for the swim and bike.

I'd hit my run target too but, more importantly, I didn't kill myself in the process.

I was one happy Phil indeed.

Since crossing the line, my mind has been buzzing with calculations pertaining to the Ironman itself.

Sunday's swim pace would see me get out of the water in under 1 hour 15 minutes in Sweden and I know that I have a sub-7 hour, 112 mile, bike ride in these legs... so that means that I could feasibly be off the bike in under 8 hours and 15 minutes - plus a smidgen more to allow for transition time.

That's not realistic, though, given the other things that will be at play so, let's consider the idea that I'll be starting the run at the 9 hour point, then... I'll have 7 hours to do a marathon, 42k, run.

Even if I only keep up Sunday's 10k pace for, say, 10k, I'll be giving myself around 6 hours to cover the remaining 32k – 5.4k per hour. That is barely faster than walking pace, surely.

Can you see why Sunday helped my confidence?!

And, to top it all off, I managed to get a chat with lots of friends after the event on Sunday – some of whom I've met on plenty of occasions but some of whom I'd never met before (although I feel like I know them, through my various social media profiles).

It was a lovely way to spend the day and, if the atmosphere of the Bristol Tri was an indicator for what Ironman Sweden will be like, I really can't wait until August!

Last…and by NO means least; a quick shout out goes to my wife, Lisa and her friend, Hayley – both of whom competed in their first 5k Park Run event on Saturday – a particularly tough local course coupled with having only recently taken up running meant that entering at all was especially courageous.

But they got it done and in a great time too – well done, Lisa, honey – I'm very proud of you!

A weekend of ups and downs – July 9th, 2014

As we edge ever closer to the big day, the number of organised events that I had yet to complete before the Ironman was down to just three as I went into the weekend that's just passed.

The last of the three will be a one mile sea-swim on the 19th July and the middle of the three will be a 120 mile bike ride this coming Saturday. I'll blog about both as and when appropriate, I'm sure!

The first of the three, though, was a 5k park-run and that took place on Saturday.

I'd never done a pure running event before Saturday.

And by "pure running event", I am referring to one in which you just run.

No swimming.

No cycling.

Just running.

My interest had been sparked only the week before whilst I was watching Lisa and her friend take part in said park-run. It takes place every Saturday morning and I had committed, there and then, to enter it myself.

I'm the first to acknowledge that, for someone about to do an Ironman, my running training has been a little... err... sparse, to say the least.

Before Saturday, I had run a cumulative total of 47 miles in the last 12 months (since entering the Ironman) and my longest run for over 15 years was 6 miles... and that was at the Standard Distance Tri just a week or so ago!

I would remind those that are now wondering what on earth I am thinking, doing so little running when I know I have a marathon to complete in just 5 weeks or so, that my having a total hip replacement "technically" means that I shouldn't attempt to run at all!!!

My non-running has been, therefore, very much borne out of necessity.

I turned up on Saturday, then, with no expectations as to my performance.

Lisa tried to push me on what my target time was for the 5k but I, as much as she didn't believe me, I hadn't even considered one.

I just wanted to get 'round, have fun and stay safe.

The build up... the pre-race chats, the event briefing and the general atmosphere... were great and, by the time the horn went to send us on our way, I could already have said that I'd had an enjoyable morning.

As the run started, I knew that the first half was essentially up-hill before then turning around and coming back down the way we had gone out.

I've cycled up that hill on a number of occasions and know it to be particularly steep so, as I approached it on foot, I tried to maintain my focus on my breathing and bouncing off of my toes rather than landing too heavily on my heels – particularly given my need to lessen any impact on my hip.

Some runners were overtaking me but I was overtaking others.

Surprisingly, having expected to feel like a "fish out of water" in a running event, I actually felt like I belonged!

I was keeping an eye on my pace, using my Garmin, despite having no target time in mind, just to get a feel for how quickly (or slowly) I was going.

On the way back down the hill, I was wondering just how quite a few people who I had overtaken going "up" were now going back past me.

I'd assumed that, if I could run faster than them up the hill, I must surely be faster on the way back down and yet, here I was, going backwards, relative to everyone else!

And then I heard one chap, who I was just about holding pace with, tell, presumably, his running mate, to "let off the brakes".

His mate immediately adjusted his running stance and leaned forward.

Both of them proceeded to leave me behind like I was stood still.

It was an important lesson in running down hill - I had been running with my brakes on!

And, as soon as I tried to copy what I had seen that other chap do, I, too, went a lot faster – catching and passing quite a few as we got nearer to the finish line.

Being that Ironman Sweden is largely flat, it's a shame that the "down-hill" running lesson won't really help me but it certainly enhanced my enjoyment of Saturday's event so I'm not complaining!

If you had told me, before the event, that I would run the 5k (3.1 miles) in sub-30 minutes, especially considering the hilly nature of the course, I would have been over the moon. Anything under a 10 minute mile average would have seemed like a bit of a dream.

So – to cross the line in a shade over 26 minutes was astonishing to me.

I know that that time wouldn't rival you serious runners out there... but it placed me (just) in the top half of the 230 strong field and I was delighted with that.

To say I wasn't pushing would only be kidding myself... maybe not to my limit, mind – but I was running hard nonetheless and I couldn't expect to maintain even nearly that pace for a marathon!

Having said that, whilst I know that I can't make running a habit, I enjoyed myself enough to take a friend up on the very kind offer to do at least one long run with me before the big day, at marathon pace – just to see how it feels.

In other training news, I was very conscious that I have a full on, sea-swim, event on the 19th July and, to date, I have only ever done one sea swim.

Ironman Sweden takes place in the Baltic and, whilst I loved my one experience of the sea, it hardly seems like great preparation for either the 19th July event OR the day itself.

With that in mind, then, I decided to venture down to join the "Clevedon Sea Swimming Nutty Nutters" (not their official name... but I've suggested it so watch this space!) who go out whenever the tide is high, whatever the conditions.

If you didn't read my earlier blog about my sea-swim experience, Clevedon is a coastal town just 5 miles from my home.

It has the second largest tidal flow in the world and a pretty fearsome undercurrent to boot – perfect training for the Ironman itself.

I've heard that Ironman Sweden is highly likely to see me encounter choppy waters and, at my last attempt in Clevedon, I remember feeling that I was swimming in conditions that would have been classed as choppy.

Oh how wrong I was!

On Sunday, the wind was quite high as I got to the sea-front with the other swimmers and the waves were crashing into the shoreline with much more "purpose" than last time!!

Thankfully, my confidence in water at the moment is high... or else I might not have wanted to venture in — as it was, I took one look at the conditions and couldn't wait to give it a go.

Let me give you some context.

As I got further into the water, the choice as to when to stop wading and start swimming was taken away from me as a wave knocked me clean off my feet.

As I swam further away from the shore, the height of the (surprisingly regular) waves was pretty impressive as I tried my hardest to swim straight through the middle of them.

The rising and falling with the waves was quite something and, at times, I was actually smiling at the ludicrousness of this situation in which I'd willingly put myself.

Despite all of that, though, I was thoroughly enjoying myself and felt that I was swimming strongly.

The issues that had previously bothered me for what seemed like ages (the front crawl stroke itself, the breathing out under water "thing" and bilateral breathing without feeling sick, to name just three) were dim and distant memories as I powered along the coast and out of sight of Lisa and the boys who, as ever, had come to watch..

I'm hoping that you are picking up on my positivity regards how the swim went.

It went well.

That's not to say that it was without negatives, though.

A couple of times, I found myself needing to just stop swimming — not because I was getting tired — more to regain a bit of the composure that the waves were knocking out of both my rhythm AND my ability to breathe!

There was also a few moments, when, every time I breathed to my right, my eyes could see nothing but the water smashing ferociously into the rocks about 50 metres to my right... and that was a little unnerving.

Lastly, of course, came the realisation of how tough the Ironman swim would be if the water is like that and how long it would take me to cover the required 2.4 miles as a result.

On that last point, though, I just have to forget that - it is out of my control and I just know that I will deal with whatever is thrown at me on the day.

So... a stunning result in the run and an absolute "party" in the sea – all in the space of 24 hours.

I'll definitely take that as I start the final build up!

Ironman blues – July 14th, 2014

I spotted a tweet from someone the other week, the day after they completed a Half-Ironman competition, alluding to the post-event blues.

The "twitterer" in question is not the only person I know to have spoken of this phenomenon and, actually, a few have specifically told me about this feeling that they have come to expect.

Now, of course, I am not yet blogging as someone who has completed an Ironman so I am going to have to take some pretty educated guesses as to how it must feel to do so.

On the one hand, I suspect that the euphoria I will experience as I cross the line will be unlike anything that I have ever felt before – and before you point out that I am on very thin ice being that I have a wife and children and that I should never seek to put any experience above that of getting married or holding my newborn sons, I know that it's politically correct to say that it will, at best, only come third behind these events in my life.

The 12 months of hard work that will have passed since I clicked "send" on my application e-mail don't even begin to tell the full story and crossing the line, to me, will mean so much more than "just" having completed an Ironman.... Just as it no doubt means so much more to every other first-timer.

That will be a special feeling indeed.

On the other hand, though, there will be that sense of a chapter of my life closing.

As it stands, the Ironman does have a tendency to dominate my thoughts when I am training.

When I am swimming, I am thinking about how my swim is going, relative to what I expect of myself on the day of the Ironman.

When I am cycling, I am thinking about how my ride is going relative to what I expect of myself on the day of the Ironman.

When I am running, I am thinking about how much I don't want to be running.... and, of course, I am thinking about how my run is going relative to what I expect of myself on the day of the Ironman.

In fact, I actually can't remember what it was like to take part in any of these activities without those thoughts being in my mind but, beyond August, I guess that this is exactly what will happen.

In a sense, then, there is a risk that completing the Ironman will leave a gaping hole – where once there was a purpose to every one of the minutes that I spent training, there will be nothing but the training itself.

I can see how that would create a sad feeling.

In terms of trying to understand whether I will suffer from these "post event blues", I have tried to think back to other days in my life which represent big achievements and attempted to recall how I felt in the days and weeks that followed.

I certainly don't remember feeling low after my wedding or the birth of my sons but then neither of these events represented the closure of a chapter without a pretty obvious opening of another one to keep me interested.

None of the training achievements en-route to August really count as single events in their own right, either, since I have mentally treated them all as just part of the journey even if, in reality, they have been pretty monumental in themselves (the 265 mile, one day, bike ride springs to mind).

No, I think I need to go back to 2002 for my last big achievement which marked the end of an era – the day I won a National Motor Racing Championship.

On that day, I kind of knew that my racing days were numbered, despite the fact that I raced on for a few more months, what with other commitments that were creeping in to my life… so it really did feel like the end of a journey and walking away with the right to sport the number "1" whilst racing was definitely the icing on the cake.

How did I feel after that?

You're asking someone who can watch a film for a second time, just weeks after the first viewing, and still be surprised at the ending to try to remember how he felt 12 years ago?

Really?

Seriously, though, I do remember feeling elated as I crossed the line, sure – it had been a tough race where I'd needed to battle through the field to clinch the title – but I really can't remember how I felt the next day, for instance.

If I tried, I suspect that I would be fabricating the memories based on how I think I should have felt.

So, without any way to mentally prepare myself for how I will feel during the days and weeks after August 16th, I guess I will just have to take it as it comes... if I feel a bit "blue" after the event then so be it.

I'm rather hoping that, with the Ironman taking place at the half-way point of a family holiday, ... in a country that I have always been intrigued to visit... there will be enough to occupy my mind to stop the "sad-gremlins" getting too strong a grip when the time comes and, inadvertently, it might turn out to be lucky that I planned it that way.

From dusk til dawn – July 17th, 2014

Sometimes, you take part in an event more to say that you've done it than for the training benefit.

The Ironman will certainly be one such event but, in the last week, I have taken part in a couple of others.

It all started when I first heard of the Dunwich Dynamo, last year - an overnight cycle from Central London to Dunwich, on the Suffolk coast – around 113 miles away.

Starting in the evening on Saturday, the aim for many of its participants seemed to be to get to the beach to see the sunrise the following morning.

I was intrigued enough to enter it as part of my 2014 training calendar and, lo and behold, the day of the event was upon us last Saturday.

As a pre-amble to the Dunwich Dynamo itself, being that we were over that side of the country anyway, Spencer (my riding buddy who I've mentioned on these pages many times before) and I decided to take on Box Hill in Surrey, just to say that we had, before hot-footing it into London in the afternoon.

So let's start there... Box Hill... a well celebrated climb in British cycling folklore which formed part of the 2012 Olympic route and which is a magnet for people and their bikes in a similar way that Alpe D'Huez is in the French Alps.

Spencer and I both parked our cars and met up at the café at the top of the climb... he'd been cycling through France and Belgium for the preceding week and was coming straight from the hotel that he'd stayed in the night before.

We proceeded to cycle an 8 mile loop which ended with a spin up Box Hill itself – in all, the ride took a shade under 30 minutes.

We pootled around at a sufficiently leisurely pace so as to mean that Spencer could tell me about his week (of which, incidentally, I am insanely jealous!)

I guess we are a little spoiled in the West Country – everywhere we go, there are hills... proper eye-bulging, lung busting, leg burning hills.

With that in mind, Box Hill was, to be perfectly frank, a little underwhelming.

It was neither long nor steep... people who live locally to me might be more inclined to call it a "lump" rather than a "hill".

That's not to say that I didn't enjoy every minute – I really did… it was a lovely "box" (pun intended) to tick and it certainly is a beautiful area.

I enjoyed the cup of tea and cake at the top too… and it was amazing to see SO many other cyclists all enjoying what is a big location on Britain's cycling map.

Anyway, on to the main event – the Dunwich Dynamo.

Spencer and I went from Box Hill into London in our separate cars, trying to stick together.

We were winging it completely - We had very little idea as to where we were going, no clue as to how easy it was going to be to park when we got there and no concept of what the set-up of the event's "Grand Depart" was going to be either.

As it happens, it was easy to find… easy to park… and the huge mass of other cyclists meant that we could hardly get the "taking part" bit wrong – we just needed to follow everyone else's lead!

The atmosphere was electric as we all gathered in London Fields ready for the off – the number of participants must have been in the thousands.

It was quite unlike any other cycling event that I have done.

There were all types of cyclists - from your serious "roadies" to one chap I saw who wasn't even on a bike! - He was on what was best described as a cross-trainer with wheels… 113 miles on a cross trainer?… kudos to him!

The Dunwich Dynamo has no "starting gun" moment – participants start drifting away from around 8pm and I suspect that a fair few hang around in the pub by the "start line" until 9pm, or even later, before venturing on to London's roads.

A good twitter friend, Fanny Marshall, whom I had never met in person, had arranged to join Spencer, Pete (another regular name on this blog who was also meeting us at the start) and me on the ride - we rolled out of the park at around 8:30pm.

For miles, it felt like we were riding in a Tour De France style peloton… we were literally (and I mean the proper, old-fashioned, meaning of the word "literally".. for those that like to be clear – you know who you are!) rubbing handlebars, and shoulders with countless others in tightly packed groups as we made our way through North London, with light fading fast.

I'm not going to pretend that the whole 113 miles were spent at quite the same level of intensity in terms of tightly packed groups – we did "thin out" as each mile passed by, of course, – but I actually can't remember one moment of the ride where I couldn't see at least one red-light ahead of me and one white light behind – for the most part, it was "groups" of lights that I had in my field of vision.

I've never seen so many bikes and, more to the point, I've rarely ever seen that many people just... well... having fun, all at the same time.

Large sections of the route genuinely did feel like they were lined with "spectators" offering their support, car horns were beeping at us in appreciation (rather than anger) and I recall drifting through one village, well into the early hours of Sunday morning, where residents were standing outside their homes, in their pyjamas, offering "high-fives" to any cyclist who was riding close enough to take them!

There were superb "official" stops, which we made good use of... AND you never felt that you were too far from an "unofficial" source of support – either from other cyclists or gazebos erected in fields to offer drinks, snacks and verbal encouragement.

All of this, remember, was taking place when anyone of sound mind would have been cosily tucked up in bed!

The sense of camaraderie was remarkable and our little foursome, once we were out of the slow-going (but exciting, nonetheless) London streets, maintained a really decent pace.

That's not to say that huge effort was being expended though.

I hope that Pete, Spencer and Fan would echo what I am saying here – the power output was fairly steady and, even by the time we'd got to the finish, at around 4:45am... just as the morning birds were starting to sing and daylight was showing its intention to replace pitch-dark... I can't say that I was feeling physically tired.

That made the whole thing feel a little more surreal... as if riding through the night wasn't surreal enough already!

Much of the sense of freshness was down to it having been a flat course, I guess – that takes me back to the "Box Hill" syndrome... we are just not used to such flat terrain in the West Country so being presented 113 climb-free miles was odd indeed.

Was I feeling "actually" tired though? By which, I mean; did I need to sleep?

Well – you'd have thought so wouldn't you?... Particularly since I only had 3 hours or so sleep on Friday night – not the best preparation for an all-night ride the following evening!

But I didn't really start to feel sleepy until the 9am coach ride back to the start, over 4 hours after finishing the ride.

The first sleep for all of us, I think, was the "power-nap" we all grabbed said coach. The bikes, incidentally, were having their own rest in a following lorry!

Again, I think I speak on behalf of the rest of our group of four to say that adrenalin probably kept us perky until that point and, for me at least, sitting on a coach will get me to sleep whether I need it or not!

All in all, I would tell anyone who can ride a bike to do the Dunwich Dynamo.

You certainly don't need to be super-fit to do it since the scope really is there to take as long as you want - I overheard two people chatting on the coach about others they knew who were not expecting to finish until after 11am.

It really is just a lovely experience.

My riding time was 6 hours 45 minutes, give or take a minute or two, but it's a little bit irrelevant really since it ended up not feeling like a "training ride" per se.

I'm not going to give any blog-words to the journey from Dunwich back to, firstly, my car or secondly, home – let's just say that traffic made it very difficult indeed and I have no intention of tarnishing a very positive review of a fantastic event with my old-man-grumpiness!

Despite it having felt less like a "training ride" and more like a "life-experience", it wasn't without learning points that I can carry forward into the Ironman.

Remember – it was an overnight ride, done on very little sleep and, as with the Buckingham Blinder Bike Ride earlier in the year, understanding what my body feels like to be exercising against that backdrop will certainly come in handy in terms of being prepared for the big day.

And with barely more than 4 weeks to go, I'm starting to feel like this whole Ironman thing is real – is it real?

Ticking off and ticking over – July 23rd, 2014

As I came into 2014, I was looking at a diary which included 13 organised events in the run up to the Ironman, not including, of course, my normal day to day training routine.

Said diary was made up of 8 Iron-distance (or longer – some of them were MUCH longer) bike rides, 2 swimming events, 1 running event and 2 triathlons.

One by one I have ticked them off and, last weekend, I swam my way across the finish line of the 13th and final event of the year before my Ironman just over 3 weeks from now.

That last event was the Clevedon Long Swim; A sea swim which took part around 5 miles from my home.

It's the only sea that I have swam in (ignoring holiday "splash-arounds") and, being that it is not for the faint-hearted, it was great from a training perspective.

With a propensity to be choppy, huge tidal flows and under-currents to trouble even the strongest swimmers, the Clevedon Long Swim, whilst only around a mile long, constitutes a great warm up event for Sweden which also takes place in the sea and which is likely to be in similar conditions.

The idea of doing a swim in that particular stretch of water would have terrified me only a few months ago.

Please remember that, until only a couple of months ago, even a comparatively calm lake swim left me feeling like I was genuinely going to drown.

But, as it now stands, my confidence in open water couldn't be much higher.

Saturday, however, was a reminder not to be too complacent – I struggled to find the place where I needed to register and, ultimately, I arrived later than ideal for the start - I had to hurriedly put my wetsuit on during the pre-race briefing.

Disorganisation and lateness are two things that I detest and, psychologically, they really do throw me so, as I got into the water, I was stressed, my heart rate was up and my breathing was already erratic.

I couldn't get comfortable in the water at all. It all felt wrong.

I was even facing the wrong way as the starting gun went off at 1pm.

From that point, for what seemed like ages, I just could not get my breathing sorted and I was back to finding it difficult to breathe out under water... my mind was becoming my biggest obstacle once again.

I was at the very back of the field... huffing, puffing and struggling.

I stopped swimming.

I simply was NOT going to let this, my last organised event before the big day, end badly.

That COULDN'T happen.

I bobbed up and down a bit whilst I regained my composure.

And then I swam on... with a renewed (and somewhat forced) confidence.

A few strokes later and it all came together... I started swimming strongly and feeling great. I got firmly into my familiar "zone". I relaxed and I was calm... my stroke felt good.

I had given up the hope of registering a quick time in the first few minutes but, nonetheless, pressed on to the very end.

I waded out of the water and Lisa showed me her watch – 1:25pm.

Had it really only taken me 25 minutes to both swim the mile course AND to find my way to Lisa?

Indeed it had – my official swim time was 22 minutes 38 seconds and, after that dreadful beginning, I still finished 37th of the 70 or so people who entered.

I can't pretend not to have been over the moon with that!

Whilst that was my last "organised event" before the big day, it wasn't the end of my weekend's notable training.

On Sunday, I finally gave in to Lisa's pleas, and those of quite a few other concerned friends, to attempt at least one long run before taking on the marathon at the end of the Ironman.

As regular readers will know, my total-hip-replacement relegates running firmly to the "don't do it" list so, cumulatively, I had run only 36 miles in the whole of 2014 before Saturday.

For additional context, the farthest I had EVER run, prior to Sunday, was 6 miles and that was only once! Outside of that 6 miler, the farthest I had run for over 15 years was just 3.5 miles.

Some while ago, on twitter, I was chatting to someone I had known on there for a while (Nicola, to give her a name!) and it transpired, unbelievably coincidentally, that she had been good friends of Lisa at school in Scotland and, moreover, she now lived down here in the Bristol area too (how bizarre is that?).

Anyway, as a strong endurance runner herself, Nicola kindly offered to do a long run with me and, a few days before, she asked me what distance we were targeting.

I had replied, without giving it much consideration, that it needed to be at least a half-marathon distance, really… just to see how my legs (and hip for that matter) coped.

By doing it 4 weeks ahead of the Ironman itself, I felt that I would be giving myself enough time to fully recover – bear in mind that I had no idea how long my body or, specifically, my hip, would take to get over that kind of shock!

Sunday was the big day, then, and it was hot hot hot… hardly ideal running conditions.

Nicola had managed to get two other nutters to join us and we set off at around quarter past 2.

The first 10 miles were actually really straightforward… we kept up a lovely pace and I was adopting a similar strategy in terms of nutrition to that which I would employ on the bike – taking on a gel every half an hour.

But the heat was starting to get to me a bit and, at mile 10, almost exactly, I had to concede that I wasn't going to be able to keep up with the others any longer.

In fact, at that same point, we all separated from each-other a little… going from running in a group to running as 4 individuals as the need for each of us to cater for our own "pace needs" took over – I was bringing up the rear - just about maintaining sight of the next person up the road.

The next 3 and a half miles were tough, there's no doubt about that… and my pace did slow…

BUT, I did it.

And, as it happens, by the end I fancied that I had got into a whole new rhythm, albeit at a much slower pace, which I felt happy with.

We ran just over half marathon distance, 13.3 miles to be precise, and, having taken around 2 hours 20 minutes, I am cock-a-hoop to have done so.

In the 48 hours that followed, I had some issues with sore toes and a nasty blister on my foot, which caused much hilarity with my boys (bless them), but, otherwise, any leg soreness that I suffered was very manageable.

The very most I could have asked for from the long run "test" was for it to have given me confidence for the Ironman rather than taken it away... and that is exactly what it did.

It gave me confidence.

So, with no more long swims, long bikes or long runs left... what now?

Well, I have just over three weeks before Ironman Sweden – when I will be hopefully piecing it all together by swimming 2.4 miles, riding 112 miles and then finishing it all off with a 26.2 mile run towards a shiny medal and a T-shirt.

Much gets written about "tapering" in the run up to such an event but I'm actually pretty rubbish at cutting down my training.

Cutting down my training tends to make me feel uncomfortable and irritable... no amount of reassurance that it is the right thing to do can shake the urge to just get out there and ride a bike, for example.

Having said that, one week before the big day will see the Collard Clan set off in the car with the caravan hitched on the back, en-route to Sweden.

It'll take a couple of days to get there and the period between arriving and taking part in the Ironman will, essentially, be a holiday so, almost by accident, I will have an enforced "tapering" period of around 7 days.

There is no doubt that, during the first week in Sweden, I will take a dip in the sea... the caravan site where we are staying is only a couple of miles from the transition area and has a Baltic Sea shoreline so I'd be wise to test the conditions.

Furthermore, I doubt I'll leave my bike alone for a whole week and am likely to head off on a short, leisurely ride at some point – but it WILL be leisurely and it WON'T be long.

To all intents and purposes, then, you are now reading a blog of someone who has finished the hard work.

You're reading the blog of someone who has two weeks of "ticking over" ahead of him followed by an enforced week of tapering.

Above all, though, you're reading the blog of someone who is already immensely proud of how far he has come in chasing this Ironman dream, whatever the outcome.

Goodness knows how I'll feel when (and IF) I hear those words... "PHIL COLLARD, YOU ARE AN...." (I can't bring myself to tempt fate by typing the final word... but you know what I mean)!

Tapertastic training – August 1st, 2014

It's now a little over one week before family-Collard head off to Sweden… and only a little over two weeks before the Ironman itself.

The week just past, then, should really have seen me starting to "taper".

As I mentioned in my last blog, tapering doesn't really sit too well with me… I find it very difficult not to get out there to train and my mind constantly ponders the syndrome that people tend to experience when they have been, say, on holiday.

You know – they get back after a 10 day break… hop on the bike (or other fitness apparatus of their choice)… and spend the first half an hour uttering phrases along the lines of – "Phew, you can tell I've been on holiday" or "This is hard work tonight" before cutting the session short and vowing to get back to their best within a week or two.

The last thing I want at the start of the Ironman is to feel below my peak so the desire to keep training is, at times, overpowering.

There was also ANOTHER reason to avoid the dreaded taper period… and it all started the day after I posted that last blog.

It was Thursday… it was 4:30am… it was time to get up for my normal Thursday morning, 3,250 metre, 130 lengths, pool swim.

My alarm went off and I struggled to open my eyes… which is unusual.

Breakfast was eaten in a daze and I think I bumped into every door in the house as I staggered around trying to get dressed… again, most unusual

I didn't read the signs, as I should have, and set off on my bike en-route to the pool.

The ride there was sluggish… again, I ignored the signs.

The swim itself started "okay" but I fatigued incredibly quickly and, at 3,225 metres, having taken almost TEN minutes longer than normal and with only one length to go, I genuinely couldn't muster the strength to swim another stroke.

I got out of the pool and was promptly (very) sick in the pool's toilets.

The onward ride to work was... well... horrible... despite my having rammed so much sugar down my throat, in an effort to recover some energy, that the share price of Tate & Lyle was rocketing as a result and Warren Buffet was wondering if he'd missed the boat a bit.

I felt "washed out" - to the point that even lifting a beloved cup of tea to my mouth was akin to doing a weights session in the gym.

I was all ready to accept that I had overtrained and that I'd finally snapped... I really was. As much as I would have hated it to have been true, it seemed like the only explanation.

That was until I started to realise that others around me (both at work and at home) had also felt like I was feeling over the last few days (although they hadn't attempted a 2 mile, high intensity, swim, whilst suffering, I should add) and, I concluded that I must have succumbed to a "bug".

My normal approach is to scare bugs off by training harder... but by the time mid-afternoon came, I was feeling even weaker, if that's possible, and I knew that this was not a bug that was going to allow me to train. Far from it... I even had to concede that I wasn't even going to be able to ride home at the end of the day.

5pm came and my ever supporting wife, Lisa, (with boys in tow) picked me and my bike up from work.

I didn't make it into work the next day and felt dreadful.

I just slept... a lot.

I felt a bit better on Saturday but, with the benefit of hindsight, I realise now that I didn't fully recover until Sunday.

How on earth could I go into a tapering period off the back of such a poor end to my "training proper"?

That bug might have gone but it had taken my confidence with it and, psychologically, I just couldn't let myself "finish" in that way.

So I sat down with Lisa on Sunday and actually wrote in the diary a sensible training plan, designed to get me from where I had found myself... all the way to the Ironman itself.

The plan needed to include at least a few days of "normal training", just to restore my confidence, before then forcing me into a taper.

287

The first "proper" session in the diary, then, was an Iron-distance open water swim on Tuesday night after work and, at 5pm on that day, I was in my car as quick as a flash to get to the lake as early as I could feasibly manage.

The swim that followed ended up being almost exactly 4,500 metres in length… so it was comfortably in excess of Iron-distance… but I certainly wasn't complaining.

From a pace perspective, taking around 1 hour 40 minutes to cover that distance in a perfectly flat lake was a little disappointing but, as I reminded myself at the time, I wasn't pushing myself to anywhere near my limit and, to all intents and purposes, I was just happy to have got the miles in – especially after how my previous swim had ended.

Wednesday night was, as always, bike night and, for the first time, Ian Connock (primarily a Twitter friend but whom I met at the Bristol Tri) joined me on what turned out to be a gorgeous evening to be out on a bike.

The club with which I ride has gone from strength to strength and on Wednesday there were an unprecedented 24 of us gathered at the start.

As with the lake swim, it was a real "restorer of confidence" – my legs were feeling good and the pace was, I would say, on the swifter side for the club… which was exactly what I needed.

We rode around 24 miles in 1 hour 24 minutes (riding time).

And, to bring this blog up to date, yesterday morning (Thursday) saw me return to the pool where, one week earlier, it had all gone horribly wrong.

This time, though, my eyes were open before the alarm went off and I bounced out of bed as I normally would.

I also felt lively on the bike ride to get me there.

This swim was going to be the start of my taper and, rather than targeting my normal 130 lengths, I had written the words "100 lengths" in the diary (2,500 metres).

I suspected that the swim was going to be tough – I was mindful that I had swam 4,500 metres in a lake only 36 hours previously AND I was coming off the back of the bike ride the night before with only a short night's sleep to recover.

It wasn't tough, though!

I felt strong and relaxed. I had to keep reminding myself that this was the start of a taper period so I should really be taking it easy. I managed to keep my effort levels in check but it was like swimming with the brakes on a bit... and I mean that in a nice way!

As I approached 100 lengths, it took an awful lot of self-control NOT to swim past that arbitrary point and on to my normal 130.

My inner voice was taunting me:

"Come on – it's only another 30... what harm can that do?"

"You can't stop now... you're feeling so good!"

"Remember last week... don't you want to 'make amends' for that failure?"

BUT... I hadn't sat down with Lisa and put together my final training plan for nothing – I was going to stick to it so I duly, and somewhat reluctantly, hauled myself out of the pool at the 2,500 metres mark.

Sometimes, you get a reminder as to how far you have come and, to go off at a tangent for a moment, the time I registered for that swim was a couple of minutes quicker than anything I could have done at a time when 100 lengths was my normal morning swim distance, towards the end of last year... that was before I started to up the distance further.

The fact that I set that pace seemed even more impressive to me when I reminded myself that I was deliberately holding myself back AND I had actually stopped for a couple of minutes mid-swim to sort out an issue with my goggles, which just weren't playing ball for some reason.

This last week, then, has seen my confidence shattered... but it's also seen my confidence restored... so in many ways I can take more pleasure from it than I would have, had it just been a "normal" week.

What's left on my training plan?

Well... I have a pootle (and I MEAN "pootle") on the bike, scheduled for Saturday evening, and one last sea-swim (again, not any real distance) on Sunday.

Next week will see one last Wednesday evening ride, although I have already warned Spencer that I might allow myself to drop off the back if the pace is a bit hot for what I am after, and, since I am off work to prepare for our departure the following day, my Thursday morning swim will take place on Friday morning... it will be further shortened to 80 lengths and, again, will be steady steady steady.

Then it's Saturday 9th August.

And that means a trip to Sweden.

Wow!

The final countdown – August 8th, 2014

The whole of the Collard Clan is setting off for Sweden tomorrow... so this will be my last blog before the Ironman – those words hardly seem real.

When I entered the event, almost exactly a year ago, I did so with a bit of a cocky mind-set... I believed that, if push came to shove, I could probably have completed it the following day.

I was wrong.

Very wrong.

I know that now.

I think the biggest struggle that I encountered between then and now was in the water.

I firstly had to transform myself from someone who was "able" to swim, but who wasn't used to doing so for more than 400 metres in a pool (I only ever really swam during Sprint Triathlons), into someone who could, firstly, breathe properly and, secondly, swim long distances without tiring. I managed that.

I then had to transform myself from a pool swimmer who, on entering a lake, had near-drowning moments, into someone who could swim those same long distances that he could in the pool... but in the open water. I managed that too.

I then had to transform myself from someone who could manage a lake swim but who really wasn't keen on replicating it in the much choppier sea, with under-currents to contend with, into someone who genuinely enjoyed the challenge. I managed that.

On the bike, the obstacles were less pronounced since I was already fairly used to cycling longer distances although I remind myself that, until the day I entered the Ironman, I had only ever ridden beyond an Iron-distance once (a single day 190 mile ride, in case you are wondering!).

And I certainly hadn't followed that with a run immediately afterwards.

I've since done another 9 Iron-distance (or beyond) bike rides... with the longest single day ride coming in at a smidgen over 265 miles... and, at the end of 2 of the 9, measuring 145 miles and a 113 miles respectively, I have thrown in a short run after a "transition-esque" footwear change.

291

I now know how very hard it is to do that.

In terms of the running, my total hip-replacement has prevented me from embarking on a running regime, as I knew it would, so I may be one of the only competitors on the Swedish start line who will be in pretty much unchartered territory from the moment I dismount my bike.

I did run a half marathon distance only a few weeks ago and, to adopt a positive outlook, it left me with the sense that I CAN get 'round a marathon... but that it will be no picnic.

Running 13.5 miles was tough with next to no specific training beforehand.

I firmly believe that, even on its own, the marathon distance that I will be looking to cover on the day is one of the toughest physical challenges that I could entertain putting my hip through... what it will feel like as the third section of an Ironman, I can't yet imagine!

In stats, then, the 12 months since I hit send on my entry e-mail have involved 83 miles of swimming, 5,499 miles of cycling and 61 miles of running...

Not including the countless Spinning sessions that I have instructed (averaging almost 3 per week) or the resistance sessions that I throw in every couple of mornings.

But I've achieved more than just simply adding hours and miles to the training log – it's been a year of learning too.

For starters, I now know what to expect of myself when I get past the point of needing sleep, which is quite possibly going to happen to me on the day... Both the 265 mile ride and the Dunwich Dynamo overnighter pushed me over that line... but I managed to keep going on both occasions and learned valuable lessons in the process.

I also have a better understanding of what my body needs in terms of nutrition, having tweaked and honed this aspect of my training continually throughout the year.

I have learned about when to push hard... and I have learned how to recognise those moments when my effort needs to be curtailed for the greater good.

For all of those challenges overcome, hours banked and lessons learned, however, I am still completely unsure as to whether I have what it takes to finish an Ironman Triathlon.

I have no idea as to whether the swim leg will echo my training – if it does, I will be fine... but throw in over 2,400 other swimmers, mix that with the anxieties that I have about what conditions I might face in the Baltic Sea, and any pre-existing confidence I might have had could well go out of the window in the first 30 seconds.

Where would that leave me?

I have no idea as to whether the bike leg will go as planned. I've heard SO many horror stories about how windy the course is in Sweden and, as long time readers of this blog will know, I really do struggle in wind.

And I mean... "really struggle".

Strong wind (coupled with torrential rain, in my defence) was a key factor in my ONLY long distance bike ride DNF to date and, psychologically, if conditions are in any way similar to that, I will have a real fight on my hands to NOT dwell on thoughts of that cold day in January when it all fell apart for me at mile 100 of a scheduled 105 (yep, I really did abort with just 5 miles to go).

I really have no idea as to whether I can cover 26 miles on foot either.

The half-marathon distance run I referred to earlier gave me confidence, sure, but, and let's make no mistake, the last 3 miles or so were very hard work. How would another 13 have felt?

I believe myself to be mentally strong, though, and that is, ultimately, what I will be relying on to get me through if my physical strength deserts me.

The question, then, is whether I am mentally and/or physically strong enough... and I'll only know the answer to that question in around 9 days' time.

Lastly, of course, any number of other things could go wrong – mechanical issues with my bike or injuries to name just two.

So... I do have doubts.

But doubts can be turned into positives.

If I "knew" I was going to finish, then I'd find it harder to summon the kind of motivation that I'll undoubtedly benefit from on the day.

If I "knew" I was going to finish, then the taking part itself would be less exciting.

If I "knew" I was going to finish, then it would somehow feel like less of an achievement if I do.

As non-committal as I'd love to be, I do want to go on record and state my targets for the day so, with no beating around the bush:

1) A sub 1 hour 30 swim

2) A sub 7 hour 30 bike

3) To finish the run within the overall 16 hour cut-off – however long it takes

My lack of a more pressing target for the run is mainly centred around my hip – I simply can't afford to put pressure on myself in that section, aside from simply saying that I want to finish.

If I hit the above targets… I'll be on top of the world… and I'll likely stay there for a long long long time – I'll be insufferable, I'm afraid!

If I don't hit the swim and/or bike targets but still finish within the 16 hours… I'll still be happy beyond belief, of course, but, in the days and weeks that follow, I suspect that there will be a small part of me that will be a tiny bit disappointed with my performance.

If I don't finish… I'll be devastated.

Simple as that.

Whatever the outcome, I can say with complete honesty that I couldn't have done more.

I can also say that I am overwhelmingly proud of what I have achieved thus far and immeasurably grateful to everyone, especially, of course, Lisa and the boys, for the support that I have enjoyed this year.

A saying that goes with me into the event is something along the lines of "The pain of success is temporary… the pain of failure is permanent".

I might well find myself reciting that under my breath for a full 16 hours on August 16th in a South Eastern corner of Sweden!

Wish me luck!

I AM an Ironman.... August 19th, 2014

It's Monday, 18th August at 6am.

I'm in the caravan.

Lisa and the boys are asleep but the adrenaline from Saturday is making it hard for me to do the same so, rather than defaulting to Twitter, Facebook or the internet, I thought I'd pen a little blog for my own amusement as much as yours!

Before I get to that, though, I'll just point out that I live, as good as makes no difference for the purposes of this blog, around an Iron-distance bike ride from London.

With that in mind let me run something by you.

What do you reckon about the idea of me taking part in the London Marathon?

But, rather than drive to the start like a normal person, I could start by swimming 2.4 miles in the sea near my house, get out of my wetsuit, ride my bike to London and, hopefully, arrive with just enough time to change my shoes and set off at the same time as all of the other entrants of the marathon itself.

AND... What about only counting my having taken part in said marathon as a success if I cross the finishing line no more than 16 hours after having started to swim.

I have no plans to act out the above mad-cap idea, of course... I thought of it the day after the Ironman and I genuinely laughed out loud at how mad it would be for anyone to try it.

But, to all intents and purposes, that's exactly what I set out to do on the 16th August in the Ironman Sweden event held in Kalmar.

And, would you believe it, I only went and finished!

Now - I'm an average swimmer, an average cyclist and the less said about my running the better.

BUT... I am... an Ironman.

Just typing that gives me goosebumps.

Please bear in mind that, not too long ago, two of my biggest physical goals (I genuinely had them written down on a list of things I'd like to achieve) were to sit in a chair like a "normal" person and to walk upstairs facing forwards.

Yep - associating the word Ironman with myself gives me goosebumps indeed.

More importantly, though, my having become an Ironman has made me realise that the realms of the possible are typically MUCH wider than we choose to believe.

I have loved and willingly accepted all of the praise and plaudits that I received through social media during and following the big day ... And there have been literally hundreds of such posts... but, seriously, I don't see myself as having done anything that the vast majority of you out there couldn't do... if you haven't already done it, that is.

Chances are that it most definitely IS within your own "realm of the possible" (that sounds like a Lord of the Rings kind of place doesn't it?!?!)

My having become an Ironman has also given me an admiration for those that do these events regularly.

I'm not just talking the professionals, either (although to be able to finish an Ironman event in under 9 hours completely blows my mind)... I mean the age-groupers, too, who go from "iron-distance" event to "iron-distance" event collecting medals as if they're going out of fashion.

I now know just how hard an Ironman is so finishers of multiple such events have my absolute respect!!

And, in a not so subtle nod to the content of an as yet "untyped" blog, my having become an Ironman has made me realise that a phrase I cheerily trot out during my Spinning classes, to those I'm instructing, is so much truer than I'd imagined.

From time to time, in said Spinning classes, I remind everyone that their legs will always tell you they've had enough long before they really have... Kind of a self defence mechanism to stop you overshooting their limit... And that the mind tends to be able to drag a bit more out of them, within reason.

I'd always thought that I had "walked the walk" when it came to that phrase but, believe me, the next time I say it, I'll be doing so with MUCH more authority on the subject!

I will blog my review of the event itself when I'm back from Sweden so stay tuned but, until then, I'm going to enjoy the next week - a long awaited family holiday!

The swim – August 27th, 2014

I considered giving you a run-down of the week's events leading up to the Ironman and was unsure as to whether me telling you all about our five days in Sweden warranted a separate blog.

In the end, I decided that I subject you to enough waffle as it is without boring you further so I'll be brief.

In that final week, I did head out on a couple of short bike rides, at a relatively leisurely rate of effort, and I also took the opportunity for a couple of similarly steady sea-swims but, aside from that, the few days before the big event were spent, in the main, either resting or walking very gingerly to preserve all of the energy that I could.

The day I registered, which was also the day that I attended the pre-race evening briefing and meal, was a big day, psychologically, as the whole thing became very real. I still have my registration band on my wrist as I type these very words and, until it bio-degrades its way off, I'm of a mind to leave it there!

Anyway, on to the event itself.

My alarm was set for 3:45am - transition was due to open from 5am and I really wanted to be there early to put the finishing touches to my bike which had been left there since the day before... Namely: pumping up the tyres, lubing the chain and dropping electrolyte tablets into the bottles which I had already been filled with water the day before.

Lisa got up with me to make me breakfast while I showered etc but, to give them a little more time to eat their own breakfasts, her and the boys made their way from the caravan, by bike, to the start area separately from me.

Once I was done in transition, I carried my wetsuit, goggles and swim hat over to where we'd all arranged to meet.

Time seemed to slow down at that point and what was only around 45 minutes between meeting up with the family and the "starting gun" seemed like hours.

The swim was a rolling start where all 2,470 of us were asked to estimate our swim times, line up with others who had similar expectations and, at the given moment, we were all going to start pushing into the water to set off on the swim itself.

I sought out the 1hr 25m group... I've maintained for some time that, all things considered, I'd be happy with anything less than 1hr 30m.

1hr 25m just happened to be slap in the middle of the options available so, again, psychologically, it felt right... The "goldilocks" estimate, if you like.

And there I was... suddenly... standing in my wetsuit... throwing a sports gel down my neck... surrounded by hundreds of other people doing the same... but feeling as alone as I ever have.

I was almost a bit sad!

I needed to talk to someone and asked the lady next to me if she spoke English.

She happened to be American.

"Nearly" English, then... close enough! (Just joking, my American friends!).

She was taking part in her 4th Ironman and just having a chat was very calming. My loneliness was, therefore, short-lived.

As our self-seeded group edged ever closer to the water, I started to feel more and more relaxed - that was until I pulled my goggles down from my forehead over my eyes and realised that, in being pressed against my hot forehead, they had misted up such that I couldn't see a thing.

A mild panic, a last minute removal of all head-gear and some "moisturising" of my goggle lenses (a nice way to say that I spat on them) later and I was back with full visibility.

Phew... crisis averted!

The ramp into the water was now in sight and it became clear that, as you descended the boards, you just kept going until walking became swimming... There was no chance for acclimatisation.

The masses behind you kept pushing like you were at the front of the queue for the latest "must have" product on release day... There was no going back and no hanging around.

The swim was exactly what everyone says an Ironman swim is like... kind of brutal... a constant physical fight with others... but great fun all the same.

I lost count, within the first few minutes, of how many potentially bruise-inducing punches and kicks that I took... and they continued for pretty much the whole of the swim because, much to my surprise, the group nature of the swimmers never did "thin out".

Before the race, I expected to find it very congested for, say, the first few hundred metres but then for the field to become almost a single-file line, with everyone focusing on the person in front.

Instead, there wasn't a single moment, when breathing to either side, where I couldn't see at least six or seven people alongside me.

I was actually using them to sight my way around the course... I figured that if I had people either side of me than I must be going the right way, so I allowed myself not to worry too much about looking forwards.

That wasn't necessarily the right strategy as I found when, with only a few hundred metres to go, I swam straight into a big solid post which was sticking out of the water near a bridge.

Hundreds of spectators witnessed me trying to coolly recover myself from this somewhat embarrassing moment!

Throughout the swim, despite the almost "boxing ring" nature of the experience, I actually felt amazingly calm and relaxed.

The water was sea-water but it tasted pretty clear - no saltiness like I've experienced nearer to home and, as if to make the swim leg more interesting, we were treated to the sights of jelly-fish, underwater foliage and other sea-life throughout!

It was, basically, a really lovely swim in the morning sun, albeit with A LOT of other people... and, as I came towards the exit ramp, nearly 4,000 metres after breaking into front-crawl, I allowed myself an underwater smile.

It didn't last long though.

As soon as my feet hit terra-firma, my legs went to jelly... Something that has never happened to me before even though I've done more than my fair share of long swims!

I stumbled to my knees on the ramp and had to use my hands and the rail to pull myself back upright, reassuring the concerned guy behind me that I was okay.

That was an odd feeling and it did shake my confidence a little, which was less than welcome but, thankfully, the "jelly-legs" sensation passed very quickly and, before I knew it, I was cheerily trotting towards the transition area, passing Lisa and the boys en-route.

It is hard to express how welcome it was to see their smiling faces... I was out of the water and on my way... It was a great feeling indeed.

My swim time as I glanced down at my watch when exiting the water: 1 hour 24 minutes... My self-seeded estimate had been spot on and, what's more, I knew that I had beaten the target that I had set myself in my last blog before the event.

As I made a bee-line for my "swim to bike" transition bag, I knew that I needed to gather my thoughts for the bike leg but, in the tradition of a Saturday night game show, you'll need to wait until "after a short break" for that blog!

The bike – August 29th, 2014

The success of the swim had put me in a good mood and as I grabbed my "swim to bike transition bag", I went through my pre-arranged transition plan in my mind:

Calmly remove wetsuit, turn off the Garmin that had been under my swim cap (logging the swim) and put it on my wrist ready for when it would next be needed in the run, switch my bike Garmin on (yes, I have two Garmins), dry feet with towel, put socks, cycling shoes and gloves on, have a sports gel, put number belt on, write the average speed that my bike leg needed to be completed at on a label (I had put an A4 sheet of paper in the bag with a whole load of scenarios based on different swim times and thought that it would be useful to know what speed I needed to maintain whilst riding to be off my bike in 9 hours, which was always my strategy). Once all that was done, I could find my bike, put my helmet on, attach my bike Garmin (which, by now, would have found its own location), stick my "average speed label" on to my Tri bars... and GO!

It sounds a lot but I'd mentally gone through it SO many times that it was going to be slick.

It WAS going to be slick... I'd promised myself that much.

I walked into the male transition changing tent and was confronted by chaos.

My beautifully crafted and mentally rehearsed plan fell down at the first hurdle – "calmly remove wetsuit".

I'm not great at getting out of my wetsuit at the best of times and, to do it quickly, I tend to need to either sit down or hold on to something for support.

There was certainly nowhere to sit and the only thing to hold on to, since I was going to be doing this standing up, was a naked, sweaty, bent over, male backside and, err, "undercarriage", onto which copious amounts of chamois cream was being applied.

I suspect that grabbing someone else's private parts to steady oneself whilst in transition is, at best, inappropriate and, at worst, against the rules.

Either way, it was not something I was about to do.

I went for the option of removing my wetsuit unaided, then, and proceeded to stumble around as if I'd had one too many glasses of wine.

That put pay to my well-formed plan, really, and, since I ended up doing it in a completely different order than intended, it was difficult to remember it all.

I ended up skipping the bit about writing down my required average speed to be off the bike in 9 hours (although I did make a mental note of it: 15.3 miles per hour).

Most annoyingly, though, I accidentally threw my swim/run Garmin into the transition bag to be dropped on exit of the tent, which I'd now not see again, rather than putting it on my wrist as had been the plan.

That played on my mind as I was mounting my bike - I now knew that, when I got to the run, I would have no way of pacing myself to the finish and that I would just be running "on feel" - that was a challenge that I REALLY hadn't wanted to face.

As I took those first few pedal strokes, literally slapping my forehead to punish my mistake, I reminded myself that I could only "control the controllables" and that the erroneous location of that Garmin was now firmly OUT of my control so I should just put it out of my head... at least for the next 112 miles anyway.

I did.

My legs felt good as I got on top of the gear that I'd pre-selected as a good one to get me going, and I was quickly up to in excess of 20mph, with the help of a following breeze.

That following breeze helped me to go through the 10 mile mark in comfortably less than 30 minutes.

I was going so quickly, in fact, that I started analysing how hard I was pushing - I wanted to resist any urge to push so hard that I had nothing in my legs for the run bit... I concluded that I was not exerting myself too much.. my legs were just ticking over... So I allowed the breeze to carry me along knowing that I was likely to encounter headwinds later.

The bike route, itself, was beautiful and, to start with, took us over a quite spectacular, 4 mile, bridge on to Öland - an island completely separate from mainland Sweden.

There were hoards of people lining big stretches of the roads - banging drums, rattling pans, ringing bells and shouting "Heja, Heja, Heja"... A Swedish phrase of encouragement.

Some of the owners of the roadside properties had music pumping out at full volume to keep us going too.

It genuinely felt like a 112 mile party... An amazing experience indeed.

The route itself, from a cycling perspective, was broadly flat and the scenery was something to behold... really it was.

So much so that I mentally drifted into a zone where I almost forgot that I was taking part in an Ironman – I even found myself singing, out loud, the song that has almost become a signature tune to this year; "On Days Like These" by Matt Monroe (that same song even gave its name to an earlier blog).

The song reflected how I was feeling.

On any normal day, it would be a ride that I would love to do with friends... Stopping from time to time for photo opportunities.

But, of course, this wasn't a normal day... This was Ironman day.

I had my normal "dark period" as I approached mile 56 - I think I've mentioned before that I always get these on longer rides and they involve me sinking into myself a little as the whole enormity of the distance to be covered becomes real.

As I know to expect these dark periods, though, I can manage my way through them and this day was no different.

The wind wasn't as bad as I thought it would be - it was windy, sure, but there was nothing that I wouldn't expect back home... That was until we turned back westwards.

The headwind became quite strong at this point and, coupled with the fact that the road, despite looking as flat as a proverbial pancake, was a very gradual and energy sapping upward gradient (something which I'd been previously warned of), my riding speed plummeted - and it dragged my average speed down with it too.

I wasn't panicking though - I was adopting what was seeming to be a satisfactory nutrition strategy (gel on the half hour, solid on the hour and drinking whenever needed) and my average speed was way above the 15.3mph that I knew I needed to maintain in order to be off the bike in 9 hours (thus giving me my desired 7 hours to complete the marathon).

Aid stations were positioned at every 12-15 miles but aside from a toilet stop or two, I was self supporting and didn't need them.

To go off on a tangent a bit, I did realise a bit of a silly dream on the bike.

I've always secretly loved the way that the professionals eject their empty drinks bottles on to the roadside and grab a full one from someone standing a few yards further on... so it was with great delight that I did the same during the bike ride... twice.

It's daft, I know, but it did feel pretty amazing to me so I wanted to mention it!

Anyway, after around 70 miles, we came back across that stunning bridge for a final 40 mile (ish) loop on the mainland.... By now, I knew that it would take a disaster for me to not have at least 7 hours to do the marathon - my average pace was looking pretty good, by my standards at least, relative to the perceived level of effort I was putting in.

I did slow a little over those last 40 miles - a combination of the wind and the fact that I saw an opportunity to go easier on the legs whilst still finishing ahead of my target – I had started to give serious thought to the run and knew that I'd find a marathon tough even with fresh legs so any opportunity to relax a little was welcomed.

The otherwise glorious sunshine gave way to a bit of a shower with around 30 miles to go but, again, it was nothing to be troubled by - if anything, it was quite refreshing.

Just as I had with the swim, I saw Lisa and the boys cheering me on as I came into transition and that lifted an already happy Phil a bit further.

Swim and bike done – and both of them within the targets I'd set myself in my final blog before the event.

I had as good as makes no difference seven and a half hours to do the marathon... Half an hour longer than I had targeted.

I hopped off my bike... My legs didn't feel "great" but they weren't too bad either.

Life was good.

My bike time: 6 hrs 49 mins (including 5 minutes total stopped time)

Now to prepare for the tough bit... The bit that I had parked in the very darkest recesses of my mind for pretty much the whole of the last year...

The RUN... (cue sinister looking lightning strikes and evil laughter noises!!!)

305

The run – September 1st, 2014

Knowing I only had a marathon left was both a lovely feeling and a terrifying one at the same time.

I had around 7hrs 30 minutes remaining until the overall 16 hour cut-off so I could have been forgiven for thinking that I'd essentially finished already... but I was taking absolutely nothing for granted.

This was the bit that I hadn't trained for, remember, aside from just a few small forays into the running world.

My first mental challenge came during the "bike to run" transition. I realised that, somewhere along the ride, my ibuprofen and anti-diarrhoea tablets had fallen out of my Tri-top back pocket.

I'm trying to be sensitive here but I had heard that anti-diarrhoea tablets, in particular, tend to be useful for an Ironman so I was fearful of what might happen without them. (It turned out to be completely fine, you'll be relieved to know!)

With that playing on my mind, I changed my shoes, grabbed my running bottle and a packet of jelly-babies before setting off on my way.

Now was time to return to those thoughts of that "run Garmin" - The one that I was hoping to rely on in terms of pacing myself to the finish but which, thanks to my having accidentally thrown it in my "swim to bike" transition bag, rather than putting it on my wrist 112 miles previously, was now unavailable to me.

It just so happened that, on the way out of the transition tent, we passed the "swim to bike" transition bags and it seemed perfectly okay to have a rummage... I was going to get my run Garmin back after all!!

A moment of hope turned into a few minutes, if not more, of frantically searching for my bag – In my haste, I couldn't see any obvious numerical logic that had been employed by the organisers in hanging them up so looking for mine, amongst over 2,400 others, was like looking for a needle in a haystack.

I gave up.

I'd wasted far too much time and resolved to run with just my normal wrist-watch for guidance.

I had been chatting with a Tri-coach the day before the big event, just after the pre-race acclimatisation swim, and had mentioned an "8 minute run, 2 minute walk" strategy.

She had broadly approved but suggested a "4 minute run, 1 minute walk" alternative.

This was the only "last minute" change to my race strategy that I had made but, as I set off on the run, I adopted her suggestion to the letter.

4 minutes running, 1 minute walking, 4 minutes running, 1 minute walking, 4 minutes running, 1 minute walking.

I kept that up for the first of the three laps - around 9 miles - but it was hard going.

Whilst my hip was feeling broadly "okay", my lack of running training was really starting to show and the realisation that I still had 17 miles to go was... well... not nice.

I'd been making good use of the aid stations (mainly taking the cola and electrolyte drinks) and it became clear to me that my water bottle and jelly babies were, essentially, dead-weight which I could look to shed at the first opportunity in an effort to give myself an easier time.

As I got to the end of the nine miles, I saw Lisa and the boys.

I had a bit of a panic.

I could sense that I was going to be cutting it fine to finish within 16 hours... Not because my pace to that point was too slow but because I could feel what my pace for the remainder might be.

My Ironman dream was still in doubt.

The idea that a whole year of effort now rested in such a fine balance was soul destroying and I started wishing that I'd pushed harder on the bike to give myself more time to get this marathon done!

I imparted my fears on Lisa and the boys (at the same time as offloading my water bottle and packet of jelly babies).

Lisa detected the despair in my voice and gave me a pep-talk, as she powered alongside me, which, basically, went something along the lines of: "man up and dig deeper".

I had "run / walked" as far as I could and now I was just power-walking... Not an ideal scenario.

The route was lined with people cheering and, during the sections which took us through the narrow cobbled streets of the city, the crowds were immense... High-fives were being thrown around left, right and centre and, as on the bike, the cries of "Heja, Heja, Heja" were sometimes drowning out even my inner voice!

The aid stations were also amazing and came along every few kilometres, which was great.

Out of the city, people were still out in their thousands to offer their support... Some even had hoses to cool you down if you gave them the nod.

But, at that same time as being surrounded by spectators and competitors alike, I was feeling very alone... Only one person had any genuine influence on whether I finished this thing or not... and that was me.

I was walking as fast as I could - lengthening my stride as much as possible and swinging my arms for momentum.

My brain was constantly calculating "distance left" versus "time remaining".

Sometimes, it was concluding that I had plenty of time... on other occassions, it was concluding that I simply couldn't hope to finish within the cut-off.

If only I'd had that Garmin to pace myself, I would have known for sure... but I didn't... and I couldn't afford to dwell on that.

As I grabbed my last "wrist band", to signify that I was on my third of the three laps, I knew that, with just under nine miles remaining, I needed to give it everything I had.

Whilst my hip wasn't hurting, as such, I was aware that it was suffering and my "fast walk" had become more of a "fast limp". It took everything I had to mentally focus on the idea of becoming an Ironman rather than on any negative thoughts I was now having.

I power-walked alongside someone else who was also limping his way around the final lap... He had injured himself early on the run and was in pain too. I'm not sure if he finished in time but he was significantly slower than me so I suspect not, sadly for him.

With around 10k to go, I started feeling tingly all over... My sugar levels were shockingly low and I was feeling faint.

My predicament, I know, was down to a lack of long distance running training but, really, I COULDN'T have prepared for this marathon any differently... risking my hip any more than I had over the last year would have been a step too far.

At the next aid station, to recover some energy, I took everything on offer! - water, cola, Red Bull, electrolytes, energy drink, crisps, fruit and a gel... I think they thought I was a mad-man but hey!

I must have been limping badly, too... the paramedic positioned just after the aid station tried to stop me: "You're limping, you're in pain, you NEED to get help here"...

"Err.. No thanks, I'm not about to stop now!!"

With 8k (5 miles) to go, a chap jogged alongside me and I started to engage with him as he slowed to a walk too.

I NEEDED reassurance that I was going to finish in time... but he couldn't give it.

Instead, he referred to his own wrist-mounted Garmin (damn him!) and told me that we were walking at 4km per hour.

We had 8km to go and only 1hr 45mins until the 16 hour cut off!

I was going to fail unless I dug EVEN deeper!!!!!!

I wasn't sure that "even deeper" existed but was desperate to do whatever I needed to do so I said goodbye to the chap I was walking with and broke into a run.

I found, to my horror, that my "run" was, by now, no quicker than my "walk" – a dozen limped strides further down the road and my new buddy was still walking alongside me! I hadn't pulled out a single metre on him in what was "full-on run mode"!

Now my predicament was even worse!!

I was going to fail AND I'd just proved that there was nothing I could do about it!!!!!

One way or another, I needed to look for more.

I looked for more... pretty hard... harder than I have ever looked before... and I found it.

I persuaded my legs to walk faster and even managed to run "faster than walking pace" for a few hundred metres at a time... It was progress and I was taking it.

I got to around 3km to go with just over an hour remaining... I refused to allow myself the luxury of a smile.

With 2km to go, I saw Lisa and the boys.

Lisa was laughing a nervous laugh: "You're going to finish... You're going to be a bloody Ironman!!!!" - she was smiling – an "ear to ear" beauty of a smile!

I talked to her but refused to either join her in her smile or to back off one iota. I wasn't convinced just yet so, as her and the boys walked the more direct route to the finish line, I headed into the maze of the cobbled streets.

The last few hundred metres, through massive crowds... all cheering, touching me, patting me on the back, high-fiving me and shaking my hand... were an intense experience and, as the finishing line came into sight, I knew I had it.

I KNEW I had it!

That Matt Monro song, "On Days Like These", that I had been singing out loud on the bike was suddenly filling my head and, instantly, I felt calmed by it.

My power walk (a "normal" walking speed on any other day) became a normal walk (a "slow" walking speed on any other day) and the finishing line music got louder as it got closer.

I was clapping my hands in wide arcs; starting by my thighs and finishing above my head, like competitors in athletic events do to get the spectators behind their next attempt at, say, the long jump.

I was cupping my hands against my ears as if to convey an "I can't hear you" message.

I was punching the air with delight.

My gestures were turning the volume up even further on the already deafeningly loud crowds in the grandstands either side of me.

I was zig-zagging down the finishing chute... taking every high-five and hand-shake I could.

And then...

PHIL COLLARD... YOU ARE... AN IRONMAN.

AMAZING!!!!!!

BEYOND WORDS, AMAZING.

But everything had been a blur and much to my immeasurable disappointment, I hadn't seen Lisa or the boys in the final few metres even though, from the photos that she took, it was clear that I had been no more than a metre or two away from them - the noise making it impossible for her shouts to be heard.

That was devastating but my mind and body were totally exhausted so I have forgiven myself for not having been compos-mentis enough to spot them.

They found me within a minute or so of my crossing the finishing line though... and the hug that I got from them was the most welcome thing a man could wish for!

I'd banked on needing 7 hours for the marathon and I took 6 hours 55 minutes : a total time for the Ironman of 15 hours, 31 minutes.

Despite the touch and go nature of the marathon, the cold hard figures show that I executed my previously devised race strategy flawlessly, which was satisfying.

I don't remember much about the minutes after finishing...

I know that a lady tried to get me wrapped in foil. I know that the same lady was essentially guiding me from one part of the finishers circle to another, putting me in front of a camera at one point and directing me to the showers and changing rooms.

I was more than a little bit dazed and jelly-legged to say the least but I was immensely happy, immensely proud and immensely satisfied.

Surprisingly, I didn't feel overly "emotional" at the finish line, though.

If you had asked me before the event what would happen as I crossed the line, I would have guessed that it would have involved an awful lot of tears on my part.

In fact, I was SO certain that I was going to be teary that I think I even tried to force a tear out when the moment actually arrived... but no tears came.

I actually think that I was SO exhausted that getting emotional would have meant calling on energy that I simply didn't have.

That was my guess as to what was happening to me... I didn't know for sure.

I knew one thing, though

I had become an Ironman.

I had the medal, the T-shirt and the pain, to prove it!

Thank you – September 4th, 2014

So... my Ironman adventure is over...

It would be wrong of me not to just drop in one last blog to thank everyone who has played their part in what has ultimately been the most amazing year I could have imagined.

Every one of the people mentioned in this blog contributed, in their own individual ways, towards me getting my hands on that finisher's medal.

So, in no particular order, and with only this very limited pre-amble, special thanks go to the following people that I know "in real life":

1. Spencer Pritchard– For being "badass" enough to train in all winds and weathers and for forming the cycle club that has enabled me to indulge my love of cycling. Also for being mad enough to join me on a ridiculous 265 miles one day ride AND a 113 mile overnight ride from London to the Suffolk coast.

2. Pete Henley – For also being "badass" enough to train in all winds and weathers and for cycling with me on that same 113 mile overnight bike ride

3. Tom Worley – For massaging my ego by pretending, in conversation, that I'm fitter than he is – and for laughing at me when I said that I wasn't going to train for the run section of the Ironman (I think it was a nervous laugh and that he was genuinely concerned for my health and sanity!)

4. Della Hudson – For ongoing support and for getting in a freezing cold lake with me in winter when most people would have been wrapped up indoors with a mug of tea.

5. Paula White – For ongoing support and her continuing confidence in my ability

6. Paula Hall – For ongoing support and her encouragement

7. Conor McGloin – For doing Ironman UK just weeks before my own big day and, in the process, making me feel all "pumped"

8. Adam Heath – For getting in a freezing cold lake with me in winter and for being someone who will apparently try anything... thus motivating me to "try anything" too!

9. Adam Watkins – For being mad enough to ride that 265 miles with me and, on the same day, for being instrumental in helping me to understand what it means to ride within your own limits.

10. Nicola Ness – For ongoing support and, in particular, for being patient enough to drag me around a half-marathon run.

11. John Wood at Tri Coaching – For turning me into an open water swimming convert in the space of one coaching session.

12. Wayne Nutland aka "Stan Hibbert" – For ongoing support and encouragement

13. Matt Elson – For ongoing support and for reminding me that it's not that mad to train at 5am

14. Fanny Marshall – For ongoing support and being mad enough to do that "through the night, 113 mile bike ride" with me.

15. Ian Connock – For ongoing support and for calming down a pretty anxious "Phil" ahead of the Bristol Tri (which was very much a warm up for the big day so crucial in terms of my preparation)

16. Chris Cooke – For ongoing support and encouragement

17. Jules Smailes – For ongoing support and encouragement

18. Evert Smith – For being the amazing surgeon who is largely responsible for my ability to move (that's quite important, I find)

19. Russell Filby – For ongoing support and encouragement.

20. Dave George – For ongoing support and encouragement

21. Nick Hall – For ongoing support and encouragement

22. Simon Hall - For ongoing support and encouragement

23. Rob Fountain - For ongoing support and encouragement

24. Simon Knott – For reminding me, from time to time, that an "Ironman in training" can be a boring individual indeed and, in the process, keeping me grounded on more than on occasion!

25. The members of the Backwell Road Cycling Club who I haven't already singled out above – for being a great bunch to ride with and a fantastic source of inspiration and encouragement to boot.

26. Everyone I work with for putting up with my insanely boring training tales!

If your name doesn't appear above but, deep down, you might have expected to see it, it's not because your support hasn't been appreciated – it's because my memory is shocking so please, don't be offended – I'm thankful to you too.

But, of course, it isn't only people that I know in "real-life" that have been part of the last year, is it?

I also need to thank those of you in the social media universe who, for one reason or another, have had a positive impact on me.

From Twitter, then, and again in no particular order, thanks to: @velohut, @RichardCBishop, @NigeWhite, @Sam_Grange, @LouxLoux71, @JackCox1901, @JonoTheTurk, @LisleDemon, @Pols80, @CarpingMick, @bluepeter1979, @davemoulding, @TheLozzatron, @Chrisoconnor06, @budjude17, @nellieh64, @BillPeterman1, @SprocketWaffle, @IronPugsley, @BrianDrought, @gaynorh1975, @Pandasotter, @DaBigOz, @G_C_Zero, @FruitMeister, @Smoker2Ironman, @Tribod, @officialrobgun, @TheBaldyGit, @KerimMorris, @AndyBirks40, @ChristinaJL_GB, @iamjasonroberts, @triathlonbox, @DarinArmstrong, @CarlSpangled, @GlenaTim, @Numberrr2, @Irongirl41, @Judithjwilliams, @annepdolphin, @anget73, @janeannenichol, @SportsMassageMo, @Supergal007, @charliemcmaster, @CromptonHoward, @ClimbingBloke, @chirebckmarkers

And from Facebook, thanks to: Jen Perrin, Matthew Pixa, Mark Llewhellin and Katerina Tanti.

Again, if your name doesn't appear above and you are a bit surprised by that, it's not because I'm not thankful – it's that blasted memory thing... trust me, I can watch a film three or even four times without remembering that I've even seen it once so, really, my rudeness is not deliberate!

The most glaringly obvious absences from the lists above, though, are my family.

So, firstly, a massive thank you to both of my boys... Angus and Evert... who have put up with a Daddy who has found himself, on occasion, needing to walk away from two children who just want to play... in favour of being on a bike or in a wetsuit.

They have had to put up with me throwing insanely sweaty or rain-soaked clothes at them as I return from a tough training session, as a joke… It's funny to me!

They have had to put up with me having the odd grumpy episode too – whether it's because I'm frustrated at a below par session or because we're running late for an event in which I'm entered.

They have even had to put up with me saying "Ten more minutes" when they have come downstairs in the morning just that bit "too early"… having to just sit on the floor and watch while I finish off a session on the Turbo Trainer.

Lastly, they have had to put up with me dragging them to events / training sessions just to watch me when, deep down, I know that waiting around for Daddy to "finish", at a location really not well suited to children, is hardly their idea of fun.

AND…

Most importantly of all, of course, I want to thank the most amazing support team member anyone could wish for; Lisa.

She has managed to be my best friend, my fantastic wife, a flawless Mummy AND "half a Daddy" for the last year… and that lot knocks my completion of a mere Ironman into a cocked hat!

Let's go straight for the jugular first, shall we?

Without Lisa, I would now be in a wheelchair – there is little doubt of that.

Without Lisa, I would never have found the confidence to have done half of the things that I have done.

And without Lisa, I would certainly never have considered the idea of entering an Ironman event!!

I have, many times throughout my numerous posts, referred to how supportive Lisa has been and, without wanting to bore you to tears, there are only so many times that I can tell you about the countless occasions where she has sacrificed a lie-in just so that I can be training.

There are only so many times I can tell you about the countless occasions where she has sacrificed her own needs, or family time, to allow me to do what I needed to do.

The list of jobs around the house that should have been done in the last 12 months, but which have taken a back seat, is huge (I dread to look), but Lisa has accepted this as part and parcel of what it is to be living with an Ironman in training.

No… her support of my goal has been plain for all to see throughout this blog.

What I have, perhaps, made less of, however, is Lisa's role in terms of pushing me to reach my own limits and I think that one example of this stands out more than any other.

I am referring to the occasion when, on lowering myself into a freezing cold lake in winter, I immediately wanted to get back out, such was the extent to which I was shivering and struggling to maintain my own composure.

Lisa refused to let me out until I'd at least "swam to the first buoy and back".

She turned out to be right.

That initial few forced yards got some warmth into me and I ended up swimming around 600 metres that day.

I've lost count of how many times Lisa has actively told me to train despite not really wanting me to… and her threatening phrase; "I'm not going all the way to Sweden for you to embarrass me by not finishing this Ironman… so get out there and train" has been trotted out on many occasions.

Even on the day of the Ironman, when it looked like it was going to fall apart for me at mile 9 of the marathon, Lisa was there to pick me up and push me on my way.

To show her appreciation of what I was doing, Lisa got me the following picture and it's the first thing I see as I wake up each morning:

As lovely as it is, though, the emotion it conveys is the wrong way around – *Lisa* inspires *me* and I should have bought it for *her*.

Lisa: I have appreciated your support hugely and so I thank you from the very bottom of my heart for everything – since words couldn't ever be enough to express what I am trying to say, that seems like a good place to stop.

So, I'll leave this, my very last blog, right there!

I have put a selection of photos below which I hope you enjoy but would like to finish the wordy bit with a heartfelt thank you to everyone who has made reading this blog a regular part of their week throughout this last 12 months... and there are a surprisingly high number of you, I know... it has been incredibly fun to write and I hope that it has been fun to read!

Phil Collard

Ironman

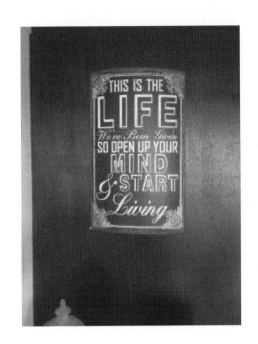